MINISTRY OF DEFENCE

UK Defence Statistics
2008

A National Statistics Publication

CARDIFF
CAERDYDD

ACC. No: 02658889

© Crown Copyright 2008

All rights reserved.

Published with the permission of the Ministry of Defence on behalf of
the Controller of Her Majesty's Stationery Office.

Copyright in the typographical arrangements and design is vested in
the Crown. Applications for reproduction should be made in writing to
the Office of Public Sector Information, Information Policy Team,
Kew, Richmond, Surrey TW9 4DU.

ISBN 978 0 11 773083 0

information & publishing solutions

Published by TSO (The Stationery Office) and available from:

Online
www.tsoshop.co.uk

Mail, Telephone, Fax & E-mail
TSO
PO Box 29, Norwich, NR3 1GN
Telephone orders/General enquiries: 0870 600 5522
Fax orders: 0870 600 5533
E-mail: customer.services@tso.co.uk
Textphone: 0870 240 3701

TSO Shops
16 Arthur Street, Belfast BT1 4GD
028 9023 8451 Fax 028 9023 5401
71 Lothian Road, Edinburgh EH3 9AZ
0870 606 5566 Fax 0870 606 5588

TSO@Blackwell and other Accredited Agents

A NATIONAL STATISTICS PUBLICATION

National Statistics are produced to high professional standards set out in the National Statistics code of Practice.
They undergo regular quality assurance reviews to ensure that they meet customer needs. They are produced free
from any political interference.

For general enquiries about National Statistics, contact the National Statistics Public Enquiry Service on
0845 6013034
Minicom: 01633812399
E-mail: info@statistics.gov.uk
Fax: 01633 652747
Letters: Customer Contact Centre, Room 1.1015, office for National Statistics, Cardiff Road, Newport. NP10 8XG

You can also find National Statistics on the internet - go to www.statistics.gov.uk

CONTENTS

CONTENTS

CONTENTS

INTRODUCTION

Welcome to the 2008 edition of UK Defence Statistics, the annual statistical compendium published by the Ministry of Defence.

The main change this year is the introduction of a new chapter on Health statistics, including tables on deaths and suicides in the Armed Forces, operational casualties, and health and safety statistics. There is also a new table in Chapter 1 regarding MOD payments on Private Finance Initiative (PFI) projects and major equipment projects; and new tables in Chapter 2 that show the strength of UK regular forces by religion, ethnicity and nationality. After consultation, statistics on aircraft air accidents, casualties and flying hours have been ceased, and the chapter which formerly covered this has been removed accordingly.

Although UK Defence Statistics is a National Statistics publication, some of the constituent tables do not constitute National Statistics. These tables have been included because they nevertheless provide useful contextual or indicative data. There are three groups of tables involved: those provided by organisations other than the UK Government, such as NATO; those from official sources that do not meet all the quality standards for National Statistics; and those which have not yet fulfilled the criteria required to be approved by the UK Statistics Authority for assignation as a National Statistic. The tables concerned are clearly marked and have further explanatory notes where necessary.

DASA also publishes a number of monthly and quarterly statistical bulletins; these are available on our web site or from the DASA contact points listed below. These contact points may also be used for any feedback that you may have.

Editorial team: Darren Barton, Laura Bates, Nick Bennett, Gary Cottrill, Julia Edwards, Kirsty Ford, Mark Gardner, Cara Grayling, Kate Harrison, Mike Lovely, Sean Mattson, Pete Newby, Tina Pursey, Sandy Rass, Hazel Rudge, Nick Sibery, Guy Tooke, Sandra White

December 2008

Defence Analytical Services and Advice
3-K-45
Main Building
Whitehall
London SW1A 2HB

Tel: 020 7807 8792
Fax: 020 7218 0969

Email: dasa-infodasa-office@mod.uk
Web site: http://www.dasa.mod.uk

If you require information which is not available in this publication, you might like to submit a Request For Information under the Freedom of Information Act 2000 to the Ministry of Defence via the following link:
http://www.mod.uk/DefenceInternet/ContactUs/FreedomOfInformationInformationRequest.htm

The main contact points within the Defence Analytical Services and Advice are:

Naval Service Manpower	02392 54 7426	Quad Service Manpower (Tri-Service and Civilian)	020 7807 8896
Army Manpower	01980 615050	Economic Statistics	0117 9134524
RAF Manpower	01494 496822	Health Information	01225 468456

SYMBOLS AND CONVENTIONS

Symbols

}	categories merged for some years
||	discontinuity in time series
~	fewer than five
*	not applicable
..	not available
p	provisional
r	revised
r p	revised but still provisional
e	estimate
-	zero or rounded to zero

Italic figures are used for percentages and other rates, except where otherwise indicated.

Rounding

Where rounding has been used, totals and sub-totals have been rounded separately and so may not equal the sums of their rounded parts. This also applies to Civilian personnel data expressed in terms of Full-Time Equivalents (FTE).

When rounding to the nearest 10, numbers ending in "5" have been rounded to the nearest multiple of 20 to prevent systematic bias.

Abbreviations

See Glossary.

CHAPTER 1 - FINANCE

INTRODUCTION

This Chapter provides details on the composition and scope of the Department's expenditure. It also provides information on the impact of defence spending on the wider economy and international comparisons.

UKDS 2008 can be found at the DASA MOD website address: http://www.dasa.mod.uk/UKDS2008/ukds.html

In addition this chapter can be found in html format at:

http://www.dasa.mod.uk/UKDS2008/chapter1.html

A pdf version of Chapter 1 is also available from:

http://www.dasa.mod.uk/UKDS2008/pdf/CHAPTER1.pdf

Other related sources on the strategy and performance of the Department include:

* The Government's Expenditure Plans 2008/2009 (Cm 7385, June 2008)
* The Ministry of Defence's Annual Report & Accounts 2007-08 (HC850-I and II, July 2008)
* HMT Public Expenditure Statistical Analyses 2008 (HC489, April 2008)

Some of these documents and other background information can be found at the MOD website:

http://www.mod.uk

Where possible, every attempt has been made to maintain the consistency of this publication with those above. Where differences do occur, this reflects differences in coverage and/or the availability of more up to date information.

This year has seen the inclusion of a new table detailing future planned financial commitments relating to MOD PFI Projects (**Table 1.12a**) as well as further improvements to existing tables including:

* the expansion of some of the industrial categories contained within **Table 1.9a**
* an update on the latest developments relating to defence related imports and exports statistics (**Tables 1.13 & 1.14**)
* a redesigned **Table 1.19** to include more information on the net direct and indirect costs incurred by MOD operations overseas.

There are five main sections within this Chapter covering:

* **Departmental Resources** – Defence Expenditure Outturn, Public Expenditure by Departmental Grouping, Principal Headings of Defence Expenditure Outturn, MOD Equipment Expenditure, MOD Resources by Budgetary Areas, MOD Resources by Departmental Aims & Objectives, MOD Fixed Assets and MOD Research & Development Expenditure Outturn.

* **Industry & Employment** – MOD spending with UK industry, Estimated UK Employment Dependent on Defence Expenditure and Exports, Estimated UK Regional Direct Employment Dependent on MOD Expenditure and MOD payments on Private Finance Initiatives (PFI) Projects.

* **Trade** – Imports, Exports and Balance of Payments for Trade in Services.

* **Contracts** – by type, major equipment projects and main suppliers (including by holding company).

* **International Defence** – MOD Operation and Peacekeeping Costs, NATO Countries Defence Expenditure and their expenditure as a percentage of GDP and the Top World-wide Military Spenders in 2007.

CHAPTER 1 - FINANCE

INTRODUCTION

Main Findings

The main findings from Chapter 1 are:

9

Departmental Resources
- In 2007/08, Defence Spending (Resource DEL plus Capital DEL minus Depreciation) totalled £37.4 billion.

- In 2007/08, the outturn against the Departmental Expenditure Limits was £43.7 billion. The Resource DEL accounted for £35.7 billion of the 2007/08 expenditure, whilst the Capital DEL accounted for £7.9 billion.

- In 2007/08 Defence is estimated to be the fourth highest area of Government expenditure (Resource DEL plus Capital DEL plus AME) behind Work and Pensions, Health, and Children, Schools and Families.

- In 2007/08, the main areas of Resource expenditure were personnel (£11.5 billion) and depreciation/impairments (£6.2 billion).

- In 2007/08, the main area of Capital expenditure was Assets under Construction (£5.4 billion), which largely consist of major weapons platforms under construction.

- Estimated MOD Equipment Expenditure has increased by some £0.7 billion for 2007/08, largely due to an increase in equipment support costs.

- The total net value of MOD Fixed Assets was £105.1 billion as at 31 March 2008.

- The largest category of assets was Single Use Military Equipment (£35.8 billion) as at 31 March 2008.

Industry & Employment
- In 2006/07, the MOD spent some £16.5 billion with UK Industry. The 'manufacturing' industries (section D) attracted nearly 50% of MOD expenditure with UK Industry. The single industry group attracting most MOD expenditure was Aircraft and Spacecraft (around 12% of the total).

- Estimated employment in UK industry and commerce dependent on MOD expenditure and defence exports has fallen slightly on last year to around 305,000.

Trade
- Total estimated UK deliveries of exports increased from £4.7 billion reported in 2006 to £5.5 billion in 2007.

- The UK identified export orders increased by £4.1 billion between 2005 and 2006 to £9.7 billion. This significant increase in export orders can be attributed to a large order from Saudi Arabia for Typhoon aircraft and orders from Oman and Trinidad and Tobago for offshore patrol vessels.

Contracts
- In 2007/08 MOD HQ placed just over 22,900 contracts with a collective value of around £14.4 billion. The number of contracts placed in 2007/08 remains roughly the same as was reported for 2006/07, whereas the value has decreased by nearly 50% (£13.8 billion) over the same period. The increase in contract value in 2006/07 was due to the placing of a multi billion pound contract with Aspire Defence Holdings and the removal of this contract from the 2007/08 calculations sees a return to historical levels of contract value. Please note that most contract payments are not made during the year in which the contract is placed.

- The largest post Main-Gate equipment project by value is the Type 45 Destroyer (£6.5 billion). This is followed by the Astute Class Submarine (£3.8 billion) and the Nimrod Maritime Reconnaissance and Attack Mk4 (£3.5 billion).

International Defence
- In 2007/08, the MOD spent around £3.0 billion on conflict prevention worldwide.
- The net additional cost incurred by the MOD as a result of operations in Iraq and Afghanistan was around £1.5 billion each.

CHAPTER 1 - FINANCE

RESOURCE ACCOUNTING & BUDGETING

Transition of Cash to Resource Accounting & Budgeting (RAB)

Up until financial year 1998/99, Government expenditure was accounted for on a cash basis. In April 1999 the introduction of Resource Accounting and Budgeting (RAB) brought in an accruals-based accounting system, although Government departments were still controlled on a cash basis. This transitional accounting regime remained for two financial years. Government expenditure has been accounted for on a resource basis only since 2001/02.

The main difference arising from the adoption of RAB is that costs are accounted for as they are incurred (the principle of accruals), rather than when payment is made (the principle of cash). This gives rise to timing differences in accounting between the cash and RAB systems and also to the recognition of depreciation, which expends the cost of an asset over its useful economic life, and the cost of capital charge, equivalent to an interest charge on the net assets held on the Balance Sheet. At the time that RAB was introduced the cost of capital charge was 6% of the net value of assets; although this was reduced to 3.5% in 2003/04.

Control regime

Under Resource Accounting, Government Departments are accountable for their spending against Resource and Capital Departmental Expenditure Limits (DELs). Spending against the Resource DEL includes current items, which are explained in the following two paragraphs. The Capital DEL, whilst part of the overall DEL, reflects investment spending that will appear on the Department's balance sheet and be consumed over a number of years, net of the receipts from sale of assets. Departments are also responsible for Annually Managed Expenditure (AME). This spending is demand led (for example, payment of War Pensions) and therefore cannot be controlled by Departments in the same way.

In **Stage 1** of RAB, which was introduced at the start of financial year 2001/02, the Resource DEL covered current costs such as in year personnel costs, equipment, maintenance of land and buildings. Non cash costs such as depreciation and the cost of capital charge fell within Annually Managed Expenditure (AME) and were not controlled to the same degree as DELs. This allowed departments an interim period to gain experience of managing the new non-cash costs and to review their holdings of stocks and fixed assets, which impact the non-cash costs, prior to the charge impacting on the more tightly controlled DELs.

Stage 2 of RAB was introduced at the start of the financial year 2003/04. This involved the movement of the primary non-cash costs (depreciation and the cost of capital charge) from AME into the Resource DEL, and reduced the cost of capital charge to 3.5% of the net value of assets.

The change in definition of the DELs combined with volatile non-cash costs over the Stage 1 period make time series comparisons over the period 2001/02 - 2003/04 complex.

From 2006/07, the MOD has transferred ownership of fixed assets into two TLBs: Defence Estates (DE) for Land and Buildings; and Defence Equipment & Support (DE&S) for Plant and Machinery, Transport, IT and Communications equipment, and Single Use Military Equipment (SUME).

Factors affecting Cash to RAB data consistency

- There are timing differences as to when payments are recognised.
- The movement of Non-Cash items of expenditure from AME into the Resource DEL from 2003/04 onwards has the 'apparent' effect of inflating the Resource DEL.
- In financial year 2003/04 the rate of interest used to calculate the cost of capital charge was reduced from 6% to 3.5%.
- The discount rate for provisions was changed from 3.5% real to 2.2% real with effect from 1 April 2005.
- The discount rate for pensions liabilities was changed from 2.8% real to 1.8% real with effect from 1 April 2007.

Further information on the introduction of RAB can be found in Chapter 1 of *UK Defence Statistics 2002* in the 'Resource Accounting & Budgeting' section. Alternatively, more information can be found on the HM Treasury website at: http://www.hm-treasury.gov.uk/about/resourceaccounts/resourceaccounts_index.cfm.

CHAPTER 1 - FINANCE

DEPARTMENTAL RESOURCES

This section examines changes in defence expenditure over time (**Table 1.1**). **Table 1.2** examines expenditure on defence within the wider public expenditure framework. **Table 1.3** gives a breakdown of defence expenditure outturn by main area. **Table 1.4** presents estimates of MOD equipment expenditure broken out by the main categories of expenditure. **Table 1.5** presents the MOD resources broken down by budgetary area. **Table 1.6** is included to show the resources consumed against departmental objectives. Following the introduction of RAB, **Tables 1.1**, **1.3** and **1.5** display the Resource, Capital and AME components separately. **Table 1.7** details actual net book values for MOD Fixed Assets broken down by budgetary area. **Table 1.8** details the MOD's annual expenditure on R&D. This is broken down into intramural (within the department) and extramural (outside of the department) expenditure.

Main Findings

Defence Spending (Table 1.1)

- In 2007/08, Defence Spending (Resource DEL plus Capital DEL minus Depreciation) totalled £37.4 billion.

- In 2007/08, the outturn against the Departmental Expenditure Limits was £43.7 billion. The Resource DEL accounted for £35.7 billion of the 2007/08 expenditure, whilst the Capital DEL accounted for £7.9 billion.

Comparison with other Government Departments (Table 1.2)

- In 2007/08 Defence is estimated to be the fourth highest area of Government expenditure (Resource DEL plus Capital DEL plus AME) behind Work and Pensions, Health, and Children, Schools and Families.

- In 2007/08 Health, Defence and Children, Schools and Families represent around 53% of Departmental Expenditure Limits (55% of Resource DEL and 39% of Capital DEL).

Principal Headings of Defence Expenditure Outturn (Resources) (Table 1.3)

- In 2007/08, the main areas of Resource expenditure were personnel (£11.5 billion) and depreciation/impairments (£6.2 billion).

- In 2007/08, the main area of Capital expenditure was Assets under Construction (£5.4 billion), which largely consist of major weapons platforms under construction.

- Between 2006/07 and 2007/08 expenditure on service personnel has increased by 2.7% while civilian personnel expenditure has increased by 2.0%.

MOD Equipment Expenditure (Table 1.4)

- MOD Equipment Expenditure has increased by some £0.7 billion for 2007/08, largely due to an increase in equipment support costs.

MOD Resources by Budgetary Area (Table 1.5)

- The largest outturn against the DEL by TLB in 2007/08 was for the Defence Equipment & Support (£22.9 billion).

- Of the operational TLBs, Commander-in-Chief Land Command had the highest outturn against the DEL in 2007/08 (£6.6 billion).

CHAPTER 1 - FINANCE

DEPARTMENTAL RESOURCES

Fixed Assets (Table 1.7)

12
- The total net value of MOD Fixed Assets was £105.1 billion as at 31 March 2008.

- The largest category of assets was Single Use Military Equipment (£35.8 billion) as at 31 March 2008.

- The value of land & buildings owned by the MOD totalled nearly £19.8 billion as at 31 March 2008.

- Defence Estates hold over 99% of the MOD's land and buildings as at 31 March 2008.

- The Defence Equipment & Support holds nearly 98% of the Department's remaining fixed assets as at 31 March 2008.

- The large holdings of Defence Estates and the Defence Equipment & Support of fixed assets reflect the policy since April 2006 to transfer tangible and intangible assets from Top Level Budgets to Single Balance Sheet Owners.

CHAPTER 1 - FINANCE

DEPARTMENTAL RESOURCES

Table 1.1 Defence Expenditure Outturn[1]

This table shows the changes in Defence expenditure over time, including the period of transition to Stage 1 and 2 of Resource Accounting & Budgeting (RAB) (see page 10). Under Stage 1 RAB, introduced in 2001/02, non-cash costs such as depreciation and cost of capital charge were held under AME, and did not form part of the Resource Departmental Expenditure Limit (DEL). This changed under Stage 2 RAB when non-cash costs moved to the Resource DEL. In order to give a single measure of spending on public services under full resource budgeting, the Defence Spending line is presented as the sum of the resource and capital budgets, net of depreciation and impairments. This reflects the resources required plus the net investment in them, but avoids double counting the writing down of the existing capital stock and the cash outlay on new assets. Control is exercised separately on gross Capital and Resource DEL which replaced Control Totals in 1999/00.

The Net Cash Requirement (NCR) is the actual money that MOD requests from the Government in order to fund its activities. The NCR takes account of movements in working capital levels (debtors, creditors, stock) whilst excluding all non-cash costs.

This table includes expenditure on Conflict Prevention (Request for Resources 2 (RfR2)).

	Cash					RAB Stage 1		RAB Stage 2				
								Inclusive of non-recoverable VAT at Current Prices (£ million)				
						Outturn	Outturn	Outturn	Outturn	Outturn	Outturn	Outturn
	1990/91	1997/98	1998/99	1999/00	2000/01	2001/02	2002/03	2003/04	2004/05	2005/06	2006/07	2007/08
Defence Spending[2]	*	*	*	*	* ||	*	* ||	30 861	32 515	33 164	34 045	37 407
Departmental Expenditure Limits	*	*	*	22 572	23 552 ||	24 456	26 148 ||	37 174	38 323	39 751	40 654	43 654
Resource DEL[3]	*	*	*	*	.. ||	18 905	19 944 ||	31 266	31 798	32 911	33 457	35 709
of which:												
Depreciation/Impairments	*	*	*	*	* ||	*	* ||	6 313	5 808	6 587	6 609	6 247
Cost of Capital Charge	*	*	*	*	* ||	*	* ||	2 770	3 026	3 106	3 242	3 371
Capital DEL[4]	*	*	*	*	.. ||	5 551	6 204 ||	5 908	6 525	6 840	7 197	7 945
Annually Managed Expenditure[5]	*	*	*	*	.. ||	14 962	19 293 ||	1 011	908	890	582	510
Cash	22 298	20 945	22 482	22 572	23 552 ||	*	* ||	*	*	*	*	*
Net Cash Requirement	*	*	*	*	.. ||	24 874	26 991 ||	29 338	29 524	30 603	31 454	33 505
Defence Spending[2] at Constant 2007/08 Prices[6]	*	*	*	*	* ||	*	* ||	34 246	35 111	35 057	35 037	37 407

Source: MOD Directorate of Performance and Analysis

1. The table includes both programme and operational expenditure on conflict prevention.
2. Also referred to as Total DEL, Defence Spending in 2003/04 to 2007/08 is the sum of the Resource DEL, less depreciation and impairments, and Capital DEL. This is consistent with HM Treasury guidance.
3. Resource DEL includes operating cost items such as pay, equipment support costs, fuel and administrative expenditure. From 2003/04 it also includes non-cash items such as depreciation and the cost of capital charge on the Department's net assets plus stock and fixed asset write offs.
4. Capital DEL includes expenditure on the purchase of fixed assets (ships, tanks, planes, buildings etc).
5. From 2003/04 Annually Managed Expenditure includes only demand led items such as war pensions.
6. Conversion to constant 2007/08 prices uses the latest available forecast GDP deflator series produced by HM Treasury dated 27 June 2008.

CHAPTER 1 - FINANCE

DEPARTMENTAL RESOURCES

Table 1.2 Public Expenditure by Departmental Grouping

This table (taken from Table 1.5 and Table 1.10 of *Public Expenditure Statistical Analyses (PESA 2008) HC 489* (http://www.hm-treasury.gov.uk/d/pesa0809_complete.pdf) produced by HMT) examines the expenditure on defence within the wider public expenditure framework. It presents Departmental Expenditure Limits, resource and capital, and Annually Managed Expenditure (AME) **by departmental groupings**. It is not possible to show figures for all individual departments separately and so departments are grouped broadly on the basis of ministerial responsibilities. A detailed list of departmental groupings can be found in *PESA 2008* Appendix B.

Annually Managed Expenditure (AME) relates to expenditure outside the Departmental Expenditure Limits (DEL) but included in Departmental Budgets. This is typically demand led items such as social security benefits, certain pension allowances and tax credits for individuals. DELs are firm plans for three years for a specific part of a department's expenditure. In general DEL will cover all running costs and all programme expenditure. DEL includes relevant non-cash items such as depreciation, cost of capital charges and provisions.

Current Prices (£ billion)

	Outturn 2002/03[1]	Outturn 2003/04	Outturn 2004/05	Outturn 2005/06	Outturn 2006/07	Estimated Outturn 2007/08
Total Government Resource DEL[2]	**229.9** r	**245.1** r	**258.8** r	**277.6** r	**291.2**	**313.1**
Of which:						
Children, Schools and Families[2]	10.6 r	11.9 r	12.6 r	14.3 r	42.1	44.9
Health	57.1	63.6	69.1	76.4	80.4	89.2
Of which: NHS England	55.4	61.9	66.9	74.2	78.5	87.1
CLG Local Government[3]	37.4	40.9	43.3	46.2	22.5	22.7
Home Office[2]	7.3 r	7.9 r	8.0 r	8.3 r	8.3	8.7
Defence[4]	36.5	31.4	31.3	33.5 r	33.5	36.7
Work and Pensions[2]	7.0 r	7.8 r	8.0 r	8.0 r	7.9	8.1

Current Prices (£ billion)

	Outturn 2002/03[1]	Outturn 2003/04	Outturn 2004/05	Outturn 2005/06	Outturn 2006/07	Estimated Outturn 2007/08
Total Government Capital DEL[2]	**27.1** r	**30.5** r	**32.8**	**35.2** r	**38.9**	**43.9**
Of which:						
Children, Schools and Families[2]	2.7 r	3.5 r	4.1 r	4.4 r	4.1	5.5
Health	2.1	2.7	2.7	2.2	3.2	3.6
Of which: NHS England	2.1	2.6	2.6	2.2	3.1	3.3
CLG Local Government[3]	0.2	0.2	0.3	0.3	0.2	0.1
Home Office[2]	0.7 r	0.7 r	0.6 r	0.6 r	0.6	0.8
Defence	6.1	6.0	6.7	6.4	7.1	8.1
Work and Pensions	0.3	0.2	0.3	0.4	0.2	0.1

Current Prices (£ billion)

	Outturn 2002/03[1]	Outturn 2003/04	Outturn 2004/05	Outturn 2005/06	Outturn 2006/07	Estimated Outturn 2007/08
Total Government AME[2,5]	**160.0** r	**164.8** r	**173.0** r	**187.5** r	**206.3**	**221.2**
Of which:						
Children, Schools and Families[2]	7.2 r	6.6 r	6.3 r	8.0 r	8.6	10.7
Health	4.7	6.3	6.7	10.1	10.5	14.6
Of which: NHS England	0.1	0.1	0.3	0.8	0.3	0.6
CLG Local Government[3]	0.2	0.4	0.5	0.5	1.0	0.9
Home Office[2]	1.7 r	-	-	-	0.3	0.4
Defence[6]	*	1.0	0.9	0.9	0.6	0.5
Work and Pensions[2]	99.9 r	103.8 r	110.7 r	115.2 r	119.3	129.6
Total Government DEL (RDEL + CDEL)[2,7]	**256.9** r	**275.6** r	**291.6** r	**312.8** r	**330.0**	**357.1**
Total Government AME[2,5]	**160.0** r	**164.8** r	**173.0** r	**187.5** r	**206.3**	**221.2**
Total Government Spend (RDEL + CDEL + AME)[2,6]	**416.9** r	**440.4** r	**464.6** r	**500.3** r	**536.3**	**578.2**

Source: HMT Public Expenditure Statistical Analyses HC 489 (Table 1.5 & Table 1.10)

1. The figures presented in this table for 2002/03 are different from the ones shown in **Tables 1.1**, **1.3** & **1.5** as the PESA figures for these years have been recast by HM Treasury on the Stage 2 RAB definition of DEL and AME whereas the MOD reported the accounts on Stage 1 definitions until 2003/04.
2. Changes in all years are a result of machinery of government changes.
3. CLG Local Government was introduced in 2006/07 but it is comparable with the "Local Government" category referred to in previous editions of UKDS. This category is due to the creation of the "Department for Communities and Local Government" established on 5 Apr 2006.
4. For 2003/04 the Defence figure includes the supplementary estimate for asset revaluation.
5. Total figures include Defence figures for AME as shown in *PESA 2008* and not as shown in this table.
6. The figures for Defence AME from 2003-04 onwards have been adjusted to align with the data contained in **Tables 1.1**, **1.3** & **1.5** which excludes contributions to the Armed Forces Pensions Scheme.
7. These figures are different from *PESA 2008*, which presents Total DEL as RDEL + CDEL less depreciation.

CHAPTER 1 - FINANCE

DEPARTMENTAL RESOURCES

Table 1.3 Principal Headings of Defence Expenditure Outturn (Resource basis)

This table provides a breakdown of defence outturn in terms of resources consumed. This is distributed between the main personnel, fixed assets and other expenditure groups. These groupings differ from those used under cash accounting and are not directly comparable. **This table includes expenditure on Conflict Prevention (RfR2).**

15

RAB Stage 2
--->

Inclusive of non-recoverable VAT at Current Prices (£ million)

		Outturn 2003/04	Outturn 2004/05	Outturn 2005/06	Outturn 2006/07	Outturn 2007/08
Defence Spending		**30 861**	**32 515**	**33 164**	**34 045**	**37 407**
Departmental Expenditure Limits		**37 174**	**38 323**	**39 751**	**40 654**	**43 654**
Resource DEL		**31 266**	**31 798**	**32 911**	**33 457**	**35 709**
of which:						
	Expenditure on Personnel	10 435	10 996	11 255	11 204	11 485
	of which: for Armed Forces	7 974	8 047	8 263	8 423	8 649
	for Civilians	2 461	2 948	2 992	2 781	2 836
	Depreciation/Impairments	6 313	5 808	6 587	6 609	6 247
	Cost of Capital	2 770	3 026	3 106	3 242	3 371
	Equipment Support[1]	3 804	3 623	3 542	3 793	4 272
	Stock Consumption[2]	1 060	1 079	1 039	1 140	1 071
	Property Management[3]	1 393	1 509	1 367	1 258	1 523
	Movements[4]	491	711	729	774	858
	Accommodation & Utilities[5]	643	581	735	786	750
	Professional Fees[6,7]	549	565	553	482 r	471
	Fuel[8]	161	239	369	416	537
	Hospitality & Entertainment	8	6	5	4	4
	PFI Service Charges	*	*	870	1 148	1 276
	IT & Communications	738	678	643	719	655
	Other Costs [9]	2 900 r	2 977 r	2 111 r	1 882 r	3 189
Capital DEL		**5 908**	**6 525**	**6 840**	**7 197**	**7 945**
of which:						
	Expenditure on Fixed Asset Categories					
	Intangible Assets[10]	1 665	1 580	1 550	1 744	1 756
	Land and Buildings[7]	54	388 r	31	45	126
	Single Use Military Equipment[7,11]	90	435 r	402	404	657
	Plant, Machinery & Vehicles	78	124	64	32	36
	IT & Communications Equipment	183	134	180	206	361
	Assets Under Construction[12]	3 931	4 335	4 879	5 099	5 450
	Transport[13]	*	73	13	33	55
	Capital Spares[13]	581	*	*	*	*
	Capital Loan Repayment	- 28	- 25	- 53	- 8	- 10
	Capital Income[14,15]	- 646	- 519	- 225	- 358	- 486
AME		**1 011**	**908**	**890**	**582**	**510**
of which:						
	War Pensions[7]	1 116	1 110	1 067	1 038 r	1 014
	Other[7,16]	- 105	- 202	- 177	- 456 r	- 504

Source: MOD Directorate of Performance and Analysis

1. Internal and contracted out costs for equipment repair and maintenance.
2. Consumption of armament, medical, dental, veterinary, oil, clothing, and general stores.
3. Estate and facilities management services and costs for buildings' maintenance.
4. Cost of transportation of freight and personnel.
5. Charges include rent, rates, gas, electricity, water and sewerage costs.
6. Fees, such as legal costs, paid to professional organisations.
7. Minor revisions in 2004/05 and 2006/07 caused by rounding.
8. Relates to fuel consumption by military vehicles, ships and aircraft.
9. Other costs can include Grants-in-aid, Exchange rate movements, Provisions, receipts, welfare, medical and legal costs, Research and Expensed Development, rentals paid under operating leases, Fixed Assets, and Stock written off.
10. Intangible Assets comprise the development costs of major equipment projects and Intellectual Property Rights.
11. SUME are assets which only have a military use, such as tanks and fighter aircrafts. Dual use items i.e. those that also have a civilian use are recorded under the other categories.
12. Assets Under Construction (AUC) largely consist of major weapons platforms under construction in the Defence Equipment & Support, and a smaller element of Buildings under construction. Once construction is complete, those platforms will transfer to the relevant Top Level Budget holder as SUME on their Balance Sheets.
13. From 2004/05 Transport has been recorded as a separate category and Capital Spares has been removed as a category, with the costs previously recorded here being incorporated into Transport or SUME.
14. Redemption of QinetiQ preference shares refers to the proceeds received from the partial redemption of the redeemable preference shares during 2004/05.
15. Capital income is receipts for the sale of fixed assets.
16. Under Stage 2 of RAB, this category now contains only demand led payments, such as cash release and cost of capital credit on nuclear provisions and QinetiQ loan repayments.

CHAPTER 1 - FINANCE

DEPARTMENTAL RESOURCES

Table **1.4** Estimated MOD Equipment Expenditure[1]

This table presents estimates of MOD equipment expenditure broken out by the main categories of expenditure. Aggregate MOD Equipment expenditure here has been used to indicate expenditure on acquisition, maintenance, repair and update of items such as plant, machinery and vehicles and fighting equipment plus associated Research & Development, and expenditure on administrative computers. It is therefore a **wider definition** than that used by the MOD Equipment and Equipment Support Plans, and covers both military and non-military equipment (including dual use equipment) used by MOD service and civilian personnel. The data are derived directly from the MOD Annual Report & Accounts.

This table is outside the scope of National Statistics because it is still under review to ensure it meets all of the high professional quality assurance standards set out in the National Statistics Code of Practice.

	Inclusive of non-recoverable VAT at Current Prices (£ million)				
	2003/04	2004/05	2005/06	2006/07	2007/08
Estimated MOD Equipment Expenditure	**10 886**	**10 754**	**10 974**	**11 672**	**12 380**
Of which:					
Capital Expenditure on Equipment[2,3]	4 404	4 555	4 913	5 146	5 401
Equipment Support[4]	3 804	3 623	3 542	3 793	4 272
Research & Development[5]	2 677	2 576	2 519	2 732	2 707

Source: MOD Annual Report & Accounts

1. These estimates are not directly comparable to the old cash equipment procurement time series last published in 2000/01 (UKDS 2002) due to the exclusion of in year stock purchases. It is not possible to identify that element of stock purchases which wholly relates to MOD equipment expenditure.
2. Capital expenditure on Equipment includes those Assets Under Construction (AUC) relating to Single Use Military Equipment (SUME) only plus in year purchases on IT and communications equipment, vehicles, SUME and plant and machinery. AUC SUME largely consist of major weapons platforms under construction in the Defence Equipment & Support (DE&S) organisation (formerly the Defence Procurement Agency and Defence Logistics Organisation), and excludes that element of Buildings under construction and Land which would fall outside the wider definition of MOD equipment procurement detailed in the commentary above. Once construction is complete, those platforms will transfer to the relevant Single Balance Sheets Owners (SBSO) as Single Use Military Equipment (SUME) on their Balance Sheets.
3. During 2007-08, the augmentation of the MOD Chart of Accounts has enabled more detailed reporting of the 'AUC-Other' classification by category type by the Defence Equipment & Support Organisation. This has improved the coverage of equipment expenditure reported in the table from 2007-08 by providing a more distinct separation of equipment (particularly dual use) from non-equipment expenditure (e.g. construction, land and buildings, and other administrative costs).
4. Internal and contracted out costs for equipment repair and maintenance.
5. The data are derived from information held on MOD accounting systems relating to expenditure on Additions to Intangible Assets and Research & Expensed Development. Development activity associated with acquiring assets is the most significant part of this expenditure. These figures do not fully align with those in **Table 1.8** which present MOD R&D expenditure on a different basis using OECD Frascati definitions. (See *Defence Statistics Bulletin No. 6*). The estimates in **Table 1.4** will include items which fall outside these definitions but nonetheless broadly relate to the wider definition of MOD equipment expenditure as described in the commentary above.

CHAPTER 1 - FINANCE

DEPARTMENTAL RESOURCES

Table 1.5 MOD Resources by Budgetary Areas[1]

This table provides a detailed breakdown of resource consumption by budgetary area for 2003/04 through to 2007/08. Under Spending Review 2002 rules, figures for financial years 2003/04 onward include non-cash items such as depreciation and cost of capital charge that previously were part of Annually Managed Expenditure (AME).

The revisions in Resource DEL and Capital DEL for the earlier years are due to 'Non Allocated' amounts being subsequently attributed to the correct TLB.

From 2007/08, changes to the MOD Top Level Budget (TLB) structure have been reflected in the figures and highlighted at footnotes 2-5.

This table includes expenditure on Conflict Prevention (RfR2).

	RAB Stage 2 -->			
				Inclusive of non-recoverable VAT at Current Prices (£ million)
	Outturn 2003/04	Outturn 2004/05	Outturn 2005/06	Outturn 2006/07	Outturn 2007/08

	Outturn 2003/04	Outturn 2004/05	Outturn 2005/06	Outturn 2006/07	Outturn 2007/08
Departmental Expenditure Limits (DEL)	**37 174**	**38 323**	**39 751**	**40 654**	**43 654**
Request for Resources 1: PROVISION OF DEFENCE CAPABILITY	**35 681**	**37 211**	**38 484**	**38 858**	**40 622**
Resource DEL	**30 033**	**30 860**	**31 855**	**32 009**	**33 513**
of which:					
Commander-in-Chief Fleet[2]	3 242	3 569	3 548	2 148	2 185
General Officer Commanding (Northern Ireland)	649	626	580	389	*
Commander-in-Chief Land Command[3]	5 079	5 341	5 632	4 322	6 495
Air Officer Commanding-in-Chief RAF Strike Command	3 385	3 503	4 043	1 924	*
Commander-in-Chief Air Command[4]	*	*	*	*	2 635
Chief of Joint Operations	524	493	570	391	475
Chief Defence Logistics[5]	7 758 r	7 452	7 588 r	12 788	*
Defence Equipment & Support[6]	*	*	*	*	16 236
2nd Sea Lord/Commander-in-Chief Naval Home Command	693	763	778	*	*
Adjutant General (Personnel and Training Command)[5]	1 743 r	1 778	1 924	1 576	*
Air Officer Commanding-in-Chief RAF Personnel and Training Command	995	1 125	904	762	*
Central[5]	2 695	3 136 r	2 458	2 172	2 317
Defence Estates[7]	*	*	1 056	2 692	2 628
Defence Procurement Agency[5]	2 850 r	2 568	2 272	2 321 r	*
Science Innovation Technology	420	506	502	524	542
Capital DEL	**5 648**	**6 351**	**6 629**	**6 849**	**7 109**
of which:					
Commander-in-Chief Fleet[2]	37	17	7	14	29
General Officer Commanding (Northern Ireland)	43	28	4	2	*
Commander-in-Chief Land Command[3]	21	153	47	75	123
Air Officer Commanding-in-Chief RAF Strike Command	40	27	10	7	*
Commander-in-Chief Air Command[4]	*	*	*	*	13
Chief of Joint Operations	22	24	19	4	34
Chief Defence Logistics	1 210	1 121	1 045	1 243	*
Defence Equipment & Support[6]	*	*	*	*	6 661
2nd Sea Lord/Commander-in-Chief Naval Home Command	28	23	11	*	*
Adjutant General (Personnel and Training Command)	41	26	17	15	*
Air Officer Commanding-in-Chief RAF Personnel and Training Command	18	24	13	11	*
Central	- 96	322	- 44	44	41
Defence Estates[7]	*	*	274	140	208
Defence Procurement Agency[5]	4 284 r	4 586	5 226 r	5 294 r	*
Science Innovation Technology	*	*	*	*	*
Request for Resources 2: CONFLICT PREVENTION	**1 493**	**1 112**	**1 266** r	**1 796** r	**3 032**
(not broken down by Top Level Budget)					
Resource DEL	1 233	938	1 055 r	1 448	2 196
Capital DEL	260	174	211	348	836
Annually Managed Expenditure (AME)	**1 011**	**908**	**890**	**582**	**510**
Request for Resources 1: PROVISION OF DEFENCE CAPABILITY[8,9]	**- 105**	**- 202**	**- 177**	**- 456** r	**-504**
Request for Resources 2: CONFLICT PREVENTION	*	*	*	*	*
Request for Resources 3: WAR PENSIONS & ALLOWANCES, etc	**1 116**	**1 110**	**1 067**	**1 038** r	**1 014**

Source: MOD Directorate of Performance and Analysis

1. Full TLB definitions are available in the **Glossary** at the back of this publication.
2. C-in-C Fleet TLB includes the former 2nd Sea Lord/C-in-C Naval Home Command TLB from 2006/07.
3. Land Command includes the former Adjutant General (Personnel and Training Command).
4. Air Command is an amalgamation of 'Air Officer Commanding in Chief RAF Personnel and Training Command' and 'RAF Strike Command'.
5. Revisions within RDEL and CDEL for the years 2003/04 to 2006/07 are caused by the attributions of costs previously classed as 'Not Allocated'. Totals for 2006/07 have been adjusted for consistency to the MOD Annual Report and Accounts.
6. Defence Equipment & Support was created from the amalgamation of the 'Defence Logistic Organisation' and 'Defence Procurement Agency'.
7. The 'Defence Estates' TLB was formed on 1 April 2005 . This was formerly part of 'Central' TLB. There is no historic data for this new TLB.
8. AME for 2003/04 onwards includes accounting charges relating to nuclear decommissioning, loan interest and cost of capital charges for self financing public corporations. The negative AME figures arise from the cash release from the nuclear decommissioning provision and the cost of capital charge calculated on a net balance sheet liability (as opposed to net assets).
9. A breakdown of AME (RfR1) figures by TLB can be viewed in the online version of UKDS.

CHAPTER 1 - FINANCE

DEPARTMENTAL RESOURCES

Table 1.6 MOD Resources by Departmental Aims & Objectives

The MOD's aim is to "deliver security for the people of the United Kingdom and the Overseas Territories by defending them, including against terrorism, and act as a force for good by strengthening international peace and security". This aim and three supporting objectives are set out in the MOD's Public Service Agreement for the years 2005 to 2008. The costs of meeting these objectives, and their enabling outputs set out below, are reported in the MOD Annual Report and Accounts. The outputs are defined more fully in Note 24 to the Accounts. Figures are net of receipts and are not comparable with those presented in Tables 1.1, 1.3 and 1.5, for example, due to the treatment of MOD Trading Funds. The Total Defence Output Cost is consistent with the net operating cost figure (excluding the payments of War Pensions and Benefits) in the statement of Operating Costs by Departmental Aim and Objectives of the MOD Annual Report & Accounts.

The sum of Resource DEL and "Other AME", which may be derived from Table 1.5, closely aligns with the total of these net operating costs. The figures do not exactly match because certain categories of MOD's interest payments and grants and other non budgetary costs are specified by HM Treasury to be outside the scope of the MOD's Departmental Expenditure Limits (DEL) and Annually Managed Expenditure (AME). Totals for 2006/07 have been adjusted for consistency to the MOD Annual Report and Accounts.

Operating costs include resource charges for capital assets through depreciation and cost of capital charges.

Inclusive of non-recoverable VAT at Current Prices (£ million)

	Outturn 2003/04	Outturn 2004/05	Outturn 2005/06[1]	Outturn 2006/07[2]	Outturn 2007/08[3]
Total Defence Output Cost	**33 415**	**31 222**	**33 325**	**32 911** ͬ	**35 209**
OBJECTIVE 1: Achieving success in the tasks we undertake	**3 481**	**3 390**	**3 564**	**3 711**	**4 050**
Operations	1 233	938	1 040	1 443	2 196
Other Military Tasks	1 659	1 764	1 698	1 525	1 086
Contributing to the Community	360	395	494	397	460
Helping to Build a Safer World	229	293	332	346	309
OBJECTIVE 2: Being ready to respond to the tasks that might arise[4]	**26 777**	**24 934**	**26 601**	**26 292**	**28 320**
Royal Navy	**9 990**	**7 310**	**7 942**	**7 037**	**7 586**
Aircraft Carriers	293	347	354	339	377
Frigates & Destroyers	1 709	1 548	1 355	1 619	1 491
Smaller Warships	284	486	413	390	360
Amphibious Ships	339	340	290	339	414
Strategic Sealift	3	38	41	46	34
Fleet Support Ships	348	408	344	366	304
Survey & Other Vessels	157	102	72	94	153
Naval Aircraft	1 393	1 193	1 139	1 083	1 123
Submarines	4 862	2 307	3 393	2 204	2 783
Royal Marines	604	540	540	557	548
Army	**8 723**	**9 252**	**10 479**	**10 706**	**11 261**
Field Units	6 372	7 517	8 492	8 822	9 671
Other Units	2 350	1 736	1 987	1 884	1 590
Royal Air Force	**7 002**	**6 825**	**6 848**	**6 987**	**7 573**
Combat Aircraft[5]	4 519	4 577	4 125	3 692	4 193
Intelligence, Surveillance, Target Acquisition and Reconnaissance Aircraft (ISTAR)[6]	350	489	606	613	899
Tankers, Transport and Communications Aircraft	1 040	1 028	1 247	1 211	1 025
Future Capability	339	15	20	44	86
Other Aircraft and RAF Units	753	716	850	1 427	1 371
Centre Grouping	**1 063**	**1 547**	**1 332**	**1 562**	**1 899**
Joint and Multinational Operations	148	523	474	425	761
Centrally Managed Military Support	236	289	400	367	606
Maintenance of War Reserve Stocks	679	734	458	770	532
OBJECTIVE 3: Building for the future	**3 156**	**2 899**	**3 160**	**2 907**	**2 838**
Research & Expensed Development	1 007	996	1 041	1 026	974
Equipment Programme	2 149	1 903	2 119	1 881	1 865

Source: MOD Annual Report & Accounts

1. The increased Total Defence Output Cost figure for 2005/06 reflects: an increased cost incurred following the change in discount rate, from 3.5% to 2.2%, applied to the Department's provisions for nuclear decommissioning of £1.1 billion; and movements in other operating costs, including staff, impairments, and depreciation as a result of the Quinquennial review of fixed assets of £1.4 billion offset by receipts from the sale of QinetiQ shares.
2. With effect from April 2006, intangible and tangible fixed assets were transferred from Top Level Budgets (TLBs) to Single Balance Sheet Owners (SBSOs). The related operating costs (e.g. depreciation and cost of capital charge) have been apportioned to outputs by the SBSOs using the percentage of costs attributed to the Management Grouping in 2005/06 as a basis for the apportionment. Where Front Line TLBs had previously allocated some asset costs directly to final outputs, the methodology used in 2006/07 has resulted in some variances in costs attributed to final outputs from those reported in 2005/06. Restructuring within RAF Strike Command resulted in a more accurate alignment of costs to outputs.
3. A working group, consisting of all TLBs and the SBSOs, was set up in 2007/08 to review the apportionment methods used. The aim was to improve consistency in the costing of final outputs; some of the variances between 2006/07 and 2007/08 are as a result of changes agreed by the group. The increase in Total Defence Output is as a result of: Operational costs due to continuing commitments in Iraq and Afghanistan £0.75Billion and costs in respect of Typhoon £0.5Billion, Apache helicopters £0.3Billion and increases to provisions in respect of nuclear decommissioning £0.5 Billion.
4. The costs of delivering the military capability to meet Objective 2 are analysed among force elements of the front line commands, including joint force units where these have been established, and a small number of centrally managed military support activities. In addition to the direct operating costs of the front line units, they include the attributed costs of logistical and personnel support. In common with all Objectives, these also contain a share of the costs of advising ministers and accountability to Parliament, and apportioned overheads for head office functions and centrally provided services.
5. Combines former titles of Strike/Attack and Offensive Support Aircraft and Defensive and Surveillance Aircraft.
6. Formerly Reconnaissance and Maritime Patrol Aircraft.

CHAPTER 1 - FINANCE

DEPARTMENTAL RESOURCES

Table 1.7 MOD Fixed Assets: 2007/08[1]

This table gives a detailed breakdown of the **net book value** of the MOD's Fixed Assets by category and budgetary area. The MOD is one of the largest owners of fixed assets in the United Kingdom. The stewardship and efficient management of the Department's assets are the responsibility of Top Level Budget (TLB) Holders. MOD Fixed Assets are formally revalued on a five-yearly basis, but are uplifted annually using indexation. This table has been modified to reflect revised asset categories. Fighting Equipment has been replaced by Single Use Military Equipment (SUME), Plant, Machinery and Vehicles has been replaced with two categories; Plant and Machinery and Transport, and the category of capital spares has been removed and incorporated into SUME and Transport.

The values contained in the table are at 31 March 2008. The valuation method complies with financial reporting standards with values being on an existing use basis and not market value at disposal. Overseas estates for which the Crown holds no legal title, but which are used for garrison and training purposes by British Forces are included in the MOD Fixed Assets Register. UK bases occupied by visiting forces are also included.

From 2006-07 the creation of Single balance sheet owners has meant that most classes of assets are now accounted for by one TLB. This accounts for changes since UKDS 2007.

Current Prices (£ million)

	Tangible Fixed Assets							Intangible Assets	Invest-ments	Total Assets
	Land & Buildings	Plant & Machinery	Transport	IT & Comms Equipment	SUME[2]	AUC[3] SUME	AUC[3] Other			
Top Level Budget[4] Total	**19 774**	**1 753**	**4 611**	**1 059**	**35 767**	**11 141**	**3 826**	**26 692**	**497**	**105 120**
Commander-in-Chief Fleet[5]	-	1	1	4	-	-	41	-	-	47
General Officer Commanding (Northern Ireland)	-	-	2	-	-	-	-	-	-	2
Commander-in-Chief Land Command	18	-	3	5	4	-	141	-	-	171
Commander-in-Chief Air Command[6]	-	-	-	1	-	-	31	-	-	32
Chief of Joint Operations	24	3	3	2	-	1	45	9	-	87
Defence Equipment & Support[7]	46	1 746	4 600	1 045	35 763	11 140	2 374	26 683	-	83 398
Central	-	2	1	2	-	-	82	-	497	583
Defence Estates	19 686	1	1	-	-	-	1 112	-	-	20 800

Source: MOD Directorate of Performance and Analysis

1. Figures provided as at 31 March 2008 are taken from MOD Fixed Assets Register. Figures relate to the net book value of the MOD fixed assets. The net value of an asset is equal to its original cost (its book value) minus depreciation and amortisation costs.
2. SUME refers to Single Use Military Equipment.
3. AUC refers to Assets Under Construction.
4. The reason for the relatively small amounts in TLBs is due to the Fixed Assets not having been transferred to the single balance sheet holder mainly because the TLBs cannot agree on the asset value or there are other difficulties over the paperwork. If the system works well they should reduce to zero.
5. C-in-C Fleet TLB includes the former 2nd Sea Lord/C-in-C Naval Home Command TLB from 2006/07.
6. Air Command is an amalgamation of 'Air Officer Commanding in Chief RAF Personnel and Training Command' and 'RAF Strike Command'.
7. Defence Equipment & Support was created from the amalgamation of the 'Defence Logistic Organisation' and 'Defence Procurement Agency'.

CHAPTER 1 - FINANCE

DEPARTMENTAL RESOURCES

Table 1.8 MOD Research & Development Expenditure Outturn

This table details the MOD's annual expenditure on Research and Development (R&D) activity. Expenditure is broken down into intramural (i.e. R&D activity undertaken within the Department) and extramural (i.e. R&D activity undertaken outside of the Department). The data included in this table are derived from an annual survey of MOD R&D expenditure conducted by DASA and information from MOD accounting systems. DASA seek to classify R&D activity within the Organisation for Economic Co-operation & Development's Frascati Guidelines which align to National Accounts definitions. Following a National Statistics Quality Review conducted during 2002/03, the MOD's R&D statistics were revised for the years 1996/97 to 2000/01. These changes are described in *Defence Statistics Bulletin No. 6*. Changes made before this date are outlined in *Defence Statistics Bulletin No.s 1 & 2*, and are described in previous editions of UK Defence Statistics. The marked shift from intramural to extramural expenditure in 2001/02 is a result of the disestablishment of the Defence Evaluation and Research Agency on 1 July 2001.

IMPORTANT NOTE: The 2006-07 figures are currently subject to a data quality review. Upon completion of this exercise, the final validated data will be updated online at www.dasa.mod.uk/UKDS2008.

Inclusive of non-recoverable VAT at Current Prices (£ million)

Research & Development	1990/91	1997/98	2001/02[1,2]	2002/03	2003/04	2004/05	2005/06	2006/07
Total Gross Expenditure on R&D	2 453	2 371	2 117	2 790	2 744	2 645	2 594	..
Of which:		-						
Intramural	902	750	419	288	380	357	365	..
Extramural	1 551	1 622	1 698	2 502	2 364	2 288	2 229	..
		-						
Receipts[3]	**116**	**57**	**60**	**56**	**68**	**69**	**75**	..
Of which used:								
Intramurally	53	39	44	46	59	61	74	..
Extramurally	63	18	16	10	9	8	1	..
Total Net Expenditure on R&D	2 337	2 314	2 057	2 734	2 677	2 576	2 519	..

Inclusive of non-recoverable VAT at Current Prices (£ million)

Research	1990/91	1997/98	2001/02[1,2]	2002/03	2003/04	2004/05	2005/06	2006/07
Total Gross Expenditure on Research	..	577	616	524	548	664	626	..
Of which:								
Intramural	..	325	229	145	164	190	171	..
Extramural	..	251	388	379	384	474	455	..
Receipts[3]	..	**13**	**60**	**9**	**24**	**26**	**28**	..
Of which used:								
Intramurally	..	12	44	9	23	25	27	..
Extramurally	..	2	16	-	1	1	1	..
Total Net Expenditure on Research	412	564	557	515	524	639	598	..

Inclusive of non-recoverable VAT at Current Prices (£ million)

Development	1990/91	1997/98	2001/02[1,2]	2002/03	2003/04	2004/05	2005/06	2006/07
Total Gross Expenditure on Development	..	1 794	1 500	2 266	2 196	1 981	1 969	..
Of which:								
Intramural	..	424	190	143	216	167	194	..
Extramural	..	1 370	1 311	2 123	1 980	1 814	1 775	..
Receipts[3]	..	**44**	-	**48**	**44**	**43**	**47**	..
Of which used:								
Intramurally	..	28	-	38	35	36	47	..
Extramurally	..	16	-	10	8	8	-	..
Total Net Expenditure on Development	1 926	1 750	1 500	2 218	2 153	1 937	1 921	..

Source: DASA (Economic Statistics)

1. Since 2000/01 the Departmental Resource Accounts (DRAc) follow Statement of Standard Accounting Practice 13, "Accounting for Research and Development". Since 2000/01 the figures are calculated on a resource basis, and are consistent with the aggregate of Research & Expensed Development plus Additions to Intangible Assets. This table therefore comprises elements from both the Operating Cost Statement and the Balance Sheet in the DRAc.

2. On 1 July 2001 DERA was split into two organisations: the Defence Science & Technology Laboratory (Dstl) (about a quarter of DERA) staying as a Trading Fund within MOD, and QinetiQ, the remainder, becoming a private (extramural) company.

3. Receipts are monies received by MOD & its Trading Funds for expenditure on R&D, for example from other government departments & private industry. This money is not necessarily spent on defence-related R&D.

CHAPTER 1 - FINANCE

INDUSTRY & EMPLOYMENT

This section provides data on the impact of MOD's spending on equipment and services in the UK. **Table 1.9** details the estimated amount of money that the MOD spent with UK industry broken down by industrial group from the cash accounts. **Table 1.9a** provides data for 2002/03 onwards against slightly different industry groupings due to the introduction of Resource Accounting and Budgeting. These numbers have been derived from administrative systems which use Resource Account Codes. The industrial groupings are based on the UK Standard Industrial Classification (SIC) 1992 and 2003 maintained by the Office for National Statistics (ONS). **Table 1.10** provides estimates of UK employment dependent on MOD expenditure and defence exports. **Tables 1.11, 1.11a** & **1.11b** provide estimates of the number of direct full time jobs in the Government Office Regions of England, Scotland, Wales, Northern Ireland and the UK as a whole, supported in industry and commerce by MOD direct expenditure. **Table 1.12** details MOD payments on PFI projects during 2007/08 whilst **Table 1.12a** lists those PFI projects which have planned unitary charge payments of over £25 million in 2008/09.

21

Main Findings

Expenditure by Industry Group (Table 1.9a)

- In 2006/07, the MOD spent some £16.5 billion with UK Industry. The 'manufacturing' industries (section D) attracted nearly 50% of MOD expenditure with UK Industry. The single industry group attracting most MOD expenditure was Aircraft and Spacecraft (around 12% of the total).

Defence Related Employment (Table 1.10 & 1.11)

- Estimated employment in UK industry and commerce dependent on MOD expenditure and defence exports has fallen slightly from last year to around 305,000.

- Regional employment directly dependent on MOD expenditure is concentrated in the South East (38,000 jobs) and the South West (37,000 jobs). Scotland, Wales and Northern Ireland account for just 11,000 jobs (7%).

MOD PFI Projects (Table 1.12)

- The PFI projects against which the highest payments were made in 2007/08 were Allenby/Connaught, Attack Helicopters Training Service - Apache, Colchester Garrison, Defence Fixed Telecommunications Service (DFTS), Main Building Redevelopment (MBR), Skynet 5 and the Tri-Service White Fleet.

CHAPTER 1 - FINANCE

INDUSTRY & EMPLOYMENT

Table 1.9 Estimated Defence Expenditure Outturn in the UK: Breakdown by Industry Group

This table, which has been prepared from the MOD's Cash Ledger, details the amount of money the MOD spent with UK industry broken down by industrial group. Figures therefore, exclude 'internal' MOD expenditure such as pay and allowances. Industrial groupings are derived from the Standard Industrial Classification (SIC) guidelines maintained by the Office for National Statistics. From 1996/97 onwards, figures are based on Standard Industrial Classification 1992 - SIC(92). Prior to this, figures are based on SIC(80). The creation of QinetiQ PLC from part of the MOD's Defence Evaluation and Research Agency (DERA) in July 2001 provides a discontinuity in 2001/02 compared to earlier years. The figures have been rounded to the nearest £10M. Differences between the totals and sums of the components are caused by this rounding. This table has been reproduced again this year to provide continuity with the time series data presented in **Table 1.9a**.

VAT exclusive at Current Prices (£ million)

SIC(92) Group		1990/91	1995/96	1997/98	1998/99	1999/00	2000/01		2001/02
Total		**8 870**	**10 030**	**11 200**	**12 170**	**11 480**	**12 060**	||	**12 760**
Solid Fuels	10	10	10	-	-	-	-	||	-
Petroleum Products	23.2	390	290	300	230	240	340	||	370
Gas, Electricity and Water Supply	40-41	250	230	270	260	250	230	||	210
Metals	27,28	*	80	140	180	200	200	||	180
Chemicals	24	*	60	40	50	40	60	||	60
Other Mechanical and Marine Engineering	29.1-29.5	800	240	370	270	220	210	||	220
Weapons & Ammunition	29.6	750	400	750	880	830	790	||	690
Data Processing Equipment	30	280	640	80	180	120	140	||	180
Other Electrical Engineering	31	170	270	180	250	210	190	||	180
Electronics & Precision Instruments	32,33	1 810	1 090	1 320	1 400	950	1 000	||	1 110
Motor Vehicles and Parts	34, 35.2, 35.4, 35.5	320	480	280	390	330	180	||	170
Shipbuilding and Repairing	35.1	780	770	790	1 180	1 090	1 100	||	1 230
Aircraft and Spacecraft	35.3	2 130	2 060	2 360	2 220	2 240	2 390	||	2 540
Food	15	160	120	110	120	120	120	||	140
Textiles, Leather Goods and Clothing	17,18,19	140	110	130	130	140	120	||	120
Office Furniture	36.1	*	70	110	60	60	60	||	70
Stationery	21,22	*	120	30	40	30	40	||	40
Construction	45	*	1 280	1 060	1 070	1 040	1 070	||	1 100
Postage	64.1	*	10	20	20	40	40	||	40
Telecommunications	64.2	*	120	180	290	260	210	||	320
Other Production Industries[1]	nes[3]	370	270	900	1 080	1 140	1 440	||	1 520
Other Industries and Services[2]	nes[3]	510	1 300	1 770	1 860	1 940	2 140	||	2 280

Source: DASA (Economic Statistics)

1. This category includes expenditure on equipment in other manufacturing industries, as well as the business and administration, education and training and operational support sectors.
2. This category includes expenditure on services in the business and administration, education and training and operational support sectors. It also includes expenditure on road and rail transport and freight.
3. Not elsewhere specified.

CHAPTER 1 - FINANCE

INDUSTRY & EMPLOYMENT

Table 1.9a Estimated Defence Expenditure Outturn in the UK: Breakdown by Industry Group

This table, which has been prepared from MOD administrative systems introduced under Resource Accounting and Budgeting (RAB), estimates the amount of money the MOD spends directly with UK industry broken down by industrial group. The RAB breakdowns do not permit the analysis that was undertaken previously. The break in series has, however, permitted the table to show all the sections of the economy that are represented in the Standard Industrial Classification (SIC). Figures exclude 'internal' MOD expenditure such as pay and allowances. Industrial groupings are based on the SIC 1992 guidelines maintained by the Office for National Statistics. The figures have been rounded to the nearest £10M. **Differences between the totals and sums of the components are caused by this rounding.**

SIC(92)/SIC(03) Section		2002/03[1]	2003/04	2004/05	2005/06	2006/07
Total		**13 810** ‖	**14 640**	**14 490**	**16 030**	**16 490**
A, B, C	Agriculture, Fishing and Mining	- ‖	-	-	-	-
D	Manufacturing, excluding those industries itemised below	1 470 ‖	1 470	1 350	1 740	1 640
	29.6 Weapons & Ammunition	790 ‖	740	820	1 030	1 080
	30 Data Processing Equipment	170 ‖	180	110	70	50
	31 Other Electrical Engineering	170 ‖	180	150	180	200
	32 Electronics	640 ‖	600	910	1 160	1 000
	33 Precision Instruments	810 ‖	760	690	750	600
	34, 35.2, 35.4, 35.5 Motor Vehicles & Parts	130 ‖	170	220	330	300
	35.1 Shipbuilding & Repairing	1 070 ‖	1 160	1 060	1 100	1 150
	35.3 Aircraft & Spacecraft	2 380 ‖	2 050	1 810	1 730	1 960
E	Electricity, Gas & Water	190 ‖	210	230	260	280
F	Construction	990 ‖	1 190	1 230	1 310	1 380
G	Wholesale, Retail & Repair of Motor Vehicles	170 ‖	180	160	180	230
H, I [2]	55 Hotels & Restaurants	200 ‖	210	200	250	230
	60.1 Transport via railways	80 ‖	70	60	70	70
	60.2,60.3 Other Land Transport (incl. via pipelines)	70 ‖	70	20	30	20
	61,62,63 Water, Air and Auxiliary/freight supply transportation	420 ‖	490	380	370	450
	64 Post & Courier Services	10 ‖	10	10	10	10
	64.2 Telecommunications	320 ‖	530	310	300	330
J, K, L, M, N, O, P	Financial Services, Business Activities, Education, Health, & Other Service Activities excluding those industries itemised below [3] [4]	2 150 ‖	2 590	2 750	2 800	2 880
	70, 71 Real Estate & Renting	950 ‖	1 000	1 230	1 460	1 500
	72 Computer Services	640 ‖	800	790	930	1 110

VAT exclusive at Current Prices (£ million)

Source: DASA (Economic Statistics)

1. The break in series between 2002/03 and 2003/04 reflects the fact that for 2002/03 the Defence Bills Agency data was still based on Internal Account Codes (used under the old cash system), and was migrated to Resource Accounting Codes one year later than the accounting systems, on 1 April 2003.
2. The "Hotels, Restaurants and Transportation" category previously published in UKDS has been expanded this year to include a more detailed breakdown of the H and I divisions of the Standard Industrial Classification. This allows for a greater disaggregation of expenditure on transportation related activities such as auxillary and freight supply transport.
3. Includes MOD payments to AWE Management Ltd, who manage the Atomic Weapons Establishment on behalf of the MOD under a Government-owned/contractor-operated arrangement.
4. The quality of data available for the service industries is insufficient to identify these SICs separately.

23

Table 1.10 Estimated UK Employment Dependent on MOD Expenditure and Defence Exports

24

This table provides estimates of the number of full-time jobs supported in the UK by MOD expenditure and defence exports. The methodology is described in *Defence Statistics Bulletin No.5*, available on the DASA website. "Direct" employment is that generated in those companies providing the product or service directly to MOD, or that within the exporter. "Indirect" employment is that provided through "the supply chain" by sub-contractors or suppliers to the "direct" contractor. The figures reflect average full time equivalent in year. The figures exclude MOD service and civilian personnel, and are shown rounded to the nearest five thousand. **Differences between the totals and sums of the components are caused by this rounding.**

From 2002/03 onwards the numbers have been calculated using expenditure data derived from the MOD administrative systems that were introduced with Resource Accounting and Budgeting. The resulting changes to the methodology are described in *Addendum No 5a to Defence Statistics Bulletin*.

This table is outside the scope of National Statistics because the Defence exports data do not meet all of the high professional quality assurance standards set out in the National Statistics Code of Practice.

Thousands

	1997/98	2001/02 [3]	2002/03	2003/04	2004/05	2005/06	2006/07
Total Employment[1]	**340**	**295 ‖**	**305**	**315**	**310**	**310**	**305**
Direct	160	155 ‖	165	170	170	165	160
Indirect	180	140 ‖	140	145	140	145	145
Employment from MOD Expenditure	**230**	**235 ‖**	**245**	**250**	**240**	**260**	**255**
Direct	115	125 ‖	135	140	135	145 [r]	135
Indirect	115	110 ‖	110	110	105	120	115
Split by:							
Equipment Expenditure							
Direct	70	75 ‖	85	85	80	85	80
Indirect	75	65 ‖	75	70	70	75	75
Non-Equipment Expenditure							
Direct	50	55 ‖	50	55	55	60	55
Indirect	45	40 ‖	35	40	35	40	40
Employment from Defence Exports[1] [2] [4]	**110**	**60 ‖**	**60**	**65**	**70**	**50**	**55**
Direct	45	30 ‖	30	30	35	25	25
Indirect	65	30 ‖	30	30	35	30	30

Source: DASA (Economic Statistics)

1. The estimates of UK employment dependent on defence exports are based on estimates of those exports which are not of sufficient quality to be badged as National Statistics.

2. Figures calculated for "exports" are not derived directly from the financial figures for exports contained in **Table 1.14**. Adjustments are made for international collaborations, electronics and vehicle exports. Please refer to *Defence Statistics Bulletin No.5* for further discussion. In aggregate the adjustments to the total export figures were £114 million in 1997, £859 million in 1998, £499 million in 1999, £49 million in 2000, -£143 million in 2001, £74 million in 2002, £48 million in 2003, £115 million in 2004, -£134 million in 2005 and £22 million in 2006.

3. In July 2001, part of the Defence Evaluation & Research Agency (DERA) was established as QinetiQ plc. These employees are now included in the "direct" employment total.

4. The increase in employment dependent on defence exports in 2004/05 reflects an increase in defence export sales, orders and deliveries identified predominantly in the aerospace, electronics and shipbuilding sectors during 2004. The methodology used to derive the defence export figures used to produce the employment estimates is described in *Defence Statistics Bulletin No.5*, available on the DASA website.

CHAPTER 1 - FINANCE

INDUSTRY & EMPLOYMENT

Table 1.11 Estimated UK Regional Direct Employment Dependent on MOD Expenditure[1,2]

Tables **1.11**, **1.11a** & **1.11b** provide estimates of the number of direct full time jobs in the Government Office Regions of England, Scotland, Wales, Northern Ireland and the UK as a whole, supported in industry and commerce by MOD direct expenditure. **Table 1.11a** provides estimates of the number of direct jobs in UK industry and commerce dependent on direct MOD equipment expenditure. **Table 1.11b** provides estimates of the number of direct jobs in UK industry and commerce dependent on direct MOD non equipment expenditure. Direct employment is that generated in those companies providing the product or service to the MOD. Equipment expenditure covers those sums spent on producing equipment for the armed forces and goods for MOD, including expenditure on Research and Development, manufacture, and equipment support. Non equipment includes expenditure on items such as utilities (gas, water and electricity) and maintaining the defence estate.

The full methodology (which includes an assessment of the quality of the underlying data used to produce these estimates) is described in *DASA Defence Statistics Bulletin No.7*, available on the DASA website.

The figures exclude MOD service and civilian personnel. Total direct UK employment has been rounded to the nearest 5000 to align to the national employment estimates in **Table 1.10**, whilst individual regional totals are shown to the nearest 1000 full time equivalent. **Differences between the totals and sums of the components are caused by this rounding. Regional percentage breakdowns are based on the unrounded UK figures.**

The data in this table are outside the scope of National Statistics because they do not meet all of the high professional quality assurance standards set out in the National Statistics Code of Practice.

	Thousands						Percentage				
	2002/03	2003/04 [3]	2004/05 [3]	2005/06 [4]	2006/07		2002/03	2003/04	2004/05	2005/06	2006/07
United Kingdom	135	140	135	145 r	135		*100%*	*100%*	*100%*	*100%*	*100%*
England	118	126 r	123 r	130 r	126		89%	89%	90% r	91%	92%
East of England	13	12	10	11	8		*10%*	*9%*	*7%*	*8%*	*6%*
East Midlands	3	3	3	5	4		*2%*	*2%*	*2%*	*3%*	*3%*
London	10	10	13	9	9		*8%*	*7%*	*10%*	*6%*	*7%*
North East	2	3	2	2	3		*2%*	*2%*	*1%*	*2%*	*2%*
North West	14	17	15	15	17		*11%*	*12%*	*11%*	*10%* r	*13%*
South East	36	36	37	41 r	38		*27%*	*26%*	*27%*	*29%* r	*28%*
South West	30	35	35	37	37		*23%*	*25%*	*26%*	*26%*	*27%*
West Midlands	6	6	5	5	7		*5%*	*4%*	*4%*	*4%*	*5%*
Yorkshire & Humber	4	4	3	4	4		*3%*	*3%*	*2%*	*3%*	*3%*
Scotland	10	10	9	9	7		*8%*	*7%*	*7%*	*6%*	*5%*
Wales	2	3	2	2	2		*2%*	*2%*	*1%*	*1%*	*1%*
Northern Ireland	2	2	2	2	2		*2%*	*1%*	*1%*	*1%*	*1%*

Source: DASA(Economic Statistics)

1. Using the average UK turnover per full time equivalent may neglect potential differences in regional turnover per head. However, regional turnover per head at the level of SIC used in the employment estimates is not currently available from the ONS: the employment estimates for a number of industries/ products use 3 digit SIC level data, and the ONS only publish (limited) regional data derived from the Annual Business Inquiry (ABI) data at 2 digit level. The impact of using national employment averages is not likely to produce a significantly different output than if regional employment averages were available.
2. Estimates have been provided from 2002-03 onwards to reflect the available expenditure data derived from the MOD adminstrative systems that were introduced with Resource Accounting and Budgeting.
3. The revisions prior to 2005-06 are due to the correction of some very minor rounding anomalies.
4. The revisions to the regional employment numbers for 2005-06 reflect updated information relating to industry turnover from the Office for National Statistics which only became available after the publication of UKDS 2007. This in turn has resulted in very minor adjustments to the percentage breakdowns.

CHAPTER 1 - FINANCE

INDUSTRY & EMPLOYMENT

Table 1.11a Estimated UK Regional Direct Employment Dependent on MOD Equipment Expenditure[1,2]

Tables **1.11**, **1.11a** & **1.11b** provide estimates of the number of direct full time jobs in the Government Office Regions of England, Scotland, Wales, Northern Ireland and the UK as a whole, supported in industry and commerce by MOD direct expenditure. **Table 1.11a** provides estimates of the number of direct jobs in UK industry and commerce dependent on direct MOD equipment expenditure. **Table 1.11b** provides estimates of the number of direct jobs in UK industry and commerce dependent on direct MOD non equipment expenditure. Direct employment is that generated in those companies providing the product or service to the MOD. Equipment expenditure covers those sums spent on producing equipment for the armed forces and goods for MOD, including expenditure on Research and Development, manufacture, and equipment support. Non equipment includes expenditure on items such as utilities (gas, water and electricity) and maintaining the defence estate.

The full methodology (which includes an assessment of the quality of the underlying data used to produce these estimates) is described in *DASA Defence Statistics Bulletin No.7*, available on the DASA website.

The figures exclude MOD service and civilian personnel. Total direct UK employment has been rounded to the nearest 5000 to align to the national employment estimates in **Table 1.10**, whilst individual regional totals are shown to the nearest 1000 full time equivalent. **Differences between the totals and sums of the components are caused by this rounding. Regional percentage breakdowns are based on the unrounded UK figures.**

The data in this table are outside the scope of National Statistics because they do not meet all of the high professional quality assurance standards set out in the National Statistics Code of Practice.

| | Thousands | | | | | Percentage | | | | |
	2002/03	2003/04	2004/05	2005/06	2006/07	2002/03	2003/04	2004/05	2005/06 [4]	2006/07
United Kingdom	**85**	**85**	**80**	**85**	**80**	*100%*	*100%*	*100%*	*100%*	*100%*
England	**74**	**74**	**73**	**78**	**76**	*89%*	*89%*	*90%*	*93%*	*93%*
East of England	9	7	6	6	5	*11%*	*8%*	*7%*	*7%*	*7%*
East Midlands	2	2	2	3	3	*2%*	*2%*	*2%*	*3%*	*4%*
London	3	2	3	3	2	*4%*	*2%*	*4%*	*3%*	*3%*
North East	2	3	2	2	1	*2%*	*4%*	*2%*	*2%*	*2%*
North West	13	15	14	14	15	*16%*	*18%*	*17%*	*16%*	*18%*
South East	21	20	21	24	21	*25%*	*24%*	*26%*	*29%*	*26%*
South West	19	20	21	22	23	*23%*	*24%*	*26%*	*26%*	*28%*
West Midlands	4	4	3	4	4	*5%*	*5%*	*4%*	*5%* [r]	*5%*
Yorkshire & Humber	1	1	1	1	1	*1%*	*1%*	*1%*	*1%*	*2%*
Scotland	7	7	6	5	4	*8%*	*8%*	*7%*	*6%*	*5%*
Wales	1	1	1	1	1	*1%*	*1%*	*1%*	*1%*	*1%*
Northern Ireland	1	1	1	-	-	*1%*	*1%*	*1%*	*-* [r]	*-*

Source: DASA(Economic Statistics)

1. Using the average UK turnover per full time equivalent may neglect potential differences in regional turnover per head. However, regional turnover per head at the level of SIC used in the employment estimates is not currently available from the ONS: the employment estimates for a number of industries/ products use 3 digit SIC level data, and the ONS only publish (limited) regional data derived from the Annual Business Inquiry (ABI) data at 2 digit level. The impact of using national employment averages is not likely to produce a significantly different output than if regional employment averages were available.
2. Estimates have been provided from 2002-03 onwards to reflect the available expenditure data derived from the MOD adminstrative systems that were introduced with Resource Accounting and Budgeting.
4. The revisions to the regional employment numbers for 2005-06 reflect updated information relating to industry turnover from the Office for National Statistics which only became available after the publication of UKDS 2007. This in turn has resulted in very minor adjustments to the percentage breakdowns.

INDUSTRY & EMPLOYMENT

Table **1.11b** Estimated UK Regional Direct Employment Dependent on MOD Non Equipment Expenditure[1,2]

Tables 1.11, **1.11a** & **1.11b** provide estimates of the number of direct full time jobs in the Government Office Regions of England, Scotland, Wales, Northern Ireland and the UK as a whole, supported in industry and commerce by MOD direct expenditure. **Table 1.11a** provides estimates of the number of direct jobs in UK industry and commerce dependent on direct MOD equipment expenditure. **Table 1.11b** provides estimates of the number of direct jobs in UK industry and commerce dependent on direct MOD non equipment expenditure. Direct employment is that generated in those companies providing the product or service to the MOD. Equipment expenditure covers those sums spent on producing equipment for the armed forces and goods for MOD, including expenditure on Research and Development, manufacture, and equipment support. Non equipment includes expenditure on items such as utilities (gas, water and electricity) and maintaining the defence estate.

The full methodology (which includes an assessment of the quality of the underlying data used to produce these estimates) is described in *DASA Defence Statistics Bulletin No.7*, available on the DASA website.

The figures exclude MOD service and civilian personnel. Total direct UK employment has been rounded to the nearest 5000 to align to the national employment estimates in **Table 1.10**, whilst individual regional totals are shown to the nearest 1000 full time equivalent. **Differences between the totals and sums of the components are caused by this rounding. Regional percentage breakdowns are based on the unrounded UK figures.**

The data in this table are outside the scope of National Statistics because they do not meet all of the high professional quality assurance standards set out in the National Statistics Code of Practice.

	Thousands					Percentage				
	2002/03	2003/04	2004/05	2005/06 [4]	2006/07	2002/03	2003/04 [3]	2004/05 [3]	2005/06 [4]	2006/07
United Kingdom	50	55	55	60 [r]	55	100%	100%	100%	100%	100%
England	44	51	51	52	51	90%	90% [r]	91% [r]	90% [r]	91%
East of England	4	5	4	6	3	8%	9%	7%	10%	5%
East Midlands	1	1	1	2	1	2%	2%	2%	3% [r]	2%
London	7	8	10	6	7	14%	14%	18%	10% [r]	12%
North East	-	-	-	-	1	-	-	-	- [r]	2%
North West	1	2	1	1	3	2%	3%	2%	2%	5%
South East	15	16	16	17 [r]	16	31%	28%	29%	29% [r]	29%
South West	11	15	14	15	15	22%	26%	25%	26%	26%
West Midlands	2	2	2	2	3	4%	3%	4%	3%	6%
Yorkshire & Humber	3	3	2	3	2	6%	5%	4%	5%	4%
Scotland	3	3	3	4	3	6%	5%	5%	7%	5%
Wales	1	2	1	1	1	2%	3%	2%	2%	2%
Northern Ireland	1	1	1	1	1	2%	2%	2%	2%	2%

Source: DASA(Economic Statistics)

1. Using the average UK turnover per full time equivalent may neglect potential differences in regional turnover per head. However, regional turnover per head at the level of SIC used in the employment estimates is not currently available from the ONS: the employment estimates for a number of industries/ products use 3 digit SIC level data, and the ONS only publish (limited) regional data derived from the Annual Business Inquiry (ABI) data at 2 digit level. The impact of using national employment averages is not likely to produce a significantly different output than if regional employment averages were available.
2. Estimates have been provided from 2002-03 onwards to reflect the available expenditure data derived from the MOD adminstrative systems that were introduced with Resource Accounting and Budgeting.
3. The revisions prior to 2005-06 are due to the correction of some very minor rounding anomalies.
4. The revisions to the regional employment numbers for 2005-06 reflect updated information relating to industry turnover from the Office for National Statistics which only became available after the publication of UKDS 2007. This in turn has resulted in very minor adjustments to the percentage breakdowns.

INDUSTRY & EMPLOYMENT

Table **1.12** MOD Payments on Private Finance Initiative (PFI) Projects: 2007/2008[1]

This table provides a listing of PFI commitments and payments made to each project by MOD during the financial year 2007/08. Values represent payments made in year against contracts relating to the project and **not the capital value**. It is based on the 'signed' projects from the PFI Project database as at 1 April 2008 and payments data drawn from the Financial Management Shared Service Centre (FMSSC). This table is split into payment groups and individual PFI projects are shown in **alphabetical order**. **Table 1.12a** shows PFI contracts where forecast payments of £25 million or over are due in 2008/09. More detailed information concerning through life planned Unitary charge payments for all currently signed PFI contracts, can be found via the HM Treasury website at: http://www.hm-treasury.gov.uk/documents/public_private_partnerships/ppp_pfi_stats.cfm.

VAT inclusive at Current Prices (£ million)

Over £50 million (7 Projects)	
Allenby/Connaught	Main Building Redevelopment (MBR)
Attack Helicopter Training Service - Apache	Skynet 5
Colchester Garrison	Tri-Service White Fleet
Defence Fixed Telecommunications Service (DFTS)	
£25 - 50 million (7 Projects)	
"C" Vehicles	MOD-Wide Water and Wastewater (Project Aquatrine) - Package C
Defence Housing Executive - Information Systems (DOMIS)	Roll-On/Roll-Off (RORO) Strategic Sealift
Joint Services Command and Staff College	Training Administration and Financial Management Information Systems (TAFMIS)
MOD-Wide Water and Wastewater (Project Aquatrine) - Package A	
£10 - £25 million (10 Projects)	
Army Foundation College (AFC)	Future Provision of Marine Services (FPMS)[2]
ASTUTE Class Training Service (ACTS)	Heavy Equipment Transporters (HET)
Defence Sixth Form College (DSFC)	Medium Support Helicopter Aircrew Training Facility (MSHATF)
Devonport Support Services - ARMADA	Northwood Headquarters
Field Electrical Power Supplies (FEPS)	Tornado GR4 Synthetic Training Service (TSTS)
£5 - 10 million (8 Projects)	
Bristol, Bath and Portsmouth Family Quarters	Material Handling Equipment (MHE) - (Follow on)
Defence Animal Centre (DAC)	MOD-Wide Water and Wastewater (Project Aquatrine) - Package B
Fire Fighting Training Units (FFTU)	Tri-Service Materials Handling Service
Marine Support to Range and Aircrew Services	VLF Naval Communications Service[3]
Up to £5 million (15 Projects)	
Central Scotland Family Quarters (HQ)	RAF Lossiemouth Family Quarters
Commercial Satellite Communication Service (INMARSAT)[4]	RAF Lyneham Sewerage
Hawk Synthetic Training Service	RAF Mail
Hazardous Stores Information System (HSIS)	RAF Sentry E3D Aircrew Training
Lynx Aircrew Training	Tidworth Water & Sewerage (Thames Water)
Portsmouth Housing 2	Wattisham & Woodbridge Married Quarters
RAF Cosford/RAF Shawbury Family Quarters	Yeovilton Family Quarters
RAF Fylingdales (Power)	

Source: MOD Private Finance Unit & DASA (Economic Statistics)

1. Future Strategic Tanker Aircraft (FSTA) project started 2007/08 but no payments made in year.
2. New PFI project added this year.
3. Previously 'Royal Navy Fleet Communications'.
4. Commercial Satellite Communication Service (INMARSAT) contract has been novated to Paradigm, with whom management responsibility now rests.

Table **1.12a** PFI Projects with Planned MOD Unitary Charge Payments[1,2] over £25 million: 2008/09

VAT inclusive at Current Prices (£ million)

Over £50 million (7 Projects)	
Allenby/Connaught	Main Building Redevelopment (MBR)
Colchester Garrison	Skynet 5
Defence Fixed Telecommunications Service (DFTS)	Tri-Service White Fleet
Future Provision of Marine Services (FPMS)	
£25 - £50 million (6 Projects)	
Attack Helicopter Training Service - Apache	MOD-Wide Water and Wastewater (Project Aquatrine) - Package A
"C" Vehicles	MOD-Wide Water and Wastewater (Project Aquatrine) - Package C
Joint Services Command and Staff College	Roll-On/Roll-Off (RORO) Strategic Sealift

Source: MOD Private Finance Unit & DASA (Economic Statistics)

1. The Unitary Charge is the regular service payment made to the private sector partner for the provision of services and is calculated in accordance with the price and payment mechanism.

2. Planned expenditure may not be directly comparable to the actual spend reported in 2008/09 because unexpected additional works and services (albeit controlled and managed by agreed control procedures) may be incurred.

CHAPTER 1 - FINANCE

TRADE

This section contains information on defence trade. This includes the estimated value of imports and exports of defence equipment, estimates of total export deliveries, orders of defence equipment and services and payments made for services consumed by MOD establishments overseas. **Table 1.13** presents the estimated value of defence equipment imports and exports split by commodity type and origin/destination. **Table 1.14** estimates total export deliveries and orders of defence equipment and services. **Table 1.15** presents the estimated value of MOD Balance of Payments for Trade in Services.

The estimate of total export deliveries is made up of 'identified defence equipment exports' and 'estimates of additional aerospace equipment and services'. Data on exports are provided by HM Revenue & Customs (HMRC) with supplementary data from the Society of British Aerospace Companies (SBAC). Information on export orders are supplied by the UK Trade & Investment Defence & Security Organisation (UKTI DSO). HMRC provide information on deliveries of military or 'other than civil' goods which cross the UK borders. All equipment exports that are reported to UK customs are classified with tariff codes and we use these to determine defence exports. SBAC data covers sales by UK aerospace companies to foreign civil customers and foreign military aerospace industries and military end-users. UKTI DSO collects data on defence export contracts and they relate to orders placed. These data are collected from the UKTI DSO publication 'The World Defence Export Market' compiled via a quarterly survey with known UK defence contractors.

MOD Trade in Services are provisions of services between UK residents and non-residents (e.g. training, cleaning services, IT support etc) and transactions in goods which are not freighted out of the country in which they take place. They are published in an ONS 'First Release' and 'The Pink Book'.

More information outlining the methodology behind these tables can be found in DASA *Defence Statistics Bulletin No 4* and in the National Statistics Quality Review, detailing Trade Statistics and MOD Balance of Payments Statistics respectively. Further information outlining recent developments with Trade Statistics and an assessment of the quality of the underlying data is given in *DASA Defence Statistics Bulletin No.8*. This is available on the DASA website.

Main Findings

Exports of Defence equipment and services (Tables 1.13 & 1.14)

- Total estimated UK deliveries of exports increased between 2006 and 2007 (from £4.7 billion in 2006 to £5.5 billion in 2007). A contributing factor to this increase has been a sharp increase in the value of identified exports in the Warships category in 2007 following an overseas delivery of three Offshore Patrol Vessels.

- The UK identified export orders increased by £4.1 billion between 2006 and 2007 to £9.7 billion. This significant increase in export orders can be attributed to a large order from Saudi Arabia for Typhoon aircraft, and orders from Oman and Trinidad & Tobago for offshore patrol vessels.

Balance of Payments: Trade in Services (Table 1.15)

- In 2007, the MOD's estimated Balance of Payments for Trade in Services was £2.3 billion in deficit made up of £2.8 billion debits and £0.4 billion receipts. The deficit has increased by £359 million compared to the previous year.

Improving the quality of defence related imports and exports data

Defence Analytical Services & Advice (DASA) publishes statistics on defence exports and imports annually in UK Defence Statistics (UKDS) (Tables **1.13** & **1.14** in 2008). Data are obtained from three different sources: HMRC, SBAC and the UKTI DSO.

There have been problems with the definition, consistency and coverage of defence related exports data over recent years. DASA has endeavoured to ensure that defence exports statistics are 'joined up' across Government. The Defence Trade Statistics Working Group (DTSWG) with representatives from across the relevant Government departments was convened in order to review the quality of the data, the issue of trade suppressions on trade statistics and to ensure consistency and definition across Government.

Subject to EU regulations, HMRC collect data on visible (goods) imports and export trade. However some data that are currently collected cannot always be segregated to indicate what is specifically military trade. Trade data are broken down using a standardised EU commodity coding system and while goods in the majority of the commodity codes that are currently employed can be identified as distinctly military or non-military, there are several codes which contain both military and civil trade (dual use). Presently there are no reliable positive identification procedures to determine what proportion of the trade reported in these commodity codes can be classed as military.

Recent developments which have continued to affect the quality of defence related imports and exports data include:

- the impact of changes to the internationally agreed tariff codes used for recording goods exports.

- the nature of a large increase in aerospace sales reported by the Society for British Aerospace Companies (SBAC).

- the feasibility of collecting export and import data via existing departmental surveys.

- the continued robustness of the current methodology.

- the simplification of the EU Intrastat System used to capture intra EU trade flows.

More information outlining progress with these developments, and an assessment of the quality of the underlying data is given in DASA *Defence Statistics Bulletin No.8*. This is available on the DASA website.

It is important to note that following the dismantling of the Defence Export Services Organisation (DESO) in July 2007, the governance framework which underpins the production and development of defence export and import (deliveries) statistics remains uncertain. These issues are currently the subject of a submission to be considered shortly by ministers in MOD, BERR, DfID and FCO.

CHAPTER 1 - FINANCE

TRADE

Table 1.13 Estimated Imports & Exports of Defence Equipment (Goods)

This table presents data on the value of defence equipment imports and exports. This information is broken down by commodity grouping and broad geographic region. Data are based on HM Revenue & Customs information relating to defence equipment reported to UK Customs. Defence equipment is identified by an agreed set of tariff codes intended to capture movements of military equipment. Over the period covered by the table, changes have been made to the list of 'identified' defence equipment by, for example, the removal of two HM Customs codes for aerospace from 1997. Further details are given in *Defence Statistics Bulletin No.4* and in the *National Statistics Quality Review on Trade Statistics*. For progress relating to improvements to the quality of defence trade statistics, please refer to the notes at the start of this section on Trade. These estimates have been subject to a variety of revisons and methodological updates in recent years including changes to the internationally agreed tariff codes used for recording goods exports. These changes are described in DASA *Defence Statistics Bulletin No.8*.

The data in this table are outside the scope of National Statistics because they do not meet all of the high professional quality assurance standards set out in the National Statistics Code of Practice.

Current Prices (£ million)

	1997	2001	2002	2003	2004	2005	2006	2007
Identified Imports	**1 288**	**1 804**	**1 645 II**	**712**	**700**	**652 II**	**1 098**	**734**
Split by Commodity:								
Armoured Fighting Vehicles and Parts	42	21	22 II	19	40	52 II	87	86
Military Aircraft and Parts	1 038	1 609	1 292 II	440	403	280 II	677	372
Warships	1	-	- II	-	2	- II	-	-
Guns, Small Arms and Parts	46	22	52 II	55	51	62 II	96	81
Guided Weapons, Missiles and Parts	113	138	217 II	163	160	231 II	188	127
Ammunition	9	1	9 II	17	20	12 II	15	30
Optical Equipment and Training Simulators	38	13	53 II	19	24	15 II	34	39
Split by Origin:								
NATO Countries and Other Europe	1 087	1 718	1 371 II	566	576	581 II	904	638
Asia and Far East	93	1	104 II	53	42	35 II	120	51
Latin America and Caribbean	6	2	20 II	2	4	1 II	2	7
Middle East and North Africa	93	80	136 II	84	70	28 II	59	24
Other Africa	9	3	15 II	7	7	7 II	13	14
Identified Exports[1]	**3 359**	**1 533**	**942**	**992**	**1 391**	**1 391 II**	**1 358**	**2 070**
Split by Commodity:								
Armoured Fighting Vehicles and Parts	201	54	77	63	62	60 II	76	76
Military Aircraft and Parts	2 296	1 207	584	734	957	740 II	866	899
Warships[2]	256	1	-	-	58	58 II	-	769
Guns, Small Arms and Parts	95	75	53	48	72	199 II	77	87
Guided Weapons, Missiles and Parts	427	175	193	121	219	291 II	250	171
Ammunition	20	9	19	5	5	6 II	3	4
Optical Equipment and Training Simulators	64	12	16	21	18	36 II	86	64
Split by Destination:								
NATO Countries and Other Europe	1 034	969	609	467	801	832 II	914	764
Asia and Far East	204	196	136	273	235	317 II	254	1 054
Latin America and Caribbean	132	19	5	6	15	5 II	6	12
Middle East and North Africa	1 985	320	185	221	250	207 II	172	196
Other Africa	3	28	8	26	90	29 II	12	44

Source: HM Revenue & Customs

1. Changes to the internationally agreed tariff codes used for recording goods exports (see Annex C of the Annual Report on Strategic Export Controls) had originally contributed to an apparent increase in the deliveries figures from 2005 to 2006. The further amalgamation of military and civil codes which has resulted in a discontinuity in the code set used to compile these data has been investigated. It was not clear how far the increase reported reflected a true increase in the value of military goods exported as opposed to the inclusion of civil goods previously excluded. Further investigation of the HMRC dataset revealed a large element of this reported increase in 2006 (recorded against one of the dual use codes) as being probably civil in nature. The 2006 figure was therefore revised prior to publication in UKDS 2007.

2. The large increase in the value of identified exports in the Warships category in 2007 is due to the overseas delivery of three Offshore Patrol Vessels.

TRADE

Table 1.14 Estimates of Total Export Deliveries & Orders: Defence Equipment & Services

This table provides an estimate of total defence export activity relating to the UK. It uses data on additional aerospace equipment and services from a survey undertaken by the Society of British Aerospace Companies. Aerospace services include training, consultancy and project support related to the export activity. The second part of the table provides data on identified export orders of defence equipment and services. This illustrates the relationship between export orders and actual export deliveries. These estimates have been subject to a variety of revisons and methodological updates in recent years including changes to the internationally agreed tariff codes used for recording goods exports. These changes are described in DASA *Defence Statistics Bulletin No.8.*

The data in this table are outside the scope of National Statistics because they do not meet all of the high professional quality assurance standards set out in the National Statistics Code of Practice.

Current Prices (£ million)

	1995	1997	2001	2002	2003	2004	2005		2006	2007
Estimated Total Export Deliveries: Equipment & Services	**4 723**	**6 684**	**4 216**	**4 120**	**4 545**	**5 162**	**4 527**	||	**4 697**	**5 474**
Of which:										
Identified Defence Equipment Exports	2 076	3 359	1 533	942	992	1 391	1 391	||	1 358	2 070
Estimates of Additional Aerospace Equipment and Services	2 647	3 325	2 683	3 178	3 553	3 771	3 136		3 339	3 404

Current Prices (£ million)

	1995	1997	2001	2002	2003	2004	2005	2006	2007 [2]
Identified Export Orders for Defence Equipment and Services[1]	**4 970**	**5 540**	**4 160**	**5 041**	**4 882**	**4 546**	**3 989**	**5 527**	**9 651**
Split by Equipment Type:									
Air Sector	3 456	3 193	3 245	3 553	3 526	3 199	2 491	4 133	7 525
Land Sector	535	656	341	509	303	475	584	670	762
Sea Sector	71	368	50	464	252	209	369	280	1 017
Not Specified	908	1 323	524	515	801	663	546	444	347

Source: UKTI Defence and Security Organisation

1. Figures for export orders are taken from the UKTI DSO survey of known Defence Contractors.

2. The large increase in the 2007 export orders figures can be attributed to a large order from Saudi Arabia for Typhoon aircraft (valued initially at £4.4 billion) and orders from Oman and Trinidad and Tobago for offshore patrol vessels.

CHAPTER 1 - FINANCE

TRADE

Table 1.15 Ministry of Defence Estimated Balance of Payments for Trade in Services

Balance of Payments is a measure of the UK's trading account with the rest of the world. Trade in Services are provisions of services (e.g. training, cleaning services, IT support etc) between UK residents and non-residents, and transactions in goods which are not freighted out of the country in which they take place; these transactions are not recorded in the official 'Trade in Goods' statistics. A detailed discussion of these concepts can by found in the latest edition of The Pink Book published by the Office for National Statistics. More details are available in *Defence Statistics Bulletin No 4* or in the *National Statistics Quality Review report* on *Balance of Payments: Trade in Services*.

The data in this table are outside the scope of National Statistics because they do not meet all of the high professional quality assurance standards set out in the National Statistics Code of Practice.

Current prices (£ million)

	1995	1997	2001	2002	2003 [1]	2004	2005	2006	2007
Net Balance	**-1 691**	**-1 394**	**-1 627**	**-1 543 II**	**-2 021**	**-1 762**	**-1 723**	**-1 979**	**-2 338**
Total Debits	**2 057**	**1 600**	**1 836**	**1 764**	**2 411**	**2 200**	**2 158**	**2 471**	**2 763**
Expenditure[2]									
Germany	1 038	848	1 035	799	974	1 190	1 237	1 244	1 501
Other Identified NATO Countries	684	406	492	731	1 139	801	573	755	881
Mediterranean	135	158	148	156	173	168	182	226	175
Far East	6	21	-	-	-	-	-	-	-
Other Areas	194	167	160	78	125	41	166	245	206
Total Credits	**366**	**206**	**209**	**221**	**390**	**438**	**435**	**492**	**425**
Receipts[3]									
Receipts from US Forces in UK	136	110	161	154	142	126	128	126	116
Other Receipts[4]	230	96	48	67 II	248	312	307	366	309

Source: DASA (Economic Statistics)

1. The increase in 'Total Debits' in 2003 was largely attributable to increased spending on services as a result of military activity in Iraq.
2. Based on drawings of foreign exchange.
3. A mix of export sales and receipts from other Government and International Organisations for services provided overseas and to overseas forces based in the UK.
4. The increase in 'Other Receipts' from 2003 is due to the improvement in the methodology used to identify receipts data.

CHAPTER 1 - FINANCE

DEFENCE CONTRACTS

This section presents an analysis of contracts placed, major equipment projects and payments made by the MOD. **Table 1.16** shows the number and value of contracts placed by type during 2007/08 and earlier years. **Table 1.17** presents more information on the MOD's major equipment projects. **Table 1.18** provides a list, by broad-banded value, of organisations paid £5 million or more during 2007/08. Following requests from UK industry, **Table 1.18a** provides a further dimension on the data contained within **Table 1.18** by presenting the individual subsidiary organisations "rolled up" into their holding companies. These data are based on information from the Financial Management Shared Service Centre (FMSSC) – formerly the Defence Bills Agency (DBA) – who are responsible for setting up and paying the majority of the MOD contracts issued each year.

Information on Major Equipment Projects comes from the "Major Projects Report". This details the largest post Main-Gate Approval Projects along with the largest pre Main-Gate Approval Projects. The full report provides a summary of each project's current status and progress to date. It also provides comparisons on current forecast costs and in-service dates. Smart Procurement stresses the importance of allocating appropriate resources in the early stages to reduce risk and increase confidence before the main investment decision is made. This is known as the Smart Procurement Acquisition Cycle. Under Resource Accounting and Budgeting all costs are at estimated outturn prices and include 'new' types of cost such as the cost of capital charge.

Main Findings

Contracts by Type (Table 1.16)

- In 2007/08 MOD HQ placed just over 22,900 contracts with a collective value of around £14.4 billion. The number of contracts placed in 2007/08 remains roughly the same as was reported for 2006/07, whereas the value has decreased by nearly 50% (£13.8 billion) over the same period. The increase in contract value in 2006/07 was due to the placing of a multi billion pound contract with Aspire Defence Holdings and the removal of this contract from the 2007/08 calculations sees a return to historical levels of contract value. Please note that most contract payments are not made during the year in which the contract is placed.

- Of the total value of MOD HQ contracts placed in 2007/08 around 47% were priced by competition.

Major Equipment Projects (Table 1.17)

- The largest post Main-Gate equipment project by value is the Type 45 Destroyer (£6.5 billion). This is followed by the Astute Class Submarine (£3.8 billion) and the Nimrod Maritime Reconnaissance and Attack Mk4 (£3.5 billion).

CHAPTER 1 - FINANCE

DEFENCE CONTRACTS

Table **1.16** Contracts Placed: By Type

This table provides an analysis of MOD new contracts and value of amendments to **existing contracts** broken down by contract type. It includes contracts set up for payment through the Financial Management Shared Service Centre (FMSSC) - formerly the Defence Bills Agency (DBA) - who are responsible for the payment of the majority of MOD contracts.

Current Prices (£ million)/Percentage

	1990/91	1997/98	2001/02	2002/03	2003/04	2004/05	2005/06	2006/07 [1]	2007/08
Total Value of MOD HQ Contracts Placed[2]	**7 000**	**8 073**	**13 136**	**12 815**	**13 107**	**14 888**	**18 242**	**28 148**	**14 388**
Percentage of Total Value:									
Contracts Priced by Competition	44	67	61	60	70	65	51	62	36
Contracts Priced by Reference to Market Forces[3]	19	8	8	8	9	8	7	7	11
Contracts Priced on Estimates at Outset or as soon as possible thereafter[4]	23	20	29	22	18	23	35	22	29
Contracts Priced on Actual Costs with Incentives to Minimise Cost[4]	13	1	2	10	3	4	7	9	24
Contracts Priced on Actual Costs plus a % Fee[4]	1	4	-	-	-	-	-	-	-

Number/Percentage

	1990/91	1997/98	2001/02	2002/03	2003/04	2004/05	2005/06	2006/07	2007/08
Total Number of MOD HQ Contracts Placed[2]	**99 000**	**91 481**	**47 892**	**45 569**	**36 610**	**27 419**	**25 865**	**22 712**	**22 910**
Percentage of Total Number:									
Contracts Priced by Competition	17	47	35	34	37	40	41	41	40
Contracts Priced by Reference to Market Forces[3]	68	37	48	37	41	28	33	31	31
Contracts Priced on Estimates at Outset or as soon as possible thereafter[4]	13	15	17	28	21	31	24	27	26
Contracts Priced on Actual Costs with Incentives to Minimise Cost[4]	1	-	-	1	1	1	2	1	3
Contracts Priced on Actual Costs plus a % Fee[4]	1	1	-	-	-	-	-	-	-

Source: MOD Commercial Project Enablement Team (CPET) and Defence Estates

1. The increase in the overall value of MOD contracts in 2006/07 and the subsequent fall in value in 2007/08 can be attributed to the placing of a £9 billion competitively let contract in 2006/07. This one contract has also impacted on the split between the value of competitively let contracts and the other categories.
2. Includes amendments which had financial implications for existing contracts.
3. Includes the use of informal competitive tendering procedures and commercial price lists.
4. Priced by reference to the Government profit formula.
5. The variation between 2001/02 and 2002/03 in number of contracts placed both by "reference to Market Forces" and "priced on estimates at outset" are due to a combination of increased requirements for Operation Telic and an internal reclassification of contracts in both of these categories.

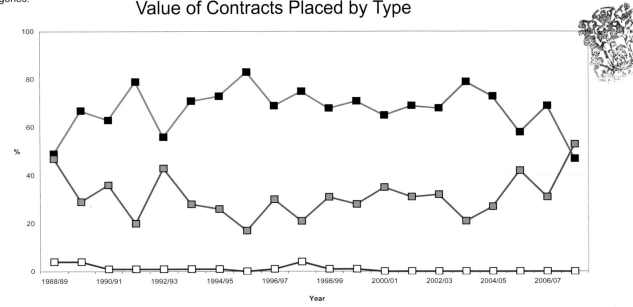

Value of Contracts Placed by Type

legend: competition | actual costs plus a % fee | other

CHAPTER 1 - FINANCE

DEFENCE CONTRACTS

Table 1.17 Major Equipment Projects

This table shows the MOD's major equipment projects as at 31 March 2007. It details the 20 largest projects on which the main investment decision has been taken (post Main-Gate) and the 10 largest projects yet to reach that point (pre Main-Gate). The information is taken from the *Major Projects Report* (http://www.nao.org.uk/publications/nao_reports/07-08/070898ii.pdf), relating to 31 March 2007, which provides a summary of each project's current status and progress to date. **The *Major Projects Report* was changed in MPR 2007 to remove forecast In Service Dates to reflect the Department's policy on public release of Assessment Phase project information.**
Costs are on a resource basis at outturn prices. Forecast costs include accruals, VAT (less recoverable elements), resource elements such as interest on capital and inflation factors. Pre 1999 figures have been uplifted to 99/00 prices. *Major Projects Report* costs relating to the pre-Main Gate projects are costs of the Assessment phase only. For post Main-Gate projects, costs are of the Demonstration and Manufacture phases.

Project Initiation Approval (Initial Gate)	Major Project Approval (Main-Gate)

The following diagram shows the CADMID cycle which is the basis for MOD Smart Procurement. The main investment decision is taken at Main-Gate, ie post assessment phase with the aim of ensuring there is a high level of confidence in achieving time, cost and performance targets. Further information is contained in the Major Projects report.

Concept > Assessment > Demonstration > Manufacture > In-Service > Disposal

As at 31 March 2007	MPR2007			
Post Main Gate Major Equipment Projects (Projects in Demonstration and Manufacture Phase only)	In-Service date Forecast or Actual	Financial Years of Peak Expenditure[1]	Forecast Cost (£ million)	Change in Cost (£ million) from MPR2006
A400M	2011	2009 & 2010	2 629	13
Astute Class Submarine	2008	2001 & 2005	3 798	142
Beyond Visual Range Air-To-Air Missile (BVRAAM)	2013	2009 & 2012	1 168	-36
Bowman	2004	2004 & 2005	2 009	- 10 [2]
Brimstone	2005	1999 & 2005	899	-1
C Vehicle Capability[3]	2006	2019 & 2020	703	-
Falcon[4]	2010	2008 & 2011	292	-
Guided Multiple Launch Rocket System	2007	2006 & 2010	91	-172
Joint Combat Aircraft (JCA)[5]	..	2005 & 2007	1 858	- 58
Merlin Mk 1 Capability Sustainment Programme[4]	2014	2009 & 2010	832	-
Next Generation Anti-Armour Weapon (NLAW)	2008	2007 & 2008	318	4
Nimrod Maritime Reconnaissance and Attack Mk4	2010	2002 & 2004	3 500	- 16
Precision Guided Bomb (PGB)	2007	2006 & 2007	277	-67 [2]
Soothsayer[4]	2008	2007 & 2010	195	-
Sting Ray Lightweight Torpedo Life Extension and Capability Upgrade	2006	2007 & 2008	577	- 12 [2]
Support Vehicle	2008	2009 & 2010	1 263	- 75
Terrier	2009	2008 & 2009	299	3
Type 45 Destroyer	2010	2003 & 2004	6 464	354
Typhoon[6]	2003	2006 & 2008	*	*
Watchkeeper[4]	2010	2009 & 2010	901	-

Source: Defence Equipment & Support

As at 31 March 2007	MPR 2007
Pre Main Gate Major Equipment Projects (Projects in Assessment Phase only)	Forecast Cost (£ million)
Future Aircraft Carrier (CVF)	299
Future Integrated Soldier Technology (FIST)	36
Future Rapid Effects System	618
Future Strategic Tanker Aircraft (FSTA)	37
Indirect Fire Precision Attack (IFPA)	67
Maritime, Airborne, Surveillance, and Control (MASC)	7
Military Afloat Reach & Sustainability (MARS)[5]	*
Search and rescue - Helicopter (SAR-H)	12
UKCEC Frigate and Destroyer Programme	55
UK Military Flying Training System (UKMFTS) - Holistic	30

Source: Defence Equipment & Support

1. Financial Year commencing 1 April - not necessarily concurrent years.
2. Forecast figures in MPR 2006 were revised after the publication of UKDS 2007. When comparing published UKDS 2007 forecast and latest MPR 2007 forecasts the differences will not align (See Pages 30, 106 and 118 of the *Major Projects Report* for further details: http://www.nao.org.uk/publications/nao_reports/07-08/070898ii.pdf.
3. PFI Service with annual service payment.
4. Cost comparison not possible as project did not appear in previous MPR.
5. The tailored Demonstration Main Gate noted but did not approve In Service Date (ISD).
6. Cost data excluded on grounds of commercial sensitivity.

CHAPTER 1 - FINANCE

DEFENCE CONTRACTS

Table 1.18 Organisations paid £5 million or more by the Ministry of Defence in 2007/08

This table shows a listing of the UK and foreign owned organisations, including defence suppliers and intermediate bodies paid through the Financial Management Shared Service Centre (FMSSC) - formally the Defence Bills Agency (DBA). The term 'defence suppliers' includes defence contractors, Defence Agencies and other Government Departments. The FMSSC is responsible for the majority of such payments (around 95% by value) made by MOD. Other payments are made, for example, via British Defence Staff (United States), MOD Trading Funds and through local cash offices. The table is split into payment groups with the organisations shown in **alphabetical order**. Company and organisation names have been reproduced (at the 1 April 2008 position) directly from the truncated entries recorded on the FMSSC database and may appear in a shortened format in places. **Where a contract is novated during the year, annual payments are shown against the new 'owner' (company or entity) of that contract.**

VAT exclusive at Current Prices (£ million)

Over £500 million (5 Organisations)

AWE Management Ltd	EDS Defence Ltd	Westland Helicopters Ltd
BAE Systems (Operations) Ltd	QinetiQ Ltd	

£250 - £500 million (10 Organisations)

BAE Systems Electronics Ltd	British Telecommunications PLC	NETMA
BAE Systems Land Systems (Munitions & Ordnance) Ltd	Debut Services Ltd[1]	Rolls Royce Power Engineering PLC
BAE Systems Land Systems (Weapons & Vehicles) Ltd	Defence Science & Technology Laboratory	
BAE Systems Surface Fleet Solutions	Devonport Royal Dockyard Ltd	

£100 - £250 million (26 Organisations)

AMEC Turner Ltd	General Dynamics United Kingdom Ltd	Purple Foodservice Solutions Ltd
Aspire Defence Ltd	Kellogg Brown & Root Ltd	Raytheon Systems Ltd
Babcock Support Services Ltd	Man Truck & Bus UK Ltd	Rolls-Royce PLC
BAE Systems Integrated System Technologies Ltd	Marshall Of Cambridge Aerospace Ltd	Serco Ltd
Carillion Enterprise Ltd	MBDA UK Ltd	Thales Air Defence Ltd
Defence Support Group (DSG)[2]	Meteorological Office	Thales UK Ltd
Europaams SAS	Modern Housing Solutions (Prime) Ltd	The Boeing Company
Flagship Training Ltd	Paradigm Secure Communications Ltd	VT Land (Whitefleet Management) Ltd
Fleet Support Ltd	Pride (Serp) Ltd	

£50 - £100 million (25 Organisations)

Aviation Training International Ltd	IBM UK Ltd	Royal & Sun Alliance Insurance PLC
Babcock Dyncorp Ltd	Landmarc Support Services Ltd	Selex Sensors and Airborne Systems Ltd
Babcock Marine (Clyde) Ltd	Lockheed Martin UK INSYS Ltd	Shell Marine Products Ltd
BAE Systems Marine Ltd	McDonnell Douglas Corporation	Sodexho Defence Services Ltd
BP International Ltd	Modus Services Ltd	Thales Naval Ltd
British Energy Direct Ltd	Northrop Grumman Overseas Service Corporation	Thales Underwater Systems Ltd
CEPSA	NP Aerospace Ltd	Ultra Electronics Ltd
Defence Aviation Repair Agency (DARA)[2]	Raytheon/Lockheed Martin Javelin Joint Venture	
HCR Ltd	RMPA Services PLC	

£25 - £50 million (44 Organisations)

Air Partner PLC	FBS Ltd	NATS (En Route) PLC
ALC (SPC) Ltd	Foreland Shipping Ltd	Northrop Grumman Information Technology International Inc
AMEC(AGL) Ltd	FR Aviation Ltd	Northwestern Shiprepairers And Shipbuilders Ltd
Annington Receivables Ltd	Fujitsu Services Ltd	OCCAR-EA
Aramark Ltd	Guy's & St Thomas NHS Foundation Trust	Reserve Forces and Cadet Association[3]
BAE Systems (Defence Systems) Ltd	Hess Energy Trading Company (UK)	Selex Communications Ltd
BAE Systems Land Systems Pinzgau Ltd	Interserve (Defence) Ltd	Serco-Denholm Ltd
Brey Utilities Ltd	Kuwait Petroleum International Aviation Company (UK) Ltd	Steria Services Ltd
Cap Gemini UK PLC	Lockheed Martin Aeronautics Company	Thales Optronics Ltd
Chapman Freeborn Airchartering Ltd	Lockheed Martin Aerospace Systems Integration Corporation	The Services Sound and Vision Corporation
Coast To Coast Water Ltd	Lockheed Martin Overseas Corporation	The United Kingdom Hydrographic Office
Compass Services (UK) Ltd	Lockheed Martin UK Ltd	Turner Facilities Management Ltd
Cooneen Watts & Stone Ltd	Logica CMG UK Ltd	VT Aerospace Ltd
Defence Management (Watchfield) Ltd	M & S Shipping (International) Ltd	VT Communications Ltd
Defense Finance and Accounting Service Columbus	Mansell Construction Services Ltd	

Source: DASA (Economic Statistics)

DEFENCE CONTRACTS

Table 1.18 Organisations paid £5 million or more by the Ministry of Defence in 2007/08 (continued)

VAT exclusive at Current Prices (£ million)

£10 - £25 million (96 Organisations)

A & P Falmouth Ltd	E2V Technologies (UK) Ltd	Paradigm Services Ltd
A & P Tyne Ltd	EADS Defence and Security Systems Ltd	Perkins Engines Company Ltd
AAH Pharmaceuticals Ltd	Eastbury Park Ltd	Qioptiq Ltd
Aerosystems International Ltd	ESSO Petroleum Company Ltd	Rail Settlement Plan Ltd
Agustawestland International Ltd	Eurocopter	Raytheon Company
Airborne Systems Ltd	Excel Aviation Ltd	Receiver General for Canada
Alfred McAlpine Business Services Ltd	Falcon Support Services Ltd	Rheinmetall Waffe Munition GmbH
Arval PHH Business Solutions Ltd	Fast Training Services Ltd	Right Management Ltd
Astrum (UK) Ltd	Fasttrax Ltd	Rockwell Collins UK Ltd
Atkins Consultants Ltd	FB Heliservices Ltd	Rolls-Royce Turbomeca Ltd
Avenance PLC	Foreign and Commonwealth Office	RUAG Ammotec
Babcock International Group PLC	GB Oils Ltd	Ryder Deutschland GmbH
BAE Systems Hagglunds AB	GE Aviation Systems Ltd	Saab AB (PUBL)
Barclays Bank PLC	Genistics Ltd	Scottish Power Energy Retail Ltd
Barloworld Handling Ltd	Goodrich Control Systems Ltd	Sellafield Ltd
Bechtel Ltd	Hawker Beechcraft Ltd	Serco Denholm Marine Services Ltd
Bovis Lend Lease Ltd	Haymills (Contractors) Ltd	SHAPE
BP Oil International Ltd	Henry Brothers (Magherafelt) Ltd	Software Box Ltd
British Gas Trading Ltd	Hesco Bastion Ltd	SSAFA Family Health Services
Britten-Norman Aircraft Ltd	Hirtenberger Defence Systems GmbH & Co Kg	SSE Energy Supply Ltd
CAE (UK) PLC	Inchcape Shipping Services Ltd	Supacat Ltd
CAE Aircrew Training Services PLC	Inviron Ltd	Systems Consultants Services Ltd
Centerprise International Ltd	Iturri SA	Thales Avionics Ltd
Central Office of Information	John Graham (Dromore) Ltd	Thales Training & Simulation (Ace) Ltd
Chemring Counter Measures Ltd	Mass Consultants Ltd	Thales Training & Simulation (Merlin) Ltd
Chevron Singapore Pte Ltd	Microsoft Ireland Operations Ltd	Ultralife Batteries (UK) Ltd
Commonwealth War Graves Commission	Minerva Education And Training Ltd	United Tool Distributors Ltd
Compass Group UK and Ireland Ltd	NAAFI	US Treasury
Cranfield University	NC3A	Vega Group PLC
David Brown Engineering Ltd	NSAF Ltd	VT Land Ltd
Defence Training Services Ltd	Office of Communications (OFCOM)	VT Maritime Affairs Ltd
DHL Global Forwarding (UK) Ltd	Organisation for Joint Armaments Cooperation Executive Admin	VT Shipbuilding Ltd

£5 - £10 million (109 Organisations)[4]

Alert Communications Ltd	CQC Ltd	KPMG LLP
Anixter Ltd	Cubic Defense Applications Inc	LA International Computer Consultants Ltd
Argyll & Bute Council	Deflog VQ Trust Ltd	Lockheed Martin Corporation
Atkins Advantage Technical Consulting Ltd	Deloitte & Touche LLP	Lockheed Martin UK Integrated Systems & Solutions Ltd
Atos Consulting Ltd	Detica Ltd	LSC Group Ltd
AWE PLC	Drive Motor Retail Ltd	M S I - Defence Systems Ltd
AXA Corporate Solutions Services UK Ltd	Drumgrange Ltd	Marlborough Communications Ltd
BAE Systems Bofors AB	Dytecna Ltd	Meggitt Aerospace Ltd
BAE Systems / Rockwell Collins Data Link Solutions LLC	Elbit Systems Ltd	Meggitt Defence Systems Ltd
Balfour Beatty Group Ltd	Enersys Ltd	Microsoft Ltd
Bayford & Co Ltd	English Welsh & Scottish Railway Ltd	Mitie Engineering Maintenance Ltd
BMT Defence Services Ltd	Flagship Fire Fighting Training Ltd	Modis International Ltd
BOC Ltd	Fluid Transfer International Ltd	NATO
Bonar Floors Ltd	Frimley Park Hospital NHS Foundation Trust	NSSL Ltd
British Embassy	Gaz De France Sales Ltd	Oshkosh Truck Corporation
Burness Corlett - Three Quays Ltd	General Dynamics Ordnance and Tactical Systems	PA Consulting Services Ltd
Cabinet Office	Government Communications HQ	Pace Petroleum Ltd
Canon (UK) Ltd	Gulf Aircraft Maintenance Company	PCG Group
Cartus Ltd	Harris Corporation	Petards Joyce-Loebl Ltd
Chemring Energetics UK Ltd	Hewlett Packard Ltd	Portsmouth Aviation Ltd
Companhia Brasileira De Cartuch	Honeywell Aerospace UK	Portsmouth Hospitals NHS Trust
Compass Contract Services (UK) Ltd	ISS Mediclean Ltd	Post Office Ltd
Computacenter (UK) Ltd	Kier Regional Ltd	Racal Acoustics Ltd
Corporate Document Services Ltd	J & S Franklin Ltd	Realm Services (DAC) Ltd
Corona Energy Ltd		

CHAPTER 1 - FINANCE

DEFENCE CONTRACTS

Table **1.18** Organisations paid £5 million or more by the Ministry of Defence in 2007/08 (continued)

VAT exclusive at Current Prices (£ million)

£5 - £10 million (109 organisations)[4]

Remotec UK Ltd	Seafast Logistics PLC	Thistle Garments Ltd
Remploy Ltd	Selex Sistemi Integrati Ltd	TNT UK Ltd
RFD Beaufort Ltd	Seyntex NV	Tricomm Housing Ltd
Ricardo UK Ltd	Shell UK Oil Products Ltd	Turbomeca Ltd
Roxel (UK Rocket Motors) Ltd	Sigma Aerospace Ltd	University Hospital Birmingham NHS Foundation Trust
Ryder PLC	Simmons & Simmons	Veolia Water Nevis Ltd
S.Com Group Ltd	Smit International (Scotland) Ltd	Veritair Ltd
Saab Bofors Dynamics AB	South Tees Hospitals NHS Trust	VT Integrated Services Ltd
Saab Training Systems AB	Systems Engineering & Assessment Ltd	Wallop Defence Systems Ltd
Saft Ltd	Terberg DTS (UK) Ltd	Wescam Inc
SCA Packaging Ltd	Thales Training and Simulation	Wiltshire and Somerset College
Scott Health & Safety Ltd	The Treasury Solicitor	Wrekin Construction Company Ltd

Source: DASA(Economic Statistics)

1. Debut Services Ltd includes payments made to Debut Services Ltd and Debut Services (South West) Ltd.

2. On 22 May 2007 it was announced that ABRO business units would merge with those of Defence Aviation Repair Agency (DARA) to form a single new Government owned organisation called Defence Support Group (DSG). Consequently payments in 2007/08 appear against both DARA and DSG prior to contract changes being made, which will attribute all payments to DSG in 2008/09.

3. Reserve Forces and Cadets Association includes payments made to: the Council of Reserve Forces and Cadets Association, Reserve Forces and Cadets Association for East Anglia, Lowland Reserve Forces and Cadets Association, Reserve Forces and Cadets Association for Wales, Reserve Forces and Cadets Association for Greater London, South East Reserve Forces and Cadets Association, The Highland Reserve Forces and Cadets Association, The Reserve Forces and Cadets Association for the North of England, The Reserve Forces and Cadets Association for Yorkshire and the Humber, The Wessex Reserve Forces and Cadets Association, West Midland Reserve Forces and Cadets Association and Reserve Forces and Cadets Association for Northern Ireland.

4. Since publication of the online version of UKDS 2008, two minor revisions have been made to this table which have resulted in a small number of companies being removed or changed category. Historical versions of the table are available on request.

CHAPTER 1 - FINANCE

DEFENCE CONTRACTS

Table 1.18a Private Sector Companies paid £50 million or more by the Ministry of Defence in 2007/08: By Holding Company

This table (which is derived from **Table 1.18**) shows a subset of the data contained within **Table 1.18**, providing a listing of the Private Sector Companies that were paid £50 million or more through the Financial Management Shared Service Centre (FMSSC) - formerly the Defence Bills Agency (DBA) - in 2007/08.

This listing details the individual subsidiaries listed in **Table 1.18** 'rolled up' by holding company and single entity private companies where no other subsidiary has been recorded by the FMSSC. The term 'holding company" refers to companies which are full or part owner of other companies (subsidiaries and joint ventures). The table includes only those subsidiaries where the MOD has made payments during 2007/08 and therefore, is not an exhaustive listing of all subsidiaries and joint ventures relating to that holding company. It also excludes those companies and/or joint ventures which work as part of a consortium. Payments to joint ventures have been allocated to their parent holding companies in proportion to their equity holdings. The table excludes all payments made to public sector bodies, government departments and agencies, local authorities, MOD trading funds, multi nation project management agencies, charities and associations.

Please note that the placement of companies by payment bandings may differ from **Table 1.18** as the sum of the annual payments made to the holding company will exceed the values for individual subsidiaries listed in **Table 1.18**. The composition of Holding Companies in terms of their subsidiaries is derived as at **31 March 2008**. A listing of each company's subsidiaries and joint ventures, who have made payments during 2007/08 can be found in the footnotes below. It is recognized that the structure and ownership of modern corporations is dynamic and changes frequently. The FMSSC are responsible for the majority of such payments (around 95% by value) made by MOD. Other payments are made, for example, via British Defence Staff (United States), MOD Trading Funds and through local cash offices. The table is split into payment groups with the companies shown in **alphabetical order**. Company and organisation names have been reproduced (at 1 April 2008 position) directly from the truncated entries recorded on the FMSSC database and may appear in a shortened format in places.

Where a contract is novated during the year, annual payments are shown against the new 'owner' (company or entity) of that contract.

VAT exclusive at current prices (£ million)

Over £500 million (8 Companies)		
Babcock International Group PLC[1]	Finmeccanica SpA[4]	Serco Group PLC[7]
BAE Systems PLC[2]	Lockheed Martin Corporation[5]	Thales SA[8]
Electronic Data Systems Corporation[3]	QinetiQ Group PLC[6]	
£250 - £500 million (5 Companies)		
BT Group PLC[9]	Rolls-Royce Group PLC[11]	VT Group PLC[13]
EADS NV[10]	The Boeing Company[12]	
£100 - £250 million (11 Companies)		
Aspire Defence Holdings Ltd[14]	Halliburton Company[18]	Marshall of Cambridge[22]
BP PLC[15]	Interserve PLC[19]	Northrop Grumman Corporation[23]
Carillion PLC[16]	Lend Lease Corporation Ltd[20]	Raytheon Company[24]
General Dynamics Corporation[17]	Man AG[21]	
£50 - £100 million (12 Companies)		
Amec PLC[25]	HCR Group Holdings Ltd[29]	Scottish and Southern Energy PLC[33]
Atkins (WS) PLC[26]	International Business Machines Corporation[30]	Sodexho[34]
British Energy Group PLC[27]	Modus Services (Holdings) Ltd[31]	Turner & Co (Glasgow) Ltd[35]
Cobham PLC[28]	Royal Dutch Shell PLC[32]	Ultra Electronics Holdings PLC[36]

Source: DASA (Economic Statistics)

1. Babcock International Group PLC includes payments made to Babcock Defence Systems Ltd, Babcock Dyncorp Ltd, Babcock International Group PLC, Babcock Marine (Clyde) Ltd, Babcock Naval Services Ltd, Babcock Support Services Ltd, Debut Services Ltd, Debut Services (South West) Ltd, Rosyth Royal Dockyard Ltd, Rosyth Royal Dockyard Pension Scheme, Devonport Royal Dockyard, Frazer-Nash Consultancy Ltd, LSC Group Ltd and Weir Strachan & Henshaw Ltd.
2. BAE Systems PLC includes payments made to Aerosystems International Ltd, BAE Systems, BAE Systems (Aviation Services) Ltd, BAE Systems (Defence Systems)Ltd, BAE Systems (Hawk Synthetic Training) Ltd, BAE Systems Land Systems Pinzgau Ltd, BAE Systems (Operations) Ltd, BAE Systems Surface Fleet Solutions, BAE Systems Bofors AB, BAE Systems Defence Ltd, BAE Systems Electronics Ltd, BAE Systems Hagglunds AB, BAE Systems Information & Electronic Systems Integration Inc, BAE Systems Information & Electronic Warfare Systems, BAE Systems Australia Ltd, BAE Systems Integrated System Technologies Ltd, BAE Systems Land Systems (Bridging) Ltd, BAE Systems Land Systems (Munitions and Ordnance) Ltd, BAE Systems Land Systems (Weapons and Vehicles) Ltd, BAE Systems Marine Ltd, BAE Systems Pension Funds Trustees Ltd, BAE Systems PLC, BAE Systems Properties Ltd, BAE Systems/Rockwell Collins Data Link Solutions LLC, Corda Ltd, Flagship Training Ltd, Fleet Support Ltd, MBDA UK Ltd and Piper Group PLC.
3. Electronic Data Systems Corporation includes payments made to EDS Defence Ltd, Electronic Data Systems Ltd and Unigraphics Solutions Ltd.
4. Finmeccanica SpA includes payments made to Agustawestland International Ltd, Aviation Training International Ltd, Galileo Avionica Spa, MBDA UK Ltd, Selex Communications Ltd, Selex Sensors & Airborne Systems Ltd, Selex Sistemi Integrati Ltd, Vega Group PLC and Westland Helicopters Ltd.
5. Lockheed Martin Corporation includes payments made to AWE Management Ltd, AWE PLC, Lockheed Martin Aeronautics Company, Lockheed Martin Aerospace Systems Integration Corp, Lockheed Martin Canada Inc, Lockheed Martin Corp, Lockheed Martin Maritime Systems & Sensors Ltd, Lockheed Martin Overseas Corp, Lockheed Martin Sippican Inc, Lockheed Martin System Integration-Owego Ltd, Lockheed Martin UK Ltd, Lockheed Martin UK Insys Ltd, Lockheed Martin UK Integrated Systems & Solutions Ltd and Raytheon/Lockheed Martin Javelin Joint Venture.

Footnotes continued on next page

CHAPTER 1 - FINANCE

INTERNATIONAL DEFENCE

Table **1.20** NATO Countries Defence Expenditure 2003 - 2007

This table shows defence payments accrued within financial years 2003-2007 as extracted from the NATO website http://www.nato.int/docu/pr/2007/p07-141e.html. Figures are based on the NATO definition of defence expenditure and are stated at 2000 prices and exchange rates.

The NATO definition of defence expenditure differs from national definitions so the figures quoted may diverge considerably from those given in national budgets. Expenditure is included for countries that provide Military Assistance. Expenditure is not included for countries receiving assistance. The financial year has been designated by the year which includes the highest number of months. For example year 2006 represents 2006/07 for Canada and the United Kingdom and 2005/06 for the United States (where the financial year for United States runs from October through to September).

Defence expenditures as of 2002 have been calculated on the basis of the revised NATO definition agreed in 2004. Most nations have reported defence expenditures according to this new definition. A few, however, continue to have difficulty meeting this requirement. Consequently figures for "NATO Total", "NATO Europe" and "North America" for 2003 are only indicative. Total figures for 2004 onwards are not calculated due to unavailability of exchange rate information, for 2000, for the countries new to the Alliance. See page 43 for more information on the new NATO definition.

The data in this table are outside the scope of National Statistics because they are provided by an organisation outside the UK Government Statistical Service.

2000 Prices and Exchange Rates

Country	Currency Unit (Million)	2003	2004	2005	2006	Estimated 2007
NATO Total[1,2]	**US Dollars**	**555 247**	..	..	..	..
NATO - Europe[1,2,3]	**US Dollars**	**162 527**	..	..	..	..
Belgium	Euro	3 245 r	3 177 r	3 062 r	3 039	3 172
Bulgaria[4]	Levas	*	821 r	850 r	835	899
Czech Republic	Czech Koruny	48 197 r	45 245 r	46 672 r	47 147	45 872
Denmark	Danish Kroner	19 457	19 387	18 421	20 180	18 635
Estonia[4]	Kroonis	*	2 004 r	2 096 r	2 265	2 787
France[5,6]	Euro	38 248	39 505 r	38 699 r ‖	38 650	38 673
Germany	Euro	29 949 r	29 264 r	29 075 r	28 776	28 612
Greece	Euro	3 863 r	4 209 r	4 604 r	4 787	5 043
Hungary	Forint	254 096 r	240 663 r	241 330 r	216 823	192 678
Italy	Euro	23 205	22 309	20 501 r	18 351	17 705
Latvia[4]	Lats	*	81	90 r	123	145
Lithuania[4]	Litai	*	908	842 r	903	977
Luxembourg	Euro	164	173	175	175	221
Netherlands	Euro	6 614	6 581	6 599	6 884	6 771
Norway	Norwegian Kroner	29 488	29 957	27 645	27 496	27 368
Poland	Zlotys	14 527 r	15 287 r	15 782 r	16 535	18 717
Portugal	Euro	1 885 r	2 010 r	2 156 r	2 085	1 997
Romania[4]	Lei - New Lei [7]	*	20 661 095 r ‖	2 123 r	2 111	2 293
Slovak Republic[4]	Slovak Koruny	*	18 806 r	20 447 r	21 093	23 166
Slovenia[4,8]	Tolars - Euro	*	74 335 r	76 369 r	87 979 ‖	381
Spain	Euro	8 461 r	8 660 r	8 552 r	9 016	9 708
Turkey	1000 Turkish Liras- New Turkish Liras [7]	5 035 733	4 486 689 ‖	4 332	4 573	4 734
United Kingdom	Pounds Sterling	24 325 r	24 053 r	26 970 r	27 725	26 415
North America[1,2]	**US Dollars**	**392 720**	..	..	..	..
Canada	Canadian Dollars	13 393 r	13 717 r	14 204 r	14 800	16 691
United States	US Dollars	383 708	416 195 r	435 883 r	439 304	441 919

Source: NATO

1. France, Italy and Luxembourg figures are based on the old NATO definition of defence expenditure, whereas all the other countries are based on the new definition agreed by the member states in 2004. The NATO totals include all countries' expenditure regardless of which definition was used.
2. In the absence of NATO data expressed at 2000 exchange rates and prices for the 'NATO', 'NATO Europe' and 'North America' totals, the individual country totals (expressed in local currencies at 2000 prices) have been converted to US dollars using the 2000 exchange rate for each country supplied by the Bank of England. Where Bank of England data were not available, comparable dollar exchange rates have been sourced from the Pacific Exchange Rate Service (http://fx.sauder.ubc.ca/data.html).
3. Iceland is a member of the Alliance but has no armed forces.
4. Bulgaria, Estonia, Latvia, Lithuania, Romania, Slovak Republic, and Slovenia joined the Alliance in 2004.
5. France is a member of the Alliance but does not belong to the integrated military structure and does not participate in collective force planning. The defence data relating to France are indicative only.
6. From 2006 onwards, following the introduction of new budgetary reform and financial law, defence expenditures are calculated with a new methodology.
7. From 2005 onwards, monetary values for Romania and Turkey are expressed in new currency units.
8. Slovenia joined the Euro in 2007, data up to this point are in Tolars.

CHAPTER 1 - FINANCE

INTERNATIONAL DEFENCE

Table 1.21 NATO Countries Defence Expenditure as % of GDP 2003 - 2007

This table shows defence payments accrued within financial years 2003-2007 as a percentage of GDP. The figures are those extracted from the NATO website http://www.nato.int/docu/pr/2007/p07-141e.html. Figures are based on the NATO definition of defence expenditure and are stated at constant prices, where the effects of inflation have been removed. Previous publications have used data in the table based on current prices but constant prices are more comparable to the data displayed in **Table 1.20**.

The NATO definition of defence expenditure differs from national definitions so the figures quoted may diverge considerably from those given in national budgets. Expenditure is included for countries that provide Military Assistance. Expenditure is not included for countries receiving assistance. The financial year has been designated by the year which includes the highest number of months. For example the year 2006 represents 2006/07 for Canada and the United Kingdom and 2005/06 for the United States (where the financial year for United States runs from October through to September).

Defence expenditures as of 2002 have been calculated on the basis of the revised NATO definition agreed in 2004. Most nations have reported defence expenditures according to this new definition. A few, however, continue to have difficulty meeting this requirement. More information on the new NATO definition can be found on page 43.

The data in this table are outside the scope of National Statistics because they are provided by an organisation outside the UK Government Statistical Service.

Constant Prices

Country	2003	2004	2005	2006	Estimated 2007
NATO - Europe[1,2]					
Belgium	1.2	1.2	1.1	1.1	1.1
Bulgaria[3]	*	2.5	2.5	2.3	2.3
Czech Republic	2.0	1.8	1.8	1.7	1.6
Denmark	1.5	1.4	1.3	1.4	1.3
Estonia[3]	*	1.6	1.5	1.4	1.6
France[4]	2.6	2.6	2.5 ‖	2.4	2.4
Germany	1.4	1.4	1.4	1.3	1.3
Greece	2.5	2.6	2.7	2.7	2.8
Hungary	1.7	1.5	1.4	1.2	1.1
Italy	1.9	1.8	1.7	1.5	1.4
Latvia[3]	*	1.3	1.3	1.6	1.7
Lithuania[3]	*	1.5	1.3	1.3	1.3
Luxembourg	0.7	0.7	0.7	0.6	0.8
Netherlands	1.5	1.5	1.5	1.5	1.4
Norway	1.9	1.9	1.7	1.6	1.6
Poland	1.8	1.8	1.8	1.8	1.9
Portugal	1.5	1.6	1.7	1.6	1.5
Romania[3]	*	2.0	2.0	1.8	1.9
Slovak Republic[3]	*	1.7	1.7	1.7	1.7
Slovenia[3]	*	1.5	1.5	1.6	1.6
Spain	1.2	1.2	1.2	1.2	1.2
Turkey	3.8	3.1	2.8	2.8	2.8
United Kingdom	2.4	2.3	2.5	2.5	2.3
North America[1]					
Canada	1.2	1.2	1.2	1.2	1.3
United States	3.7	3.9	4.0	3.9	3.8

Source: NATO

1. France, Italy and Luxembourg figures are based on the old NATO definition of defence expenditure, whereas all the other countries are based on the new definition agreed by the member states in 2004.
2. Iceland is a member of the Alliance but has no armed forces.
3. Bulgaria, Estonia, Latvia, Lithuania, Romania, Slovak Republic and Slovenia joined the Alliance in 2004.
4. France is a member of the Alliance but does not belong to the integrated military structure and does not participate in collective force planning. The defence data relating to France are indicative only.

CHAPTER 1 - FINANCE

INTERNATIONAL DEFENCE

Table 1.22 Top World-wide Military Spenders: 2007

This table shows the Top 15 World-wide Military Spenders in 2007. Figures are in US billion Dollars and at **2005 Prices and Exchange Rates**. Countries are ranked separately using Market Exchange Rates and Purchasing Power Parity (PPP rates). If a different base year were used, the rankings could change due to fluctuations in exchange rates.

Conversion into a common currency using Market Exchange Rates (MER) tends to undervalue the currency and hence the scale of expenditure of lower income countries, although this may also be because a large part of the economy of a lower income country is domestically based and not based on internationally traded goods and services. Attempts are often made to circumvent this problem using Purchasing Power Parity (PPP) measures. These use currency conversion rates which equalise the overall price of a bundle of goods and services in each country. However PPP measures can be highly inaccurate because of the difficulty of allowing for differences in quality and devising appropriate and relevant "weighting" of individual goods and services. Civilian based PPPs may also not be representative of defence goods and services. As such, this table must be regarded as providing only an illustrative ranking of world-wide military spending.

The data in this table are outside the scope of National Statistics because they are provided by an organisation outside the UK Government Statistical Service.

At constant 2005 Prices and Exchange Rates

Market Exchange Rates		Spending	Spending Per Capita	World Share	Purchasing Power Parity Rates[1]		Spending
Rank	Country	US$ Billions	US$	%	Rank	Country	US$ Billions
1	USA	546.8	1 799	45	1	USA	546.8
2	UK	59.7	995	5	2	China	[140.3]
3	China	[58.3]	[44]	[5]	3	Russia	[78.8]
4	France	53.6	880	4	4	India	72.7
5	Japan	43.6	339	4	5	UK	54.7
Sub-total Top 5		**762.0**		**63**	**Sub-total Top 5**		**893.3**
6	Germany	36.9	447	3	6	Saudi Arabia[2]	52.8
7	Russia	[35.4]	[249]	[3]	7	France	47.9
8	Saudi Arabia[2]	33.8	1 310	3	8	Japan	37.0
9	Italy	33.1	568	3	9	Germany	33.0
10	India	24.2	21	2	10	Italy	29.6
Sub-total Top 10		**925.4**		**76**	**Sub-total Top 10**		**1 093.6**
11	South Korea	22.6	470	2	11	South Korea	29.4
12	Brazil	15.3	80	1	12	Brazil	26.7
13	Canada	15.2	461	1	13	Iran[3]	22.1
14	Australia	15.1	733	1	14	Turkey	16.5
15	Spain	14.6	336	1	15	Taiwan	15.8
Sub-total Top 15		**1 008.2**		**83**	**Sub-total Top 15**		**1 204.1**
World Total		**1 214**	**183**	**100**	**World Total**		**. .**

Source: Stockholm International Peace Research Institute (SIPRI)

1. The figures in PPP dollar terms are converted at PPP rates (for 2005), based on prices comparisons of the components of GDP.

2. The figures for Saudi Arabia include expenditure for public order and safety and might be slight overestimates.

3. The figure for Iran is for national defence and does not include spending on the Revolutionary Guards Corps, which constitutes a considerable part of Iran's total military expenditure.

[ ] Indicates SIPRI estimate.

CHAPTER 2 - PERSONNEL

INTRODUCTION

Chapter 2 is divided into six main sections

- **Personnel summary** (**Tables 2.1 to 2.6**) - overall statistics relating to both civilians and Armed Forces personnel, including numbers overseas.

- **UK Armed Forces** (**Tables 2.7 to 2.28**) – summaries of the main trends in strengths, intakes and outflows of personnel in the UK Armed Forces. A chart setting out the equivalent ranks between the Services and civilians is included as **Table 2.28**.

- **Civilian personnel** (**Tables 2.29 to 2.38**) - summaries of the main trends in strengths, intakes and outflows of civilian personnel.

- **War Pensions** (**Table 2.39**) – statistics on the numbers receiving various types of war pension.

- **Compensation claims made against the MOD (Tables 2.40 and 2.41)** - statistics on the numbers of new and settled claims made against the MOD.

- **International** (**Table 2.42**) - manpower holdings and ceilings by member countries of the Conventional Armed Forces in Europe (CFE) Treaty.

Key trends and summaries precede the **UK Armed Forces** and **Civilian Personnel** sections. These can be found on pages 58 and 85 respectively.

New Tables

Chapter 2 includes three tables presented for the first time: **Table 2.14 (**Strength of UK Regular Forces by Service and **ethnic origin** at 1 April each year); **Table 2.15** (Strength of UK Regular Forces by Service and **religion** at 1 April each year); and **Table 2.16** (Strength of the Trained UK Regular Forces by **nationality** and Service at 1 April each year). The deaths in the armed forces (formerly tables **2.24** and **2.25** in previous editions of UKDS) and civilian sickness absence tables (formerly table **2.36**) are no longer featured in this chapter - due to the inclusion of the new Health Chapter, these tables have now moved to **Chapter 3**. **Tables 2.14** to **2.36** as presented in UKDS 2007 have been renumbered to allow for the inclusion of new tables and the transfer of health related tables to Chapter 3.

Data sources

The principal sources of data for personnel information presented in UKDS Chapter 2 are the civilian and Armed Forces administrative databases.

Armed Forces statistics to 2005 are compiled from pay records (Naval Service) or personnel records (Army and RAF) held by the Service Personnel and Veterans Agency (SPVA, formerly the Armed Forces Personnel Administration Agency). In March 2006 the transfer of all Service personnel records to the Joint Personnel Administration (JPA) system began. Statistics are compiled from JPA in the RAF from April 2006, in the Naval Service from November 2006 and in the Army from April 2007. All statistics before these points are derived from single Service legacy systems.

Civilian statistics are compiled from several sources. Data for MOD staff are taken from personnel systems; CIPMIS prior to April 2003, HRMS from April 2004 onwards and a combination of the two in the year in between.

The MOD has four Trading Funds[1] that provide DASA with monthly extracts from their personnel systems. The Royal Fleet Auxiliary (RFA) data are taken from the MOD pay system and locally engaged civilians (LEC) data are derived from quarterly head counts provided to DASA by administrators in each Top Level Budget (TLB).

Data quality

Armed Forces data on JPA are a combination of mandatory and non-mandatory fields populated by unit administrators and voluntary fields such as **ethnic origin** that Armed Forces personnel can choose to complete based on their self-perceptions. In 2002 the ethnicity categories were aligned with the new classifications in the 2001 Census of Population. Analysis conducted by DASA indicates that the percentage of ethnic minority Service personnel in the unknown or undeclared population is higher than in the declared population. If the percentage of personnel with unknown or undeclared ethnicity exceeds 40% DASA consider the risk of misrepresenting ethnicity percentages is too high to publish.

CHAPTER 2 - PERSONNEL

INTRODUCTION

Due to ongoing validation of data from JPA some data are provisional. This is indicated by a superscript p next to the figure and means that the data are sufficiently accurate to be published but that further validation may lead to small revisions that should not materially affect the information presented.

Civilian data on HRMS are a combination of fields mandated by the People Pay and Pensions Agency (PPPA), such as grade, with voluntary fields such as **disability status**. Civilian personnel complete these fields based on their self perceptions. If personnel that consider they have a disability are more or less likely to record their status than those who consider they are not disabled, the percentages of disabled persons presented will be too high or too low depending on the direction of the bias. It is not possible for DASA to measure this bias without surveying a random sample of the unknown or undeclared group.

Most tables presented in Chapter 2 meet the high standards of quality and integrity demanded by the National Statistics code of practice. The following tables require further validation of data and methods before they attain National Statistics status: **Table 2.40**, **Table 2.41** and **Table 2.42**.

[1] Defence Support Group (formerly Army Base Repair Organisation and the Defence Aviation and Repair Agency)
Defence Science and Technology Laboratory
Hydrographic Office
Meteorological Office

CHAPTER 2 - PERSONNEL

PERSONNEL SUMMARY

Table 2.1 Recent trends in Service and civilian personnel[1] strengths at 1 April each year

Thousands: FTE

	1990 [2]		1997		2003	2004	2005	2006 [3]	2007 [3]	2008
Total personnel[4]	**487.3**	||	**348.5**	||	**321.0**	**322.4**	**315.3**	**304.8** r	**293.8** rp ||	**282.6** p
Service	**314.8**		**215.1**		**213.4**	**213.3**	**206.9**	**201.4**	**196.1** p	**193.1** p
UK Regulars	305.8		210.8		206.9	207.0	201.1	195.9	190.4 p	187.1 p
FTRS	-		-		2.4	2.2	1.7	1.5	1.6 p	1.8 p
Gurkhas[5]	} 9.0		4.3 {		3.8	3.7	3.7	3.7	3.7 p	3.9 p
Locally entered/engaged[5]					0.4	0.4	0.4	0.4	0.4	0.4
Civilian Level 0[1,4]	**172.5**	||	**133.3**	||	**107.6**	**109.0**	**108.5**	**103.4** r	**97.7** r ||	**89.5**
Level 1[1]	141.4	||	101.9	||	81.5	82.2	82.0	78.1	73.8	69.0
Trading Funds[4]	-		15.5	||	12.2	11.4	10.8	10.7	10.1 ||	9.2
Locally engaged civilians	31.1	||	15.9	||	13.8	15.4	15.7	14.5 r	13.8 r	11.2

Excluded from the above table:

Royal Irish (Home Service)	6.2		4.8		3.5	3.4	3.2	3.1	2.1	- [6]

Source: DASA (Quad-Service)

1. Civilian Level 0 and Level 1 are defined in the Glossary.
2. Data using the definition of civilians updated in April 2004 are not available for 1990 - figures are as published in UK Defence Statistics 1990. The 1990 figure excludes casual staff and those not directly funded by the MOD.
3. LEC figures for April 2006 and 2007 have been revised due to the inclusion of previously unavailable data on personnel based in Brunei and in the CJO
4. The following changes have affected the continuity of the civilian data: removal of GCHQ personnel from April 1994 and the contractorisation of the Atomic Weapons Establishment (6,000) in 1993. In 2001 the QinetiQ portion of the Defence Evaluation and Research Agency (8,000) was established as a private company. At 1 April 2008 the Defence Aviation Repair Agency and the Army Based Repair Organisation merged to form the Defence Support Group and around 1,000 personnel transferred to the Vector Aerospace Corporation.
5. Gurkhas are included in the locally entered service personnel figures until 1997 after which they are shown separately.
6. The Home Service of the Royal Irish Regiment was officially disbanded on 31 March 2008.

Due to ongoing validation of data from the Joint Personnel Administration System, Service strength statistics for 1 April 2007 and 1 April 2008 are provisional and subject to review.

CHAPTER 2 - PERSONNEL

PERSONNEL SUMMARY

Table 2.2 Civilian personnel[1] by budgetary area, at 1 April 2008

Due to ongoing validation of data from a new personnel administration system, Service personnel figures broken down by budgetary area at 1 April 2008 are currently unavailable.

Thousands: FTE

	Total	Non-industrial	Industrial
Civilian Level 0[1,2]	**89.5**	*	*
Royal Navy Areas			
Commander-in-Chief Fleet[2]	**4.6**	*	*
Fleet	2.3	1.8	0.5
Royal Fleet Auxiliary Service[2]	2.3	*	*
Army Areas			
Commander-in-Chief Land Forces[3]	**17.2**	**12.2**	**5.0**
Chief of Staff Land Forces	3.2	3.0	0.2
Regional Forces	11.8	7.5	4.3
Field Army	0.9	0.6	0.3
Joint Helicopter Command	0.4	0.2	0.2
Service Children's Education Agency	1.0	1.0	-
Royal Air Force Areas			
Air Officer Commanding-in-Chief	**8.7**	**5.7**	**3.0**
HQ Air Command	8.7	5.7	3.0
Defence Equipment & Support			
Defence Equipment & Support	**18.0**	**15.2**	**2.8**
Defence Equipment Support Management Group	14.9	14.2	0.6
Future Defence Supply Chain	3.2	1.0	2.2

Source: DASA(Quad-service)
Continued overleaf

PERSONNEL SUMMARY

Table **2.2** Civilian personnel[1] by budgetary area, at 1 April 2008 (continued)

Thousands: FTE

	Total	Non-industrial	Industrial
MoD Head Office, HQ and centrally managed expenditure			
Central Top Level Budget	**16.9**	**16.4**	**0.5**
Chief of Defence Intelligence	1.6	1.5	0.1
Defence Academy	0.4	0.4	-
Defence Export Services Organisation	0.1	0.1	-
Deputy Chief of the Defence Staff (Health)	0.7	0.6	0.1
Finance Director	1.0	1.0	-
Ministry of Defence Police and Guarding Agency	7.8	7.7	-
Personnel Director	2.3	2.3	-
Policy and Commitments	0.8	0.6	0.2
Central Other[4]	2.2	2.1	0.1
Chief of Joint Operations	**0.3**	**0.3**	**-**
Commander of British Forces Cyprus	0.1	0.1	-
Commander of British Forces Falklands	-	-	-
Commander of British Forces Gibraltar	-	-	-
Permanent Joint Headquarters	0.1	0.1	-
Defence Estates	**2.7**	**2.6**	**0.1**
Science Innovation & Technology	**0.3**	**0.3**	**-**
Unallocated	**0.3**	**0.2**	**0.1**
Civilian Level 1[1,2]	**69.0**	*	*
MOD owned Trading Funds[2]			
Defence Science & Technology Laboratories	**3.3**	*	*
Meteorological Office	**1.7**	*	*
UK Hydrographic Office	**1.0**	*	*
Defence Support Group[5]	**3.1**	*	*
Locally engaged civilians[2]	**11.2**	*	*
Civilian Level 0[1,2]	**89.5**	*	*

Source: DASA(Quad-Service)

1. Civilian Level 0 and Level 1 are defined in the Glossary.
2. A breakdown of industrial and non-industrial personnel is unavailable for Royal Fleet Auxiliary, Trading Funds and locally engaged civilian personnel.
3. As at 1 April 2008, Land Command and Adjutant General combined to form Land Forces.
4. This budgetary area contains personnel from the following working level management groups: Service Personnel and Veterans Agency, Programme Costs, Strategy Director and any residual from budgetary areas closed in Central TLB.
5. As at 1 April 2008, the Defence Aviation Repair Agency and the Army Base Repair Organisation merged to form the Defence Support Group and around 1 000 personnel transferred to the Vector Aerospace Corporation.

PERSONNEL SUMMARY

Table 2.3 Location of Service and civilian personnel[1,2] in the United Kingdom

Thousands: FTE

At 1 July each year		1990	1997	1999	2000		2005	2006	2007
United Kingdom		..	**276.9**	**272.0**	**267.7**	||	**254.5**	**245.6**	**236.8** p
	Service	215.9	171.6	171.8	170.3		169.6	164.4	159.7 p
	Civilian	..	105.3	100.2	97.4	||	84.9	81.2	77.1
England		..	**229.4**	**226.5**	**222.6**	||	**216.2**	**209.8**	**205.8** p
	Service	179.6	142.6	144.4	143.0		145.0	141.6	140.3 p
	Civilian	..	86.8	82.2	79.5	||	71.2	68.2	65.5
Wales		..	**8.4**	**8.4**	**8.3**	||	**6.2**	**5.4**	**5.0** p
	Service	5.3	3.3	3.3	3.2		2.9	2.5	2.6 p
	Civilian	..	5.1	5.2	5.0	||	3.4	2.9	2.4
Scotland		..	**24.2**	**24.6**	**24.7**	||	**20.2**	**19.7**	**18.9** p
	Service	19.3	13.9	14.9	15.1		13.2	12.9	12.4 p
	Civilian	..	10.3	9.7	9.6	||	7.0	6.8	6.5
Northern Ireland		..	**14.6**	**12.2**	**11.6**	||	**10.4**	**9.1**	**7.3** p
	Service	11.5	11.5	9.0	8.4		7.0	5.9	4.5 p
	Civilian	..	3.1	3.2	3.2	||	3.4	3.2	2.8

Source: DASA (Quad-Service)

Service and Civilian personnel[1,2] by Government Office Region

Number: FTE

	Service			Civilian		
At 1 April each year	2007	2008	% change[3]	2007	2008	% change[3]
United Kingdom	**161 390** r p	**158 660** p	**-1.7**	**68 230**	**63 960**	**-6.3**
England	**141 390** r p	**140 310** p	**-0.8**	**57 880**	**54 880**	**-5.2**
East of England	18 070 r p	17 950 p	-0.7	6 430	6 400	-0.5
East Midlands	9 270 r p	9 230 p	-0.4	2 410	2 390	-0.7
London	6 790 r p	5 900 p	-13.2	6 040	5 370	-11.1
North East	1 490 r p	1 450 p	-2.8	510	510	0.6
North West	1 720 r p	1 710 p	-0.9	2 640	2 530	-4.2
South East	44 880 r p	45 610 p	1.6	13 630	12 660	-7.1
South West	39 160 r p	39 030 p	-0.3	18 290	17 630	-3.6
West Midlands	6 190 r p	5 900 p	-4.7	4 330	3 820	-11.7
Yorkshire and The Humber	13 790 r p	13 530 p	-1.9	3 590	3 560	-1.0
Wales	**2 590** r p	**2 640** p	**1.7**	**1 420**	**1 230**	**-13.1**
Scotland	**12 640** r p	**11 970** p	**-5.3**	**6 020**	**5 730**	**-4.7**
Northern Ireland	**4 770** r p	**3 740** p	**-21.6**	**2 920**	**2 120**	**-27.6**
Unallocated	580 r p	370 p	-36.2	540	370	-32.1
Royal Fleet Auxiliaries	*	*	*	2 360	2 270	-3.5
Overseas	**27 990** r p	**27 630** p	**-1.3**	**2 650**	**2 450**	**-7.7**
Civilian Level 1	*	*	*	**73 780**	**69 050**	**-6.4**
Trading Funds	*	*	*	**10 060**	**9 210**	**-8.5**
Trading Funds United Kingdom	*	*	*	9 870	8 930	-9.5
Trading Funds Overseas	*	*	*	40	30	-11.4
Trading Fund Unallocated	*	*	*	160	250	57.7
Locally Engaged Civilians	*	*	*	**13 840** r	**11 240**	**-20.9**
Civilian Level 0	*	*	*	**97 690** r	**89 500**	**-8.7**

Source: DASA (Quad-Service)

1. Service personnel figures are for UK Regular Forces, and therefore exclude Gurkhas, Full Time Reserve Service personnel and mobilised reservists.
2. Civilian Level 0 and Level 1 are defined in the Glossary.
3. Percentage change is calculated from unrounded data.

Due to ongoing validation of data from the Joint Personnel Administration System, Service strength statistics for 1 April 2007, 1 July 2007 and 1 April 2008 are provisional and subject to review.

PERSONNEL SUMMARY

Table 2.4 Global locations of Service[1] and civilian personnel, at 1 April each year

Number: FTE

		1997		2003	2004	2005	2006	2007	2008
Global Total		**344 120**	||	..	..	**309 570**	**299 240** e,r	**288 080** r p	**276 560** p
	Service	210 820		..	..	201 100	195 870 e	190 400 r p	187 060 p
	Civilian	133 290	||	107 580	109 050	108 470	103 380 r	97 690 r	89 500
	Level 0[2]								
United Kingdom	Service	166 080		..	..	171 870	167 330 e	161 390 r p	158 660 p
	Civilian	107 480	||	84 760	86 210	84 740	83 000	78 110	72 840
Overseas Total		**60 420**	||	..	..	**47 500**	**45 820** r	**44 520** r p	**41 340** p
	Service	42 700		..	..	29 130	28 540	27 990 r p	27 630 p
	Civilian	17 730	||	16 030	17 810	18 270	17 280 r	16 530 r	13 710
Mainland European States		**41 160**	||	..	..	**34 040**	**32 710** e	**32 650** r p	**31 200** p
Germany	Service	21 900		..	..	22 170	21 960 e	21 710 r p	21 690 p
	Civilian	12 130	||	9 440	9 780	9 700	8 700	8 790	7 910
Balkans[3]	Service	5 100		..	..	170	30 e	50 r p	20 p
	Civilian	20	||	980	640	660	680	710	230
Remainder	Service	1 920		..	..	1 200	1 180 e	1 160 r p	1 130 p
	Civilian	100	||	130	130	140	160	230	220
Mediterranean		**8 690**	||	..	..	**7 430**	**7 630** e	**6 740** r p	**5 670** p
Cyprus	Service	4 090		..	..	3 170	3 040 e	2 950 r p	2 780 p
	Civilian	2 930	||	2 760	2 880	2 790	3 230	2 280 r	1 850
Gibraltar	Service	480		..	..	360	340 e	310 r p	280 p
	Civilian	1 200	||	1 090	1 200	1 100	1 010	1 190	750
Middle East[4]	Service	670		..	..	390	390 e	270 r p	320 p
	Civilian	40	||	120	1 610	1 650	1 380 r	1 490	1 020
Far East/Asia	Service	2 210		..	..	260	260 e	220 r p	260 p
	Civilian	770	||	710	730	730	960 r	750	740
Africa		**560**	||	..	..	**950**	**560** e	**610** r p	**660** p
Sierra Leone	Service	-		..	..	100	90 e	90 p	80 p
	Civilian	-	||	-	-	610	230	220	220
Remainder	Service	550		..	..	70	70 e	70 p	70 p
	Civilian	-	||	160	160	170	180	230	280

Continued on the next page

54

PERSONNEL SUMMARY

Table **2.4** **Global locations of Service[1] and civilian personnel, at 1 April each year (continued)**

Number: FTE

		1997		2003	2004	2005	2006	2007	2008
North America		**2 260**	‖	..	..	**910**	**870** e	**850** r p	**890** p
USA	Service	1 310		..	..	400	410 e	390 r p	420 p
	Civilian	100	‖	200	200	200	180	180	180
Canada[5]	Service	840		..	..	290	260 e	270 r p	270 p
	Civilian	10	‖	–	10	20	20	10	20
Central/South America	Service	300		..	..	100	110 e	90 r p	90 p
	Civilian	10	‖	150	150	150	170	180	190
Falkland Islands[6]	Service	1 790		..	..	320	310 e	290 r p	130 p
	Civilian	40	‖	50	50	50	60	60	50
Elsewhere[7]	Service	1 550		..	..	230	90 e	100 r p	110 p
	Civilian	390	‖	240	280	280	340	220 r	60
Unallocated		**7 910**	‖	..	..	**3 110**	**750** e	**1 270** r p	**980** p
	Service	2 040		..	..	–	– e	580 r p	370 p
	Civilian	5 870	‖	4 340	2 710	3 110	750	690	610
Royal Fleet Auxiliaries	Civilian	**2 210**		**2 450**	**2 310**	**2 350**	**2 340**	**2 360**	**2 270**

Source: DASA(Quad-Service)

1. Data for the global locations of Service personnel were suspended between 2003 - 2004 because of concerns over quality of the source data. Figures for 1997 showed where Service personnel were deployed. From 2005 data show where Service personnel are stationed.
2. Civilian Level 0 and Level 1 are defined in the Glossary.
3. Consists of Bosnia-Herzegovina, Croatia, the Former Yugoslav Republic of Macedonia, Kosovo, Montenegro, and Serbia.
4. Including Egypt, Iraq and Libya. Service personnel figures for 1 April 2005 and 1 April 2006 include Naval Parties, but exclude all other personnel deployed on operations from 1 April 2007. Figures exclude all personnel deployed on operations.
5. Excluding British troops training in Canada at the British Army Training Unit, Suffield.
6. Whilst the Falkland Islands figure appears to have fallen between 2007 and 2008, the number of personnel located in the Falkland Islands has remained constant. The apparent fall is due to changes in the way administrative systems record the type of assignment of personnel in the Falklands Islands. Those on temporary assignments are shown against their permanent stationed location.
7. Includes personnel in transit and those in any other geographic region that is not specifically identified above.

Due to ongoing validation of data from the Joint Personnel Administration System, Service strength statistics for 1 April 2007 and 1 April 2008 are provisional and subject to review.

PERSONNEL SUMMARY

Table 2.5 Strength of locally entered personnel including Gurkhas by global location, at 1 April each year

	1990	1997	2003	2004	2005	2006	2007 [1]	2008
Total	**40 160**	**20 190**	**17 970**	**19 510**	**19 740**	**18 560** r	**17 940** r	**15 480** p
Naval Service	310	190	-	-	-	-	-	-
Army	8 710	4 140	4 130	4 080	4 080	4 010	4 100	4 240 p
of which Gurkhas	..	*3 760*	*3 760*	*3 720*	*3 690*	*3 660*	*3 710*	*3 860* p
Royal Air Force	-	-	-	-	-	-	-	-
Civilian	31 140	15 860	13 840	15 430	15 660	14 540 r	13 840 r	11 240
by location								
United Kingdom								
Army	1 300	2 000	2 600	2 550	2 520	2 550	2 770	3 020 p
of which Gurkhas	..	*2 000*	*2 600*	*2 550*	*2 520*	*2 550*	*2 770*	*3 020* p
Continental Europe								
Civilian	23 290	10 790	8 070	8 290	8 050	7 040	7 210	6 350
Mediterranean								
Gibraltar								
Army[2]	70	350	370	360	390	350	400	380 p
Civilian	1 530	1 130	1 030	1 140	1 040	940	1 130	700
Malta								
Civilian	10	-	-	-	-	-	-	-
Cyprus								
Civilian[3]	2 460	2 660	2 440	2 510	2 430	2 870	1 960 r	1 550
Far East								
Hong Kong								
Naval Service	310	190	-	-	-	-	-	-
Army	5 310	140	-	-	-	-	-	-
of which Gurkhas	..	*120*	-	-	-	-	-	-
Civilian	2 630	190	-	-	-	-	-	-
Brunei								
Army	840	780	790	730	770	800	840	790 p
of which Gurkhas	..	*780*	*790*	*730*	*770*	*800*	*840*	*790* p
Civilian	200	230	300	300	300	290 r	290	290
Nepal[4]								
Army	1 190	860	370	440	400	300	90	40 p
of which Gurkhas	..	*860*	*370*	*440*	*400*	*300*	*90*	*40* p
Civilian		300	360	370	370	360	360	360
Elsewhere	} 290 {							
Civilian		40	20	20	20	40	40	40
Other areas								
Falkland Islands								
Army	-	-	-	-	-	10	10	- p
of which Gurkhas	..	-	-	-	-	*10*	*10*	- p
Elsewhere								
Civilian[5]	730	530	1 620	2 790	3 440	2 990 r	2 850	1 950

Source: DASA(Quad-Service)

1. Due to the introduction of the Joint Personnel Administration system, locally entered Service personnel figures by location for 1 April 2007 are not available and therefore shown as at 1 March 2007.
2. Gibraltar Army figures comprise the Gibraltar Permanent Cadre and Gibraltar Volunteer Reserve.
3. From 1996, includes the locally employed dependents of Service personnel.
4. In March 2007 Gurkha terms and conditions of service were changed, and, among other things, this involved replacing Nepal Long Leave (five months' unpaid leave every three years) with the same leave entitlement as UK Regular soldiers (30 days paid leave each year). As a result, the number of Gurkhas recorded as being in Nepal is lower from 1 April 2007 onwards than in previous years.
5. The increase in 2002 reflects the engagement of local personnel in Bosnia-Herzegovina and Kosovo and the increase in 2004 of the engagement of personnel in Iraq.

Due to ongoing validation of data from the Joint Personnel Administration System, Service strength statistics for 1 April 2008 are provisional and subject to review.

CHAPTER 2 - PERSONNEL

PERSONNEL SUMMARY

Table **2.6** Civilian personnel[1] in UK Defence Agencies and MOD-owned Trading Funds, at 1 April 2008

Due to ongoing validation of data from a new personnel administration system, the number of Service personnel in UK Defence Agencies and Trading Funds at 1 April 2008 are currently unavailable.

Number: FTE

		Grand Total	England	Scotland	Wales	N.Ireland	Elsewhere
Total Agencies and Trading Funds		**23 510**	**18 590**	**2 200**	**1 230**	**50**	**1 440**
As a percentage of total MOD personnel in category		*26*	*30*	*37*	*57*	*3*	*8*
Agencies[2, 3]							
Service Personnel and Veterans Agency	Total	940	880	50	10	-	-
	Non-industrial	900	840	50	10	-	-
	Industrial	50	50	-	-	-	-
Defence Storage and Distribution Agency	Total	3 160	2 520	530	80	10	10
	Non-industrial	1 000	770	180	50	-	10
	Industrial	2 150	1 760	360	30	10	-
Defence Vetting Agency	Total	380	240	-	-	-	140
	Non-industrial	380	240	-	-	-	140
	Industrial	-	-	-	-	-	-
Ministry of Defence Police and Guarding Agency	Total	7 760	6 150	1 350	200	-	50
	Non-industrial	7 710	6 120	1 340	200	-	50
	Industrial	50	30	10	-	-	-
People Pay and Pensions Agency	Total	1 110	1 080	10	-	10	10
	Non-industrial	1 110	1 080	10	-	10	10
	Industrial	-	-	-	-	-	-
Service Childrens Education	Total	960	-	-	-	-	960
	Non-industrial	960	-	-	-	-	960
	Industrial	-	-	-	-	-	-
Trading Funds[5,6]							
Defence Support Group[4]		3 120	2 000	160	920	20	20
Defence Scientific and Technology Laboratories		3 350	3 110	-	-	-	230
Meteorological Office		1 740	1 590	100	20	10	30
UK Hydrographic Office		1 010	1 010	-	-	-	-
MOD Total excluding Agencies and Trading Funds		**52 470**	**44 000**	**3 790**	**940**	**2 090**	**1 650**
Locally engaged civilian staff[5]		**11 240**	-	-	-	-	**11 240**
Royal Fleet Auxiliary (RFA) staff[5]		**2 270**	-	-	-	-	**2 270**
Civilian Level 0		**89 500**	**62 590**	**5 990**	**2 170**	**2 150**	**16 600**

Source: DASA(Quad-Service)

1. Civilian Level 0 and Level 1 are defined in the Glossary.
2. Data are drawn from the Resource Accounting and Budgeting system.
3. The following Agencies formally ceased to be Defence Agencies as at 1st April 2008: Defence Analytical Services Agency and the Defence Medical And Education Training Agency.
4. Defence Support Group was formed in April 2008 from the merger of the Army Base Repair Organisation and Defence Aviation Repair Agency Trading Funds.
5. A breakdown of industrial and non-industrial personnel is unavailable for Royal Fleet Auxiliary, Trading Funds and locally engaged civilian personnel.
6. Data are drawn from personnel records.

CHAPTER 2 - PERSONNEL

UK ARMED FORCES

Armed Forces personnel key points and trends

Strength and requirement
Both the required size and actual strength of the UK's Armed Forces have decreased.

- At 1 April 2008 the total strength of the UK Regular Forces was 187,060 (see **Table 2.7**), a decrease of 38.8% from the 1 April 1990 strength of 305,750.

- The 2008 strength is 1.8% lower than the 190,400 serving in 2007.

- Four fifths of the total decrease in strength from 1990 to 2008 took place during the period 1990 to 1997 as the Armed Forces were restructured following the end of the Cold War (see **Chart 2.7**).

- The requirement for the UK's full time trained Armed Forces officers has decreased 4.0% from 30,280 in 2003 to 29,070 in 2008. The equivalent decrease for the other ranks is 8.9% from 164,850 in 2003 to 150,190 in 2008 (see **Table 2.9**).

- At 1 April 2008 the strength of the full-time trained Armed Forces was 173,960, 5,310 below the requirement of 179,270.

Intake and outflow
More people are leaving the Armed Forces than joining.

- Intake and outflow figures over the time series presented are affected by the drawdown in strength from 1990 to 1997 after the Cold War.

- Intake of civilians into the UK Regular Armed Forces has decreased 31.7% from 31,210 in the financial year 1990/91 to 21,330 in 2007/08 (see **Table 2.19**). The largest decrease took place between 1990/91 and 1997/98. From 1997/98 to 2007/08 intake figures have ranged between 17,590 and 23,610.

- Total intake during the financial year 2007/08 intake was 7.8% higher than 2006/07; 21,330 compared with 19,790.

- Outflow from the trained strength of the UK Regular Forces (see **Table 2.24**) has exceeded the number of new entries to the trained strength (Gains to Trained Strength) (see **Table 2.22**) for each of the last four financial years - 2004/05 to 2007/08.

- Outflow from the UK Regular Forces to civil life has decreased by 36.8% from 39,080 in 1990/91 to 24,690 in 2007/08 (see **Table 2.23**). From 1997/98 to 2007/08 the number of personnel leaving has been relatively stable.

Ethnic Minorities
The percentage of ethnic minorities serving in the Armed Forces is increasing

- The percentage of ethnic minorities in the UK Regular Forces has increased every year from 4.3% in 2003 to 6.1% in 2008, mostly due to an increase in the percentage of ethnic minorities in ranks Corporal and below (see **Table 2.11**).

- The percentage of ethnic minorities joining the Army other ranks (the largest component of the UK Armed Forces) was 11.0% in 2007/08 – the highest of the five financial years shown.

Females
The percentage of females serving in the Armed Forces is increasing

- The percentage of females in the UK Regular Forces has increased from 5.7% in 1990 to 9.4% in 2008 (see **Table 2.13**). The RAF has the highest percentage of female personnel (13.2% in 2008) followed by the Naval Service (9.5% in 2008) then the Army (7.8% in 2008) (see **Table 2.13**).

- The percentage of people joining the untrained strength of the UK Regular Forces that are female has been steadily decreasing from 14.3% in 1997/98 to 9.9% in 2007/08 (see **Table 2.21**). The rate of the decline has been faster for other ranks (13.9% down to 9.2%) compared with officers (18.8% down to 17.1%).

- The percentage of officers leaving in the UK Regular Forces that are female has increased from 9.9% from 1997/98 to 12.3 % in 2007/08. In contrast the percentage of other ranks leaving the UK Regular Forces that are female has decreased from 10.3% to 8.4% over the same period (see **Table 2.26**). As the percentage of females in the Armed Forces increases the percentage of females leaving will also increase.

CHAPTER 2 - PERSONNEL

UK ARMED FORCES

Location

The percentage of MOD personnel based outside the UK is stable.

- The percentage of civilian and Service personnel[1] stationed outside the UK has changed from 18.6% (60,420) in 1997 to 16.0% (41,340) in 2008 (see **Table 2.4**).

Reserve Forces

The strength of the Reserve Forces has remained more stable than the Regular Forces.

- The strength of the cadet forces has decreased from 136.0 thousand in 1990 to 127.6 thousand in 2008. There was an increase in the strength of Army cadets but this was offset by larger net decreases in the number of Naval Service and RAF cadets (see **Table 2.18**).

[1] Excluding personnel of unallocated location

UK ARMED FORCES

Table 2.7 Strength of UK Regular Forces by Service and whether trained or untrained, at 1 April each year

Thousands

	1990	1997	2003	2004	2005	2006	2007	2008
All Services	**305.8**	**210.8**	**206.9**	**207.0**	**201.1**	**195.9**	**190.4** [p]	**187.1** [p]
Officers	42.9	32.7	33.2	33.4	33.0	32.7	32.1 [p]	31.7 [p]
Other Ranks	262.9	178.1	173.8	173.6	168.1	163.2	158.3 [p]	155.3 [p]
Trained	**277.6**	**193.6**	**182.8**	**184.6**	**182.8**	**178.3**	**172.9** [p]	**168.6** [p]
Officers	37.9	29.8	29.4	29.9	29.9	29.7	29.3 [p]	28.8 [p]
Other Ranks	239.6	163.9	153.3	154.7	152.9	148.6	143.6 [p]	139.9 [p]
Untrained	**28.2**	**17.2**	**24.1**	**22.4**	**18.3**	**17.6**	**17.5** [p]	**18.4** [p]
Officers	4.9	2.9	3.7	3.6	3.1	3.0	2.8 [p]	3.0 [p]
Other Ranks	23.2	14.3	20.4	18.9	15.2	14.5	14.7 [p]	15.5 [p]
Naval Service	**63.3**	**45.1**	**41.5**	**40.9**	**39.9**	**39.4**	**38.9**	**38.6** [p]
of which: Royal Marines	*7.5*	*6.7*	*7.3*	*7.2*	*7.3* [r]	*7.4*	*7.5*	*7.7* [p]
Officers	10.1	7.9	7.8	7.8	7.7	7.7	7.6	7.5 [p]
of which: Royal Marines	*0.7*	*0.7*	*0.7*	*0.7*	*0.7*	*0.8*	*0.8*	*0.8* [p]
Other Ranks	53.1	37.2	33.8	33.1	32.2	31.7	31.3	31.1 [p]
of which: Royal Marines	*6.9*	*6.0*	*6.5*	*6.5*	*6.6*	*6.7*	*6.7*	*6.9* [p]
Trained	**56.7**	**41.7**	**36.6**	**36.4**	**35.5**	**34.9**	**34.3**	**34.5** [p]
Officers	8.3	7.0	6.6	6.7	6.7	6.6	6.7	6.5 [p]
Other Ranks	48.4	34.7	30.0	29.7	28.8	28.3	27.7	28.1 [p]
Untrained	**6.6**	**3.5**	**4.9**	**4.5**	**4.4**	**4.5**	**4.5**	**4.0** [p]
Officers	1.9	1.0	1.2	1.1	1.0	1.0	0.9	1.0 [p]
Other Ranks	4.7	2.5	3.7	3.4	3.4	3.5	3.6	3.1 [p]
Army	**152.8**	**108.8**	**112.1**	**112.7**	**109.3**	**107.7**	**106.2** [p]	**105.1** [p]
Officers	17.4	13.7	14.4	14.7	14.7	14.7	14.6 [p]	14.6 [p]
Other Ranks	135.4	95.1	97.7	98.0	94.6	93.0	91.5 [p]	90.5 [p]
Trained	**137.4**	**97.8**	**97.6**	**99.4**	**98.5**	**96.8**	**95.4** [p]	**93.8** [p]
Officers	16.2	12.7	13.2	13.5	13.6	13.8	13.8 [p]	13.7 [p]
Other Ranks	121.2	85.0	84.4	85.9	84.9	83.1	81.6 [p]	80.2 [p]
Untrained	**15.4**	**11.1**	**14.5**	**13.3**	**10.8**	**10.9**	**10.8** [p]	**11.3** [p]
Officers	1.2	1.0	1.2	1.2	1.0	1.0	0.8 [p]	0.9 [p]
Other Ranks	14.2	10.1	13.3	12.1	9.8	10.0	10.0 [p]	10.4 [p]
Royal Air Force	**89.7**	**56.9**	**53.2**	**53.4**	**51.9**	**48.7**	**45.4**	**43.4** [p]
Officers	15.3	11.0	11.0	11.0	10.6	10.3	9.9	9.7 [p]
Other Ranks	74.4	45.8	42.3	42.4	41.2	38.4	35.5	33.7 [p]
Trained	**83.5**	**54.2**	**48.5**	**48.7**	**48.8**	**46.6**	**43.2**	**40.3** [p]
Officers	13.4	10.1	9.7	9.7	9.6	9.3	8.9	8.6 [p]
Other Ranks	70.1	44.1	38.9	39.1	39.3	37.3	34.3	31.7 [p]
Untrained	**6.2**	**2.7**	**4.7**	**4.7**	**3.0**	**2.1**	**2.2**	**3.1** [p]
Officers	1.9	1.0	1.3	1.3	1.0	1.0	1.0	1.1 [p]
Other Ranks	4.3	1.7	3.4	3.4	2.0	1.1	1.1	2.1 [p]

Source: DASA (Quad-Service)

UK Regular Forces includes all trained and untrained personnel. Gurkhas, Full Time Reserve personnel, and mobilised reservists are excluded.

Due to ongoing validation of data from the Joint Personnel Administration System, Army strength statistics for 1 April 2007 and 1 April 2008, and Naval Service and RAF strength statistics for 1 April 2008 are provisional and subject to review.

CHAPTER 2 - PERSONNEL

UK ARMED FORCES

Chart to Table 2.7 **Percentage change in UK Regular strength compared with 1990**

61

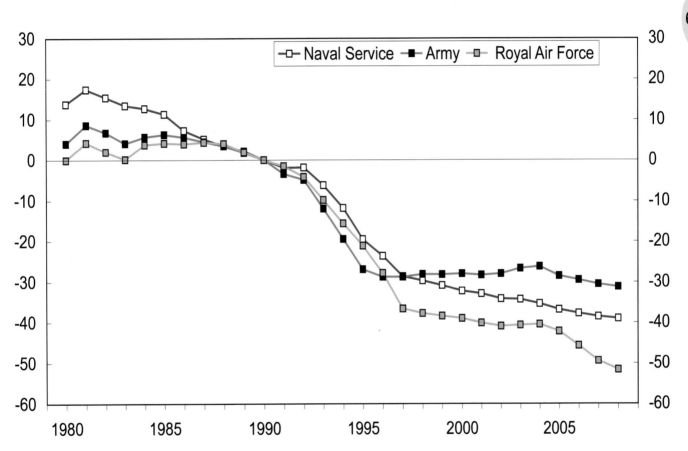

CHAPTER 2 - PERSONNEL

UK ARMED FORCES

Table 2.8 Strength of UK Regular Forces by age and rank, at 1 April each year

	1990	1997	2003	2004	2005	2006	2007	2008
Officers	**42 860**	**32 680**	**33 150**	**33 450**	**33 000**	**32 700**	**32 100** P	**31 710** P
by age:								
Under 18	-	-	-	-	-	-	- P	- P
18-19	680	150	290	280	110	80	120 P	110 P
20-24	6 020	2 970	3 240	3 200	3 020	2 550	2 570 P	2 490 P
25-29	8 240	6 490	5 820	5 970	6 060	6 210	6 280 P	6 240 P
30-34	6 340	6 040	5 630	5 610	5 490	5 180	5 030 P	4 920 P
35-39	5 420	5 490	6 060	6 000	5 790	5 700	5 580 P	5 440 P
40-44	7 160	4 540	5 360	5 470	5 540	5 730	5 520 P	5 470 P
45-49	5 320	4 030	3 820	4 000	4 140	4 300	4 300 P	4 320 P
50 and over	3 680	2 950	2 940	2 920	2 850	2 940	2 690 P	2 730 P
Average age (years)	**36**	**36**	**37**	**37**	**37**	**37**	**37** r, P	**37** P

	1990	1997	2003	2004	2005	2006	2007	2008
Other Ranks	**262 890**	**178 140**	**173 760**	**173 570**	**168 090**	**163 150**	**158 290** P	**155 340** P
by age:								
Under 18	11 330	4 600	7 510	6 690	5 140	4 920	4 650 P	4 450 P
18-19	30 060	10 520	16 030	16 030	14 110	12 490	11 650 P	11 250 P
20-24	81 610	41 490	46 410	47 100	45 320	43 670	41 760 P	40 580 P
25-29	60 110	51 890	30 220	30 550	31 430	32 460	33 530 P	34 230 P
30-34	37 910	33 760	32 590	30 780	28 500	25 800	23 380 P	22 010 P
35-39	25 150	25 100	27 150	27 230	27 480	27 840	27 350 P	26 500 P
40-44	11 210	6 600	9 970	11 040	11 540	11 200	11 050 P	11 200 P
45-49	3 630	2 810	2 820	3 130	3 490	3 660	3 800 P	3 940 P
50 and over	1 880	1 370	1 060	1 030	1 070	1 110	1 120 P	1 190 P
Average age (years)	**27**	**29**	**29**	**29**	**29**	**29**	**29** P	**29** P

	1990	1997	2003	2004	2005	2006	2007	2008
Officers	**42 860** [1]	**32 680**	**33 150**	**33 450**	**33 000**	**32 700**	**32 100** P	**31 710** P
by rank[2]:								
Major General and above	200	150	140	140	150	140	140 P	140 P
Brigadier	390	350	360	370	350	350	350 P	350 P
Colonel	1 510	1 120	1 190	1 210	1 210	1 200	1 190 P	1 180 P
Lieutenant Colonel	4 610	3 870	4 050	4 110	4 130	4 060	4 070 P	4 070 P
Major	11 800	9 960	10 130	10 120	10 010	9 950	9 760 P	9 600 P
Captain	14 780	12 370	11 820	12 020	12 310	12 290	12 120 P	11 900 P
Lieutenant and below	9 310	4 860	5 450	5 470	4 840	4 700	4 480 P	4 460 P
Other Ranks	**262 890**	**178 140**	**173 760**	**173 570**	**168 090**	**163 150**	**158 290** P	**155 340** P
by rank[2]:								
Warrant Officer	11 560	8 790	8 860	9 010	9 540	9 410	9 150 P	9 080 P
Staff Sergeant	22 750	17 010	15 450	15 310	14 470	14 110	13 810 P	13 570 P
Sergeant	35 440	25 300	22 820	23 090	22 920	22 590	21 950 P	21 310 P
Corporal[3]	55 980	37 020 ‖	32 320	32 470	32 510	31 710	30 650 P	30 300 P
Lance Corporal[3]	23 840	16 370 ‖	16 740	16 770	16 410	16 350	16 560 P	16 700 P
Private (including juniors)	113 330	73 660	77 580	76 920	72 250	68 980	66 160 P	64 390 P

Source: DASA (Quad-Service)

UK Regular Forces includes all trained and untrained personnel. Gurkhas, Full Time Reserve personnel, and mobilised reservists are excluded.

1. Includes 260 Naval Service personnel of unknown rank.
2. Figures are for paid rank. Includes the equivalent ranks for the Naval Service and RAF. See **Table 2.28**.
3. Royal Marines with a substantive rank of Marine but acting as Corporal are presented as Lance Corporal from 1 April 2003 onwards. Before this point they are presented as Corporal.

Due to ongoing validation of data from the Joint Personnel Administration System, Service strength statistics for 1 April 2007 and 1 April 2008 are provisional and subject to review.

UK ARMED FORCES

Table **2.9** Full-time trained strength[1] and requirement, at 1 April each year

	2003	2004	2005	2006	2007	2008
All Services						
Officers						
Requirement	30 280	30 730	30 970	30 070	29 840	29 070
Strength[2]	30 380	30 740	30 670	30 380	30 070 P	29 580 P
Surplus/Deficit	90	10	- 300	310	230 P	500 P
Surplus/Deficit as percentage of requirement[3]	0.3	-	-1.0	1.0	0.8 P	1.7 P
Other Ranks						
Requirement	164 850	164 620	160 120	155 850	153 770	150 190
Strength[2]	158 140	159 450	157 380	152 800	147 750 P	144 380 P
Surplus/Deficit	-6 710	-5 160	-2 740	-3 050	-6 020 P	-5 810 P
Surplus/Deficit as percentage of requirement[3]	-4.1	-3.1	-1.7	-2.0	-3.9 P	-3.9 P
Naval Service						
Officers						
Requirement	6 860	6 940	6 980	6 830	6 840	6 670
Strength[2]	6 790	6 900	6 880	6 800	6 800	6 630 P
Surplus/Deficit	- 80	- 40	- 100	- 30	- 50	- 40 P
Surplus/Deficit as percentage of requirement[3]	-1.1	-0.6	-1.5	-0.4	-0.7	-0.7 P
Other Ranks						
Requirement	31 640	31 780	31 210	30 000	29 960	29 590
Strength[2]	30 820	30 610	29 520	28 820	28 120	28 440 P
Surplus/Deficit	- 820	-1 170	-1 690	-1 190	-1 830	-1 150 P
Surplus/Deficit as percentage of requirement[3]	-2.6	-3.7	-5.4	-4.0	-6.1	-3.9 P
Army						
Officers						
Requirement	13 760	13 710	13 860	13 350	13 350	13 480
Strength[2]	13 730	13 940	14 020	14 150	14 260 P	14 210 P
Surplus/Deficit	- 30	230	170	800	900 P	730 P
Surplus/Deficit as percentage of requirement[3]	-0.2	1.7	1.2	6.0	6.8 P	5.4 P
Other Ranks						
Requirement	93 220	93 020	90 320	88 450	88 450	88 320
Strength[2]	88 270	89 610	88 420	86 470	85 090 P	84 060 P
Surplus/Deficit	-4 940	-3 410	-1 900	-1 980	-3 350 P	-4 260 P
Surplus/Deficit as percentage of requirement[3]	-5.3	-3.7	-2.1	-2.2	-3.8 P	-4.8 P
Royal Air Force						
Officers						
Requirement	9 650	10 070	10 140	9 890	9 640	8 920
Strength[2]	9 850	9 890	9 770	9 430	9 020	8 740 P
Surplus/Deficit	200	- 180	- 370	- 460	- 620	- 180 P
Surplus/Deficit as percentage of requirement[3]	2.1	-1.8	-3.6	-4.7	-6.5	-2.0 P
Other Ranks						
Requirement	39 990	39 820	38 590	37 400	35 370	32 290
Strength[2]	39 040	39 230	39 440	37 510	34 530	31 880 P
Surplus/Deficit	- 950	- 590	850	120	- 840	- 410 P
Surplus/Deficit as percentage of requirement[3]	-2.4	-1.5	2.2	0.3	-2.4	-1.3 P

Source: DASA (Quad-Service)

1. The Full Time Trained Strength comprises Trained UK Regular Forces, Trained Gurkhas and FTRS (Full Time Reserve Service) personnel. It does not include mobilised reservists.
2. FTRS Strength figures include Full Commitment (FC), Home Commitment (HC) and Limited Commitment (LC) individuals. For the RAF, FC individuals serve against the regular requirement whilst HC and LC individuals fill posts specifically for FTRS personnel. All Naval Service and Army FTRS personnel serve against the regular requirement. See **Glossary** for further information.
3. Percentages are calculated from unrounded data.

Due to ongoing validation of data from the Joint Personnel Administration System, Army strength statistics for 1 April 2007 and 1 April 2008, and Naval Service and RAF strength statistics for 1 April 2008 are provisional and subject to review.

UK ARMED FORCES

Table **2.10** Strength of UK Regular Forces by Service, ethnic origin and rank[1], at 1 April 2008

	All Personnel	White		Ethnic Minorities		Unknown[2]		Ethnic minorities as a percentage[3] of total (exc.unknown)
		Number	Percent[3]	Number	Percent[3]	Number	Percent[3]	
All Services	187 055 p	164 250 p	87.8 p	10 600 p	5.7 p	12 210 p	6.5 p	6.1 p
						-		
Officers	31 715 p	28 610 p	90.2 p	730 p	2.3 p	2 380 p	7.5 p	2.5 p
Lieutenant Colonel and above	5 750 p	5 405 p	94.0 p	100 p	1.8 p	245 p	4.2 p	1.8 p
Major and below	25 965 p	23 205 p	89.4 p	625 p	2.4 p	2 135 p	8.2 p	2.6 p
Other Ranks	155 340 p	135 640 p	87.3 p	9 870 p	6.4 p	9 830 p	6.3 p	6.8 p
Sergeant and above	43 960 p	40 235 p	91.5 p	895 p	2.0 p	2 830 p	6.4 p	2.2 p
Corporal and below	111 385 p	95 410 p	85.7 p	8 975 p	8.1 p	7 000 p	6.3 p	8.6 p
Naval Service	38 575 p	35 690 p	92.5 p	1 125 p	2.9 p	1 760 p	4.6 p	3.1 p
Officers	7 480 p	7 060 p	94.4 p	110 p	1.5 p	310 p	4.2 p	1.5 p
Commander and above	1 490 p	1 440 p	96.6 p	20 p	1.3 p	30 p	2.1 p	1.3 p
Lieutenant Commander and below	5 990 p	5 620 p	93.8 p	90 p	1.5 p	280 p	4.7 p	1.6 p
Other Ranks	31 090 p	28 630 p	92.1 p	1 015 p	3.3 p	1 450 p	4.7 p	3.4 p
Petty Officer and above	10 495 p	10 115 p	96.4 p	145 p	1.4 p	235 p	2.3 p	1.4 p
Leading Rate and below	20 595 p	18 510 p	89.9 p	870 p	4.2 p	1 215 p	5.9 p	4.5 p
Army	105 090 p	89 625 p	85.3 p	8 610 p	8.2 p	6 860 p	6.5 p	8.8 p
Officers	14 560 p	13 220 p	90.8 p	410 p	2.8 p	930 p	6.4 p	3.0 p
Lieutenant Colonel and above	2 605 p	2 440 p	93.7 p	45 p	1.7 p	120 p	4.6 p	1.8 p
Major and below	11 955 p	10 775 p	90.1 p	370 p	3.1 p	810 p	6.8 p	3.3 p
Other Ranks	90 530 p	76 405 p	84.4 p	8 195 p	9.1 p	5 930 p	6.5 p	9.7 p
Sergeant and above	22 475 p	20 185 p	89.8 p	530 p	2.4 p	1 760 p	7.8 p	2.6 p
Corporal and below	68 055 p	56 220 p	82.6 p	7 665 p	11.3 p	4 165 p	6.1 p	12.0 p
Royal Air Force	43 390 p	38 935 p	89.7 p	865 p	2.0 p	3 590 p	8.3 p	2.2 p
Officers	9 670 p	8 330 p	86.1 p	205 p	2.1 p	1 135 p	11.7 p	2.4 p
Wing Commander and above	1 655 p	1 525 p	92.1 p	40 p	2.3 p	95 p	5.6 p	2.4 p
Squadron Leader and below	8 015 p	6 805 p	84.9 p	170 p	2.1 p	1 040 p	13.0 p	2.4 p
Other Ranks	33 720 p	30 605 p	90.8 p	660 p	2.0 p	2 455 p	7.3 p	2.1 p
Sergeant and above	10 985 p	9 930 p	90.4 p	220 p	2.0 p	835 p	7.6 p	2.2 p
Corporal and below	22 735 p	20 675 p	90.9 p	440 p	1.9 p	1 620 p	7.1 p	2.1 p

Source: DASA(Quad-Service)

UK Regular Forces includes all trained and untrained personnel. Gurkhas, Full Time Reserve personnel, and mobilised reservists are excluded.

1. Figures are for paid rank. All Services totals include equivalent ranks in the Naval Service and RAF. See **Table 2.28**.

2. Includes those with an unrecorded ethnic origin and those who chose not to declare.

3. Percentages are calculated from unrounded data.

Due to ongoing validation of data from the Joint Personnel Administration System, Service strength statistics for 1 April 2008 are provisional and subject to review.

Table 2.11 Strength of UK Regular Forces by ethnic origin and rank[1] at 1 April each year

	2003	2004	2005	2006	2007	2008
White	**181 655**	**182 060**	**177 665**	**173 710**	**167 315** P	**164 250** P
Full coverage estimates[2]	*198 010*	*196 965*	*190 520*	*185 035*	*179 380* P	*175 720* P
Officers	**29 725**	**29 890**	**29 720**	**29 615**	**28 700** P	**28 610** P
Lieutenant Colonel and above	5 370	5 455	5 460	5 400	5 395 P	5 405 P
Major and below	24 355	24 435	24 260	24 215	23 305 P	23 205 P
Other Ranks	**151 930**	**152 170**	**147 945**	**144 095**	**138 610** P	**135 640** P
Sergeant and above	43 260	43 435	43 035	42 310	41 055 rp	40 235 P
Corporal and below	108 670	108 740	104 915	101 785	97 555 rp	95 410 P
Ethnic minorities	**8 175**	**9 320**	**9 885**	**10 180**	**10 360** P	**10 600** P
Full coverage estimates[2]	*8 905*	*10 055*	*10 580*	*10 815*	*11 015* P	*11 335* P
Officers	**750**	**745**	**740**	**735**	**730** P	**730** P
Lieutenant Colonel and above	120	120	120	110	115 P	100 P
Major and below	630	625	620	620	615 P	625 P
Other Ranks	**7 425**	**8 575**	**9 145**	**9 450**	**9 630** P	**9 870** P
Sergeant and above	1 095	1 080	1 070	1 005	955 rp	895 P
Corporal and below	6 330	7 495	8 075	8 445	8 675 P	8 975 P
Unknown[3]	**17 085**	**15 640**	**13 545**	**11 955**	**12 725** P	**12 210** P
Officers	**2 680**	**2 810**	**2 545**	**2 350**	**2 670** P	**2 380** P
Lieutenant Colonel and above	255	255	265	235	240 P	245 P
Major and below	2 425	2 555	2 280	2 115	2 430 P	2 135 P
Other Ranks	**14 405**	**12 830**	**11 000**	**9 605**	**10 055** P	**9 830** P
Sergeant and above	2 770	2 900	2 825	2 795	2 905 rp	2 830 P
Corporal and below	11 635	9 930	8 175	6 810	7 150 rp	7 000 P

Ethnic minorities as a percentage of total (excluding unknowns)[4]

	2003	2004	2005	2006	2007	2008
All	*4.3*	*4.9*	*5.3*	*5.5*	*5.8* P	*6.1* P
Officers	**2.5**	**2.4**	**2.4**	**2.4**	**2.5** P	**2.5** P
Lieutenant Colonel and above	*2.2*	*2.2*	*2.2*	*2.0*	*2.1* P	*1.8* P
Major and below	*2.5*	*2.5*	*2.5*	*2.5*	*2.6* P	*2.6* P
Other Ranks	**4.7**	**5.3**	**5.8**	**6.2**	**6.5** P	**6.8** P
Sergeant and above	*2.5*	*2.4*	*2.4*	*2.3*	*2.3* P	*2.2* P
Corporal and below	*5.5*	*6.4*	*7.1*	*7.7*	*8.2* P	*8.6* P

Source: DASA (Quad-Service)

UK Regular Forces includes all trained and untrained personnel. Gurkhas, Full Time Reserve personnel, and mobilised reservists are excluded.

1. Figures are for paid rank and include equivalent ranks in the Naval Service and RAF. See **Table 2.28**.
2. Full coverage estimates show the expected number of personnel in each ethnicity category if ethnicity were known for all personnel.
3. Includes those with an unrecorded ethnic origin and those who chose not to declare.
4. Percentages are calculated from unrounded data.

Due to ongoing validation of data from the Joint Personnel Administration System, Service strength statistics for 1 April 2007 and 1 April 2008 are provisional and subject to review.

65

CHAPTER 2 - PERSONNEL

UK ARMED FORCES

Table 2.12 Strength of UK Regular Forces by sex and rank[1], at 1 April each year

	1990	1997	2003	2004	2005	2006	2007	2008
Female Officers	2 780 [2]	2 380	3 350	3 520	3 600	3 680	3 720 [P]	3 760 [P]
by rank:								
Major General and above	-	-	-	-	-	-	- [P]	- [P]
Brigadier	7	2	3	3	4	3	2 [P]	2 [P]
Colonel	24	16	31	34	39	41	39 [P]	39 [P]
Lieutenant Colonel	66	80	140	150	170	180	200 [P]	210 [P]
Major	370	420	670	730	760	820	890 [P]	920 [P]
Captain	1 140	1 180	1 540	1 630	1 720	1 770	1 800 [P]	1 810 [P]
Lieutenant and below	920	680	970	980	900	860	790 [P]	780 [P]
Male Officers	40 080	30 300	29 800	29 920	29 410	29 020	28 380 [P]	27 950 [P]
by rank:								
Major General and above	200	150	140	140	150	140	140 [P]	140 [P]
Brigadier	380	350	360	370	350	350	340 [P]	350 [P]
Colonel	1 490	1 110	1 160	1 180	1 170	1 160	1 150 [P]	1 140 [P]
Lieutenant Colonel	4 550	3 790	3 910	3 960	3 960	3 880	3 870 [P]	3 860 [P]
Major	11 420	9 540	9 460	9 400	9 250	9 130	8 860 [P]	8 680 [P]
Captain	13 640	11 190	10 280	10 400	10 580	10 520	10 320 [P]	10 090 [P]
Lieutenant and below	8 390	4 180	4 490	4 490	3 940	3 840	3 680 [P]	3 680 [P]
Female Other Ranks	14 690	12 450	14 560	14 870	14 560	14 190	13 920 [P]	13 860 [P]
by rank:								
Warrant Officer	140	170	280	300	320	320	350 [P]	350 [P]
Staff Sergeant	360	370	520	550	560	590	570 [P]	610 [P]
Sergeant	1 390	1 170	1 340	1 420	1 500	1 640	1 700 [P]	1 740 [P]
Corporal[3]	2 980	2 360 ‖	2 960	3 210	3 350	3 370	3 400 [P]	3 450 [P]
Lance Corporal[3]	1 290	1 080 ‖	1 570	1 510	1 520	1 550	1 500 [P]	1 500 [P]
Private (including juniors)	8 530	7 300	7 900	7 880	7 310	6 730	6 400 [P]	6 210 [P]
Male Other Ranks	248 210	165 690	159 200	158 700	153 530	148 960	144 380 [P]	141 480 [P]
by rank:								
Warrant Officer	11 420	8 610	8 580	8 710	9 230	9 090	8 800 [P]	8 730 [P]
Staff Sergeant	22 390	16 640	14 930	14 770	13 910	13 520	13 240 [P]	12 970 [P]
Sergeant	34 050	24 130	21 480	21 670	21 410	20 950	20 260 [P]	19 570 [P]
Corporal[3]	53 000	34 660 ‖	29 360	29 260	29 150	28 340	27 250 [P]	26 850 [P]
Lance Corporal[3]	22 550	15 290 ‖	15 170	15 260	14 890	14 790	15 060 [P]	15 200 [P]
Private (including juniors)	104 800	66 360	69 680	69 040	64 940	62 260	59 770 [P]	58 180 [P]
Females as a percentage of total[4]								
Officers	6.5 [2]	7.3	10.1	10.5	10.9	11.3	11.6 [P]	11.9 [P]
by rank:								
Major General and above	-	-	-	-	-	-	- [P]	- [P]
Brigadier	1.8	0.6	0.8	0.8	1.1	0.9	0.6 [P]	0.6 [P]
Colonel	1.6	1.4	2.6	2.8	3.2	3.4	3.3 [P]	3.3 [P]
Lieutenant Colonel	1.4	2.1	3.5	3.7	4.1	4.5	4.8 [P]	5.2 [P]
Major	3.2	4.3	6.6	7.2	7.6	8.3	9.2 [P]	9.6 [P]
Captain	7.7	9.5	13.0	13.5	14.0	14.4	14.8 [P]	15.2 [P]
Lieutenant and below	9.9	13.9	17.7	17.9	18.6	18.4	17.7 [P]	17.5 [P]
Other Ranks	5.6	7.0	8.4	8.6	8.7	8.7	8.8 [P]	8.9 [P]
by rank:								
Warrant Officer	1.2	2.0	3.1	3.4	3.3	3.4	3.8 [P]	3.9 [P]
Staff Sergeant	1.6	2.2	3.4	3.6	3.9	4.2	4.1 [P]	4.5 [P]
Sergeant	3.9	4.6	5.9	6.2	6.6	7.3	7.7 [P]	8.1 [P]
Corporal[3]	5.3	6.4 ‖	9.2	9.9	10.3	10.6	11.1 [P]	11.4 [P]
Lance Corporal[3]	5.4	6.6 ‖	9.4	9.0	9.3	9.5	9.1 [P]	9.0 [P]
Private (including juniors)	7.5	9.9	10.2	10.2	10.1	9.8	9.7 [P]	9.6 [P]

Source: DASA (Quad-Service)

UK Regular Forces includes all trained and untrained personnel. Gurkhas, Full Time Reserve personnel, and mobilised reservists are excluded.

1. Figures are for paid rank and include equivalent ranks in the Naval Service and RAF. See **Table 2.28**.
2. Includes 260 female Naval Officers of unknown rank.
3. Royal Marines with a substantive rank of Marine but acting as Corporal are presented as Lance Corporal from 1 April 2003 onwards. Before this point they are presented as Corporal.
4. Percentages are calculated from unrounded data.

Figures fewer than 100 have been left unrounded so as not to obscure the data.

Due to ongoing validation of data from the Joint Personnel Administration System, Service strength statistics for 1 April 2007 and 1 April 2008 are provisional and subject to review.

UK ARMED FORCES

Table **2.13** Strength of UK Regular Forces by sex and Service, at 1 April each year

	1990	1997	2003	2004	2005	2006	2007	2008
Females: total	**17 470**	**14 830**	**17 910**	**18 390**	**18 160**	**17 870**	**17 640** ᴾ	**17 620** ᴾ
Naval Service	3 660	3 250	3 690	3 730	3 690	3 670	3 650	3 680 ᴾ
Army	7 050	6 680	8 290	8 420	8 210	8 180	8 180 ᴾ	8 240 ᴾ
RAF	6 760	4 900	5 930	6 240	6 260	6 020	5 810	5 710 ᴾ
Officers	**2 780**	**2 380**	**3 350**	**3 520**	**3 600**	**3 680**	**3 720** ᴾ	**3 760** ᴾ
Naval Service	420	440	610	640	660	680	680	700 ᴾ
Army	1 230	1 060	1 470	1 520	1 550	1 590	1 630 ᴾ	1 640 ᴾ
RAF	1 140	880	1 270	1 360	1 390	1 410	1 410	1 420 ᴾ
Other Ranks	**14 690**	**12 450**	**14 560**	**14 870**	**14 560**	**14 190**	**13 920** ᴾ	**13 860** ᴾ
Naval Service	3 250	2 810	3 080	3 090	3 030	3 000	2 970	2 980 ᴾ
Army	5 820	5 620	6 820	6 890	6 660	6 590	6 550 ᴾ	6 600 ᴾ
RAF	5 620	4 020	4 660	4 880	4 870	4 600	4 400	4 290 ᴾ
Males: total	**288 280**	**195 990**	**189 000**	**188 630**	**182 940**	**177 980**	**172 760** ᴾ	**169 430** ᴾ
Naval Service	59 590	41 900	37 860	37 150	36 250	35 720	35 210	34 900 ᴾ
Army	145 760	102 120	103 840	104 330	101 080	99 550	97 990 ᴾ	96 860 ᴾ
RAF	82 920	51 970	47 310	47 150	45 610	42 710	39 560	37 680 ᴾ
Officers	**40 080**	**30 300**	**29 800**	**29 920**	**29 410**	**29 020**	**28 380** ᴾ	**27 950** ᴾ
Naval Service	9 730	7 480	7 180	7 130	7 070	6 980	6 900	6 780 ᴾ
Army	16 210	12 660	12 940	13 190	13 110	13 140	13 000 ᴾ	12 920 ᴾ
RAF	14 140	10 160	9 680	9 600	9 230	8 900	8 480	8 250 ᴾ
Other Ranks	**248 210**	**165 690**	**159 200**	**158 700**	**153 530**	**148 960**	**144 380** ᴾ	**141 480** ᴾ
Naval Service	49 860	34 420	30 670	30 020	29 180	28 740	28 310	28 110 ᴾ
Army	129 560	89 460	90 900	91 140	87 970	86 410	84 980 ᴾ	83 940 ᴾ
RAF	68 790	41 810	37 630	37 540	36 380	33 810	31 080	29 430 ᴾ
Females as a percentage of total[1]	*5.7*	*7.0*	*8.7*	*8.9*	*9.0*	*9.1*	*9.3* ᴾ	*9.4* ᴾ
Naval Service	*5.8*	*7.2*	*8.9*	*9.1*	*9.2*	*9.3*	*9.4*	*9.5* ᴾ
Army	*4.6*	*6.1*	*7.4*	*7.5*	*7.5*	*7.6*	*7.7* ᴾ	*7.8* ᴾ
RAF	*7.5*	*8.6*	*11.1*	*11.7*	*12.1*	*12.3*	*12.8*	*13.2* ᴾ
Officers	*6.5*	*7.3*	*10.1*	*10.5*	*10.9*	*11.3*	*11.6* ᴾ	*11.9* ᴾ
Naval Service	*4.1*	*5.5*	*7.9*	*8.2*	*8.6*	*8.8*	*9.0*	*9.4* ᴾ
Army	*7.1*	*7.7*	*10.2*	*10.4*	*10.6*	*10.8*	*11.1* ᴾ	*11.3* ᴾ
RAF	*7.4*	*8.0*	*11.6*	*12.4*	*13.1*	*13.7*	*14.3*	*14.7* ᴾ
Other Ranks	*5.6*	*7.0*	*8.4*	*8.6*	*8.7*	*8.7*	*8.8* ᴾ	*8.9* ᴾ
Naval Service	*6.1*	*7.6*	*9.1*	*9.3*	*9.4*	*9.4*	*9.5*	*9.6* ᴾ
Army	*4.3*	*5.9*	*7.0*	*7.0*	*7.0*	*7.1*	*7.2* ᴾ	*7.3* ᴾ
RAF	*7.6*	*8.8*	*11.0*	*11.5*	*11.8*	*12.0*	*12.4*	*12.7* ᴾ

Source: DASA (Quad-Service)

UK Regular Forces includes all trained and untrained personnel. Gurkhas, Full Time Reserve personnel, and mobilised reservists are excluded.

1. Percentages are calculated from unrounded data.

Due to ongoing validation of data from the Joint Personnel Administration System, Service strength statistics for 1 April 2007 and 1 April 2008 are provisional and subject to review.

67

UK ARMED FORCES

Table 2.14 Strength of the UK Regular Forces by Service and ethnic origin, at 1 April each year[1,2]

68

	2003 Number	2003 Percentage[1] of total (exc. unknown)	2004 Number	2004 Percentage[1] of total (exc. unknown)	2005 Number	2005 Percentage[1] of total (exc. unknown)	2006 Number	2006 Percentage[1] of total (exc. unknown)	2007 Number	2007 Percentage[1] of total (exc. unknown)	2008 Number	2008 Percentage[1] of total (exc. unknown)
All Services	206 915		207 020		201 100		195 850		190 395 P		187 055 P	
Ethnic Minorities[2]	8 175	*4.3*	9 320	*4.9*	9 885	*5.3*	10 180	*5.5*	10 360 P	*5.8* P	10 600 P	*6.1* P
Asian	740	*0.4*	790	*0.4*	905	*0.5*	970	*0.5*	1 025 P	*0.6* P	1 090 P	*0.6* P
Black	4 020	*2.1*	5 065	*2.6*	5 535	*3.0*	5 790	*3.1*	5 990 P	*3.4* P	6 270 P	*3.6* P
Chinese	150	*0.1*	155	*0.1*	160	*0.1*	150	*0.1*	140 P	*0.1* P	145 P	*0.1* P
Mixed	2 295	*1.2*	2 320	*1.2*	2 275	*1.2*	2 275	*1.2*	2 250 P	*1.3* P	2 155 P	*1.2* P
Other	970	*0.5*	995	*0.5*	1 010	*0.5*	995	*0.5*	955 P	*0.5* P	940 P	*0.5* P
White	181 655	*95.7*	182 060	*95.1*	177 665	*94.7*	173 710	*94.5*	167 315 P	*94.2* P	164 250 P	*93.9* P
Unknown[3]	17 085	*	15 640	*	13 545	*	11 955	*	12 725 P	*	12 210 P	*
Naval Service	41 550		40 880		39 945		39 390		38 860		38 575 P	
Ethnic Minorities[2]	880	*2.3*	920	*2.4*	960	*2.5*	995	*2.6*	985	*2.7*	1 125 P	*3.1* P
Asian	75	*0.2*	75	*0.2*	85	*0.2*	85	*0.2*	70	*0.2*	80 P	*0.2* P
Black	290	*0.7*	310	*0.8*	335	*0.9*	385	*1.0*	405	*1.1*	540 P	*1.5* P
Chinese	25	*0.1*	25	*0.1*	25	*0.1*	25	*0.1*	25	*0.1*	25 P	*0.1* P
Mixed	350	*0.9*	360	*0.9*	365	*0.9*	360	*0.9*	345	*0.9*	340 P	*0.9* P
Other	145	*0.4*	145	*0.4*	145	*0.4*	145	*0.4*	140	*0.4*	135 P	*0.4* P
White	38 005	*97.7*	37 630	*97.6*	37 465	*97.5*	37 260	*97.4*	35 485	*97.3*	35 690 P	*96.9* P
Unknown[3]	2 660	*	2 330	*	1 520	*	1 135	*	2 385	*	1 760 P	*
Army	112 125		112 745		109 285		107 730		106 170 P		105 090 P	
Ethnic Minorities[2]	6 070	*5.9*	7 200	*6.9*	7 780	*7.6*	8 150	*8.0*	8 435 P	*8.4* P	8 610 P	*8.8* P
Asian	495	*0.5*	540	*0.5*	655	*0.6*	735	*0.7*	820 P	*0.8* P	885 P	*0.9* P
Black	3 405	*3.3*	4 435	*4.2*	4 890	*4.8*	5 140	*5.1*	5 345 P	*5.3* P	5 515 P	*5.6* P
Chinese	90	*0.1*	95	*0.1*	95	*0.1*	90	*0.1*	85 P	*0.1* P	90 P	*0.1* P
Mixed	1 460	*1.4*	1 475	*1.4*	1 460	*1.4*	1 495	*1.5*	1 510 P	*1.5* P	1 445 P	*1.5* P
Other	625	*0.6*	655	*0.6*	675	*0.7*	690	*0.7*	670 P	*0.7* P	670 P	*0.7* P
White	97 280	*94.1*	97 745	*93.1*	94 595	*92.4*	93 490	*92.0*	92 000 P	*91.6* P	89 625 P	*91.2* P
Unknown[3]	8 775	*	7 805	*	6 910	*	6 090	*	5 730 P	*	6 860 P	*

Continued overleaf

CHAPTER 2 - PERSONNEL

UK ARMED FORCES

Table 2.17 Strength of the Reserve Forces[1] at 1 April each year

Thousands

	1990		1997	2003	2004	2005	2006	2007	2008
Total Reserve	**341.4**	||	**322.1**	**257.2**	**244.4**	**233.6**	..	..	..
Regular reserve	**250.8**		**259.4**	**212.3**	**201.0**	**191.3**	..	..	..
Naval Service[2]	**27.2**		**24.1**	**23.2**	**22.8**	**22.2**	..	..	**19.6**
Royal Fleet Reserve[3]	13.6		10.0	10.3	10.7	10.5	..	..	8.0
of which mobilised	-		-	-	-	-	..	..	-
Individuals liable to recall	13.6		14.1	12.8	12.0	11.7	..	..	11.6
Army[4]	**183.5**		**190.1**	**151.4**	**141.8**	**134.2**	**127.6**	**121.8**	..
Army Reserve	65.8		41.2	32.3	31.1	31.4	32.1	33.8	..
of which mobilised	..		..	0.4	0.1	0.2	0.3	0.1	..
Individuals liable to recall	117.7		148.9	119.1	110.7	102.8	95.5	88.1	..
Royal Air Force	**40.1**		**45.3**	**37.7**	**36.4**	**35.0**	**34.4**	**33.4** [p]	..
Royal Air Force Reserve	10.1		16.2	10.2	9.3	8.2	7.8	7.3 [p]	6.1 [p]
of which mobilised	..		..	-	-	-	-	- [p]	0.1 [p]
Individuals liable to recall	30.1		29.0	27.5	27.1	26.7	26.6	26.0 [p]	..
Volunteer reserve	**90.6**	||	**62.6**	**44.9**	**43.4**	**42.3**	..	**41.0** [p]	**39.2** [p]
Naval Service[5]	7.0		3.6	4.1	3.8	3.6	..	3.0	2.9
of which mobilised	-		-	0.4	0.1	-	..	0.1	0.2
Army[6,7,8,9]	81.9	||	57.7	39.3	38.1	37.3	38.5	36.8	35.0 [p]
of which mobilised	-		0.1	4.1	2.9	1.5	1.1	1.0	1.4 [p]
Royal Air Force[10]	1.7		1.4	1.5	1.4	1.4	1.4	1.3 [p]	1.3 [p]
of which mobilised	-		-	0.8	-	-	0.1	0.2 [p]	0.1 [p]

Sources: DASA (Quad-Service), Single Services

1. Figures exclude FTRS personnel.
2. Naval Service Regular reserve data for 2006 and 2007 were not compiled as a result of Naval Service restructuring and so are not available.
3. Comprises Royal Fleet Reserve, Naval and Royal Fleet Reserve and Marine.
4. Army Regular reserve data for 2008 have not been compiled and so are not available.
5. Excludes University Royal Navy Unit personnel.
6. Army Volunteer reserve data are as at 1 June 2008 since 1 April 2008 have not been compiled and so are not available.
7. Includes the Ulster Defence Regiment prior to 1 July 1992, when it merged with the Royal Irish Rangers and became the Home Service element of the Royal Irish Regiment. Full details can be found in **Table 7.1**.
8. Between 1983 and 1993 includes the Home Service Force.
9. Includes Officer Training Corps and Non-Regular Permanent Staff.
10. Excludes University Air Squadron personnel.

Table 2.18 Strength of the cadet forces at 1 April each year

Thousands

	1990		1997	2003	2004	2005	2006	2007	2008
Total cadet forces[1]	**136.0**	||	**127.5**	**132.8**	**132.2**	**130.3**	..	**127.4**	**127.6**
Naval Service[2]	26.2	||	20.7	18.7	18.2	17.5	..	14.9	15.2
Army	65.7		65.1	69.8	71.3	71.6	71.9	72.2	73.0
Royal Air Force	44.2		41.8	44.3	42.7	41.1	39.5	40.3	39.4

Sources: DRFC, Single Services

1. The figures for each service include both single service cadet forces and an element of the Combined Cadet Force. Figures exclude officers, training and administrative staff except for Naval Service figures before 1993 where separate figures are not available.

2. Prior to 1993 includes officers and training staff.

UK ARMED FORCES

Table **2.19** Intake[1] to UK Regular Forces from civil life[2] by sex and Service

	1990/91	1997/98	2003/04	2004/05	2005/06	2006/07	2007/08
All Services	**31 210**	**23 610**	**23 540**	**17 590**	**18 150**	**19 790** p	**21 330** p
Officers	**2 780**	**1 760**	**1 800**	**1 450**	**1 520**	**1 580** p	**1 740** p
Male	..	1 380	1 450	1 150	1 230	1 280 p	1 440 p
Female	..	380	350	300	290	310 p	300 p
Other Ranks	**28 420**	**21 850**	**21 730**	**16 140**	**16 630**	**18 210** p	**19 590** p
Male	..	18 870	19 360	14 540	15 180	16 560 p	17 790 p
Female	..	2 980	2 370	1 600	1 450	1 650 p	1 800 p
Naval Service	**6 910**	**4 600**	**4 120**	**3 690**	**3 940**	**3 770** p	**3 860** p
Officers	**550**	**370**	**340**	**370**	**370**	**320** p	**290** p
of which: Royal Marines	..	*40*	*40*	*50*	*50*	*50* p	*30* p
Male	..	300	290	300	320	280 p	240 p
of which: Royal Marines	..	*40*	*40*	*50*	*50*	*50* p	*30* p
Female	..	70	50	60	50	50 p	50 p
of which: Royal Marines	..	*-*	*-*	*-*	*-*	*-* p	*-* p
Other Ranks	**6 360**	**4 230**	**3 780**	**3 320**	**3 570**	**3 450** p	**3 580** p
of which: Royal Marines	..	*980*	*1 050*	*1 030*	*1 190*	*1 080* p	*1 080* p
Male	..	3 660	3 240	2 930	3 160	3 030 p	3 160 p
of which: Royal Marines	..	*960*	*1 040*	*1 010*	*1 180*	*1 070* p	*1 070* p
Female	..	560	530	390	410	420 p	420 p
of which: Royal Marines	..	*10*	*10*	*20*	*10*	*10* p	*10* p
Army	**17 500**	**15 480**	**15 260**	**11 720**	**12 730**	**14 300** p	**14 540** p
Officers	**1 450**	**990**	**940**	**790**	**820**	**900** p	**1 060** p
Male	..	780	780	640	680	720 p	890 p
Female	..	200	160	140	140	170 p	170 p
Other Ranks	**16 050**	**14 500**	**14 310**	**10 940**	**11 910**	**13 400** p	**13 480** p
Male	..	12 660	13 210	10 160	11 060	12 440 p	12 500 p
Female	..	1 830	1 110	770	850	970 p	980 p
Royal Air Force	**6 800**	**3 530**	**4 160**	**2 180**	**1 480**	**1 720**	**2 930** p
Officers	**780**	**400**	**520**	**290**	**330**	**370**	**390** p
Male	..	290	380	200	230	280	300 p
Female	..	110	140	100	100	90	80 p
Other Ranks	**6 010**	**3 130**	**3 640**	**1 880**	**1 150**	**1 360**	**2 540** p
Male	..	2 540	2 910	1 440	960	1 090	2 140 p
Female	..	590	730	440	190	270	400 p

Source: DASA (Quad-Service)

UK Regular Forces includes all trained and untrained personnel. Gurkhas, Full Time Reserve personnel, and mobilised reservists are excluded.

1. Figures show intake to UK Regular Forces including re-enlistments and rejoined reservists but excludes movements between services.

2. Includes trained entrants. Trained entrants are excluded from **Tables 2.20** and **2.21**.

Due to ongoing validation of data from the Joint Personnel Administration System, all Naval Service and Army flow statistics for financial year 06/07 and 07/08 and all RAF flow statistics for financial year 07/08 are provisional and subject to review.

Table 2.20 Intake to untrained strength of UK Regular Forces by Service and ethnic origin

	2003/04	2004/05	2005/06	2006/07	2007/08
All Services	**23 040**	**17 200**	**17 810**	**19 260** [p]	**20 910** [p]
Officers	**1 950**	**1 510**	**1 600**	**1 640** [p]	**1 910** [p]
White	1 580	1 375	1 490	..	..
Ethnic minorities	35	35	35	..	..
Unknown[1]	335	95	75	..	..
Other ranks	**21 090**	**15 700**	**16 210**	**17 630** [p]	**19 000** [p]
White	18 675	13 940	14 650	.. [r]	..
Ethnic minorities	1 870	1 290	1 015	.. [r]	..
of which: Commonwealth 'Block recruits'[2]	315	225	110	.. [r]	..
Unknown[1]	545	465	545	.. [r]	..
Naval Service	**4 050**	**3 660**	**3 870**	**3 780** [p]	**4 000** [p]
Officers	**420**	**470**	**440**	**400** [p]	**420** [p]
White	360	380	385	..	330
Ethnic minorities	~	5	10	..	10
Unknown[1]	60	80	50	..	80
Other ranks	**3 630**	**3 190**	**3 430**	**3 380** [p]	**3 580** [p]
White	3 000	2 670	2 810	.. [r]	..
Ethnic minorities	115	100	115	.. [r]	..
of which: Commonwealth 'Block recruits'[2]	-	-	-	.. [r]	..
Unknown[1]	515	420	505	.. [r]	..
Army	**14 700**	**11 300**	**12 360**	**13 700** [p]	**13 840** [p]
Officers	**880**	**680**	**730**	**810** [p]	**990** [p]
White	850	650	710	770 [p]	..
Ethnic minorities	30	20	20	30 [p]	..
Unknown[1]	~	5	~	10 [p]	..
Other ranks	**13 820**	**10 620**	**11 620**	**12 890** [p]	**12 840** [p]
White	12 115	9 470	10 740	11 590 [p]	9 415 [p]
Ethnic minorities	1 695	1 150	880	1 040 [p]	1 160 [p]
of which: Commonwealth 'Block recruits'[2]	315	225	110	- [p]	..
Unknown[1]	10	~	10	260 [p]	2 265 [p]
Royal Air Force	**4 290**	**2 240**	**1 580**	**1 790**	**3 070** [p]
Officers	**650**	**360**	**430**	**430**	**500** [p]
White	370	345	395	..	445
Ethnic minorities	10	10	5	..	5
Unknown[1]	270	10	25	..	40
Other ranks	**3 640**	**1 880**	**1 150**	**1 360**	**2 580** [p]
White	3 560	1 800	1 100	1 155	2 195 [p]
Ethnic minorities	55	45	20	20	45 [p]
Unknown[1]	25	40	30	185	340 [p]

Ethnic minorities as a percentage[4] of total (exc. unknown)

	2003/04	2004/05	2005/06	2006/07	2007/08
All personnel[4]	*7.3*	*6.7*	*5.5*	*..*	*..*
Officers	*2.3*	*2.6*	*2.4*	*..*	*..*
Naval Service	*0.3*	*1.6*	*2.0*	*..*	*2.4* [p]
Army	*3.2*	*3.1*	*2.9*	*3.6* [p]	*..*
Royal Air Force	*2.1*	*2.8*	*1.7*	*..*	*1.5* [p]
Other ranks[4]	*7.7*	*7.1*	*5.8*	*..* [r]	*..*
Naval Service	*3.8*	*3.5*	*3.9*	*..* [r]	*..*
Army[4]	*10.2*	*8.9*	*6.7*	*8.2* [p]	*11.0* [p]
Royal Air Force	*1.6*	*2.3*	*1.8*	*1.5*	*1.9* [p]

Source: DASA(Quad-Service)

UK Regular Forces excludes Gurkhas, Full Time Reserve personnel, and mobilised reservists. Officer figures include intake from the ranks and re-entrants.

Fluctuations in intake reflect changes in recruiting targets as well as the degree of success in meeting them.

Ethnicity figures are based on those with a known ethnic origin. Where more than 40% of ethnicity data are unknown, figures are suppressed to reduce the possibility of presenting misleading information. All service totals are also surpressed when comprised of single service figures of varying coverage to prevent bias towards services with higher coverage.

1. Includes those with an unrecorded ethnic origin and those who choose not to declare.
2. Ethnic minorities recruited *en bloc* include Fijians, Vincencians and St Lucians for 2003/04. From April 2004, only Fijians are included. From April 2006 there are no block recruits.
3. Percentages are calculated from unrounded data.
4. Excludes Fijians, Vincencians and St Lucians recruited *en bloc*.

Due to ongoing validation of data from the Joint Personnel Administration System, all Naval Service and Army flow statistics for financial year 06/07 and 07/08 and all RAF flow statistics for financial year 07/08 are provisional and subject to review.

UK ARMED FORCES

Table 2.21 Intake to untrained strength of UK Regular Forces by Service and sex

	1997/98	2003/04	2004/05	2005/06	2006/07	2007/08
Females: total	**3 280**	**2 660**	**1 810**	**1 660**	**1 880** p	**2 070** p
Officers: total	360	360	280	270	280 p	330 p
Naval Service	80	60	80	60	50 p	50 p
Army	160	140	100	100	140 p	170 p
Royal Air Force	120	160	100	110	100	100 p
Other ranks: total	2 920	2 300	1 530	1 390	1 590 p	1 750 p
Naval Service	560	510	380	390	410 p	420 p
Army	1 780	1 060	710	800	920 p	930 p
Royal Air Force	590	730	440	190	270	400 p
Males: total	**19 650**	**20 390**	**15 390**	**16 150**	**17 380** p	**18 840** p
Officers: total	1 540	1 590	1 230	1 330	1 350 p	1 580 p
Naval Service	380	370	390	380	350 p	370 p
Army	720	740	580	630	670 p	820 p
Royal Air Force	440	490	260	310	330	390 p
Other ranks: total	18 110	18 800	14 160	14 820	16 040 p	17 260 p
Naval Service	3 650	3 120	2 810	3 040	2 970 p	3 160 p
Army	11 930	12 760	9 910	10 820	11 970 p	11 910 p
Royal Air Force	2 540	2 910	1 440	960	1 090	2 180 p
Females as a percentage of total[1]	**14.3**	**11.5**	**10.5**	**9.3**	**9.7** p	**9.9** p
Officers: total	18.8	18.3	18.5	17.1	17.4 p	17.1 p
Naval Service	17.2	13.2	16.1	12.9	12.5 p	12.9 p
Army	17.8	16.1	14.6	14.0	17.1 p	17.2 p
Royal Air Force	21.6	24.7	28.8	26.8	22.6	20.4 p
Other ranks: total	13.9	10.9	9.8	8.6	9.0 p	9.2 p
Naval Service	13.2	13.9	11.9	11.5	12.1 p	11.7 p
Army	13.0	7.7	6.7	6.9	7.1 p	7.2 p
Royal Air Force	18.9	20.1	23.3	16.8	19.7	15.4 p

Source: DASA (Quad-Service)

UK Regular Forces excludes Gurkhas, Full Time Reserve personnel, and mobilised reservists.

1. Percentages are calculated from unrounded data.

Due to ongoing validation of data from the Joint Personnel Administration System, all Naval Service and Army flow statistics for financial year 06/07 and 07/08 and all RAF flow statistics for financial year 07/08 are provisional and subject to review.

Table 2.22 Gains to trained strength[1] of UK Regular Forces by Service

	2003/04	2004/05	2005/06	2006/07	2007/08
All Services	**19 070**	**16 780**	**14 780**	**14 670** r,p	**15 500** p
Officers: total	2 150	2 020	1 840	1 990 p	1 790 p
Naval Service	480	410	370	430 p	300 p
Army	1 070	1 050	1 090	1 160 p	1 040 p
Royal Air Force	600	550	380	400	440 p
Other ranks: total	16 920	14 760	12 940	12 670 r,p	13 700 p
Naval Service	2 840	2 310	2 470	2 320 p	3 270 p
Army	10 920	9 580	8 610	9 350 r,p	9 260 p
Royal Air Force	3 160	2 870	1 860	1 010	1 170 p

Source: DASA (Quad-Service)

UK Regular Forces excludes Gurkhas, Full Time Reserve personnel, and mobilised reservists.

1. Gains to Trained Strength (GTS) represent those who are added to the trained strength, usually having just completed their training and thus transferring from the untrained strength. Because of the nature of the data, this has been inferred by adding trained outflow to the net change in trained strength. Personnel who have transferred from the untrained to trained strength and back again (or vice versa) within the period shown are thus excluded. Direct entries to the trained strength are included in GTS, such as trained re-entrants, Professionally Qualified Officers (PQO) and FTRS. Fluctuations in GTS reflect changes in GTS targets as well as the degree of success in meeting them.

Due to ongoing validation of data from the Joint Personnel Administration System, all Naval Service and Army flow statistics for financial year 06/07 and 07/08 and all RAF flow statistics for financial year 07/08 are provisional and subject to review.

UK ARMED FORCES

Table **2.23** Outflow[1] from UK Regular Forces by Service and whether trained or untrained

	1990/91	1997/98	2003/04	2004/05	2005/06	2006/07	2007/08
All Services	39 080 ||	24 350	23 400	23 430	23 260	25 160 r, p	24 690 p
Officers[2]	3 710 ||	2 280	2 040	2 310	2 290	2 680 p	2 820 p
Trained	.. ||	2 040	1 740	1 970	2 080	2 310 p	2 340 p
as a percentage of trained strength[3]	.. ||	6.9	5.8	6.6	7.0	7.9 p	8.1 p
Untrained	.. ||	240	310	340	220	370 p	480 p
Other ranks	35 370	22 070	21 360	21 120	20 980	22 480 r,p	21 860 p
Trained	..	16 350	14 730	15 640	16 070	16 560 p	15 670 p
as a percentage of trained strength[3]	..	10.1	9.6	10.1	10.6	11.4 p	11.1 p
Untrained	..	5 720	6 640	5 490	4 910	5 920 p	6 190 p
Naval Service	8 110	5 270	4 770	4 630	4 490	4 320 p	4 340 p
Officers	800	620	470	510	520	500 p	580 p
Trained	..	500	380	420	430	400 p	460 p
as a percentage of trained strength[3]	..	7.3	5.7	6.3	6.5	6.0 p	7.0 p
Untrained	..	120	90	90	90	100 p	120 p
Other ranks	7 310	4 650	4 300	4 130	3 960	3 820 p	3 760 p
Trained	..	3 560	3 060	3 170	2 870	2 800 p	2 660 p
as a percentage of trained strength[3]	..	10.4	10.3	10.8	10.1	10.0 p	9.5 p
Untrained	..	1 080	1 250	960	1 100	1 020 r,p	1 110 p
Army	22 820 ||	14 470	14 600	15 070	14 190	15 770 p	15 330 p
Officers[2]	1 860 ||	1 040	950	1 100	1 070	1 330 p	1 490 p
Trained	.. ||	960	780	900	980	1 110 p	1 160 p
as a percentage of trained strength[3]	.. ||	7.5	5.8	6.6	7.1	8.1 p	8.4 p
Untrained	.. ||	80	170	200	90	220 p	330 p
Other ranks	20 960	13 430	13 640	13 970	13 120	14 440 p	13 830 p
Trained	..	9 250	8 790	9 840	9 520	9 820 p	9 310 p
as a percentage of trained strength[3]	..	10.9	10.3	11.4	11.3	12.0 p	11.6 p
Untrained	..	4 180	4 850	4 130	3 600	4 620 p	4 530 p
Royal Air Force	8 150	4 610	4 040	3 730	4 590	5 070	5 020 p
Officers	1 050	620	620	700	700	850	760 p
Trained	..	580	580	640	670	800	720 p
as a percentage of trained strength[3]	..	5.9	6.0	6.7	7.1	8.9	8.3 p
Untrained	..	40	40	60	30	50	30 p
Other ranks	7 090	3 990	3 410	3 020	3 890	4 220	4 270 p
Trained	..	3 540	2 880	2 630	3 670	3 930	3 710 p
as a percentage of trained strength[3]	..	8.2	7.4	6.7	9.6	11.1	11.3 p
Untrained	..	450	530	400	220	280	560 p

77

Source: DASA (Quad-Service)

UK Regular Forces includes all trained and untrained personnel. Gurkhas, Full Time Reserve personnel, and mobilised reservists are excluded.

Outflow from UK Regular Forces includes death and outflow to civil life including recalled reservists on release and outflow to the Home Service battalions of the Royal Irish Regiment, which was disbanded on 31 March 2008.

1. Does not include promotion to officer from other ranks.

2. From 1997/98 onwards, Army officer outflow figures include miscellaneous outflow.

3. Calculated as a percentage of the average trained strength over the year.

Due to ongoing validation of data from the Joint Personnel Administration System, all Naval Service and Army flow statistics for financial year 06/07 and 07/08 and all RAF flow statistics for financial year 07/08 are provisional and subject to review.

Charts to Tables **2.19** & **2.23** Intake and Outlow of UK Regular Forces

Intake and Outflow of UK Regular Officers

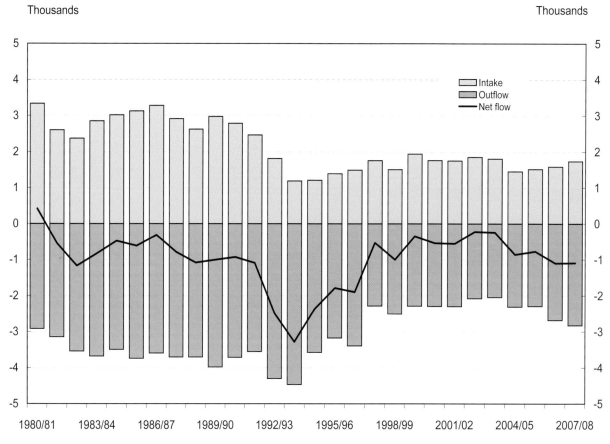

Intake and Outflow of UK Regular Other Ranks

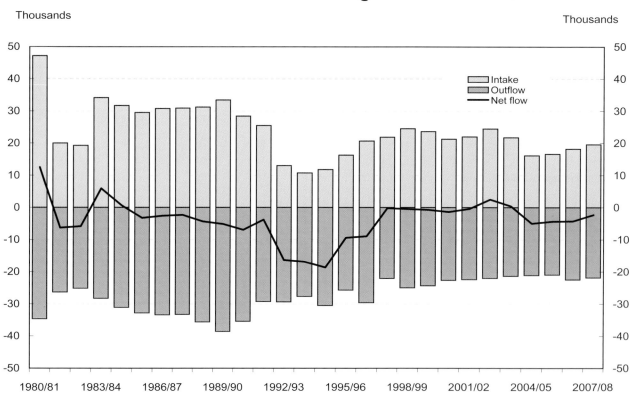

78

UK ARMED FORCES

Table 2.24 Outflow[1] from trained UK Regular forces by Service and ethnic origin[2]

	1997/98	2003/04	2004/05	2005/06	2006/07	2007/08
All Services	**18 390**	**16 460**	**17 600**	**18 140**	**18 870** [P]	**18 010** [P]
Officers[3]	**2 040**	**1 740**	**1 970**	**2 080**	**2 310** [P]	**2 340** [P]
White	2 015 ||	1 565	1 770	1 880	2 095 [P]	2 125 [P]
Ethnic minorities	20 ||	40	45	55	45 [P]	70 [P]
Unknown[4]	5 ||	135	150	140	170 [P]	145 [P]
Other ranks	**16 350**	**14 730**	**15 640**	**16 070**	**16 560** [P]	**15 670** [P]
White	16 060 ||	12 640	13 695	14 250	14 720 [P]	13 840 [P]
Ethnic minorities	190 ||	425	475	560	740 [P]	1 000 [P]
Unknown[4]	100 ||	1 660	1 465	1 260	1 095 [P]	835 [P]
Naval Service	**4 060**	**3 440**	**3 590**	**3 300**	**3 200** [P]	**3 110** [P]
Officers	**500**	**380**	**420**	**430**	**400** [P]	**460** [P]
White	495 ||	350	390	410	375 [P]	435 [P]
Ethnic minorities	5 ||	5	~	5	10 [P]	10 [P]
Unknown[4]	- ||	25	25	15	15 [P]	15 [P]
Other ranks	**3 560**	**3 060**	**3 170**	**2 870**	**2 800** [P]	**2 660** [P]
White	3 540 ||	2 725	2 770	2 670	2 620 [P]	2 510 [P]
Ethnic minorities	25 ||	50	60	75	65 [P]	65 [P]
Unknown[4]	- ||	285	345	125	120 [P]	80 [P]
Army	**10 210**	**9 570**	**10 740**	**10 500**	**10 930** [P]	**10 470** [P]
Officers[3]	**960**	**780**	**900**	**980**	**1 110** [P]	**1 160** [P]
White	950 ||	705	805	875	1 005 [P]	1 060 [P]
Ethnic minorities	5 ||	15	25	25	20 [P]	35 [P]
Unknown[4]	~ ||	60	75	80	85 [P]	65 [P]
Other ranks	**9 250**	**8 790**	**9 840**	**9 520**	**9 820** [P]	**9 310** [P]
White	9 065 ||	7 410	8 640	8 355	8 590 [P]	8 020 [P]
Ethnic minorities	105 ||	320	350	385	580 [P]	845 [P]
Unknown[4]	80 ||	1 060	850	785	645 [P]	445 [P]
Royal Air Force	**4 120**	**3 460**	**3 270**	**4 340**	**4 740**	**4 430** [P]
Officers	**580**	**580**	**640**	**670**	**800**	**720** [P]
White	575 ||	510	575	595	710	630 [P]
Ethnic minorities	5 ||	15	20	25	15	25 [P]
Unknown[4]	~ ||	50	50	45	75	65 [P]
Other ranks	**3 540**	**2 880**	**2 630**	**3 670**	**3 930**	**3 710** [P]
White	3 455 ||	2 505	2 285	3 220	3 505	3 305 [P]
Ethnic minorities	60 ||	55	65	100	95	90 [P]
Unknown[4]	20 ||	320	270	350	335	310 [P]

Ethnic minorities as a percentage[5] of total (excluding Unknown)

	1997/98	2003/04	2004/05	2005/06	2006/07	2007/08
All personnel	**1.1** ||	**3.2**	**3.3**	**3.7**	**4.5** [P]	**6.3** [P]
Officers	**0.9** ||	**2.4**	**2.6**	**2.8**	**2.1** [P]	**3.3** [P]
Naval Service	1.2 ||	2.0	~	1.7	2.3 [P]	2.2 [P]
Army[3]	0.6 ||	2.1	3.0	2.7	2.0 [P]	3.3 [P]
Royal Air Force	1.0 ||	3.2	3.0	3.7	2.1	4.0 [P]
Other ranks	**1.2** ||	**3.3**	**3.3**	**3.8**	**4.8** [P]	**6.7** [P]
Naval Service	0.7 ||	1.8	2.1	2.7	2.4 [P]	2.5 [P]
Army	1.1 ||	4.2	3.9	4.4	6.3 [P]	9.5 [P]
Royal Air Force	1.8 ||	2.1	2.8	3.0	2.6	2.7 [P]

Source: DASA (Quad-Service)

UK Regular Forces excludes Gurkhas, Full Time Reserve personnel, and mobilised reservists.

Outflow from UK Regular Forces includes death and outflow to civil life including recalled reservists on release and outflow to the Home Service battalions of the Royal Irish Regiment, which was disbanded on 31 March 2008.

1. Does not include promotions to officer from other ranks or flows between Services.
2. From 2002 onwards ethnicity classifications were changed in line with the 2001 census of population so that the new ethnicity classifications used in the 2001 Census of Population could be used. These classifications are the basis of the figures from 2002 onwards.
3. Army officer outflow figures include miscellaneous outflow.
4. Includes those with an unrecorded ethnic origin and those who chose not to declare.
5. Percentages are calculated from unrounded data.

~ denotes fewer than 5 or a percentage based on fewer than 5.
Due to ongoing validation of data from the Joint Personnel Administration System, all Naval Service and Army flow statistics for financial year 06/07 and 07/08 and all RAF flow statistics for financial year 07/08 are provisional and subject to review.

UK ARMED FORCES

Table 2.25 Outflow[1] from trained UK Regular Forces by sex and reason for leaving

	1990/91	1997/98	2003/04	2004/05	2005/06	2006/07[2]	2007/08[2]
All trained personnel	28 820 ||	18 390	16 460	17 600	18 140	18 870 ᴾ	18 010 ᴾ
Trained officers	2 760 ||	2 040	1 740	1 970	2 080	2 310 ᴾ	2 340 ᴾ
Male	2 450 ||	1 860	1 580	1 760	1 880	2 090 ᴾ	2 080 ᴾ
Age, option point and time[3]	1 130	980	710	800	810	..	..
Full career: age[4]	440	420	430	470	..	..	..
Full career: option point[5]	190	160	180	190	..	..	..
Short career: time[6]	460	380	90	130	..	..	..
Short career: option[7]	40	20	-	-	..	..	..
Redundancies	-	-	-	-	40	..	..
Voluntary Outflow	1 180	790	760	820	900	..	..
Medical reasons and death	100	70	60	100	70	..	..
Other reasons[8,9]	40 ||	20	40	40	70	..	..
Female	310 ||	180	160	200	200	220 ᴾ	260 ᴾ
Age, option point and time[3]	180	100	50	80	70	..	..
Full career: age[4]	10	-	-	10	..	..	..
Full career: option point[5]	10	20	20	20	..	..	..
Short career: time[6]	150	80	30	40	..	..	..
Short career: option[7]	-	-	-	-	..	..	..
Redundancies	-	-	-	-	-	..	..
Voluntary Outflow	120	60	100	110	110	..	..
Medical reasons and death	-	10	10	10	10	..	..
Other reasons[8,9]	10 ||	-	-	-	-	..	..
Trained other ranks	26 060	16 350	14 730	15 640	16 070	16 560 ᴾ	15 670 ᴾ
Male	24 070	14 880	13 390	14 260	14 700	15 190 ᴾ	14 360 ᴾ
End of engagement	5 330	4 240	3 030	2 960	3 440	..	..
Redundancies	-	-	-	-	490	..	..
Voluntary Outflow	15 640	7 970	6 720	7 310	7 260	..	..
Service no longer required, disciplinary and other reasons[8]	1 850	1 500	2 760	2 940	2 430	..	..
Medical reasons and death	1 120	1 110	830	1 020	1 020	..	..
Compassionate release	130	60	50	40	50	..	..
Female	1 990	1 470	1 330	1 380	1 360	1 360 ᴾ	1 320 ᴾ
End of engagement	160	150	110	110	140	..	..
Redundancies	-	-	-	-	10	..	..
Voluntary Outflow[3]	1 650	1 090	910	920	900	..	..
of which:							
Marriage	540	-	-	-	..	..	..
Pregnancy	350	180	170	190	..	..	..
Service no longer required, disciplinary and other reasons[8]	150	110	200	210	200	..	..
Medical reasons and death	30	110	100	120	120	..	..
Compassionate release	10	20	20	10	10	..	..

Source: DASA (Quad-Service)

UK Regular Forces excludes Gurkhas, Full Time Reserve personnel, and mobilised reservists.

Outflow from UK Regular Forces includes death and outflow to civil life including recalled reservists on release and outflow to the Home Service battalions of the Royal Irish Regiment, which was disbanded on 31 March 2008.

1. Does not include promotions to officer from other ranks or flows between Services.
2. Due to ongoing validation of data from the Joint Personnel Administration System, breakdowns of outflow by exit reason are not currently available from 1 April 2006.
3. Due to the introduction of the Joint Personnel Administration System, there are no further breakdowns of this category available from 2005/06.
4. Naval Service: completion of Full Term Commission; Army: completion of Regular Career Commission; RAF: exit at Normal Retirement Date.
5. Naval Service: completion of Career Commission; Army: completion of Intermediate Regular Commission; RAF: exit at Initial or Optional Retirement Date (typically aged 38-44 years).
6. Naval Service: completion of an Initial Commission (Short Career Commission before 1999); Army/RAF: Short Service Commission.
7. RAF only: 8 year break-point in Short Service Commission or 8 or 12 year breakpoint in other commissions.
8. Includes dismissal.
9. From 1997/98, Army Officer outflow figures include miscellaneous outflow.

Due to ongoing validation of data from the Joint Personnel Administration System, all Service flow statistics for financial year 06/07 and 07/08 are provisional and subject to review.

80

UK ARMED FORCES

Table 2.26 Outflow[1] from UK Regular Forces by sex and Service

	1990/91	1997/98	2003/04	2004/05	2005/06	2006/07	2007/08
Females: total	3 060 ‖	2 490	2 200	2 100	1 980	2 160 P	2 170 P
Officers: total	360 ‖	230	220	250	240	300 P	350 P
Naval Service	40	60	30	50	40	50 P	50 P
Army[2]	180 ‖	100	110	130	110	140 P	190 P
Royal Air Force	140	60	70	80	90	100	100 P
Other ranks: total	2 700	2 260	1 990	1 840	1 730	1 870 P	1 830 P
Naval Service	640	560	510	440	440	440 P	420 P
Army	1 060	1 180	980	960	840	960 P	900 P
Royal Air Force	1 000	530	500	450	450	460	500 P
Males: total	36 020 ‖	21 860	21 200	21 330	21 290	23 000 r, P	22 510 P
Officers: total	3 350 ‖	2 060	1 830	2 050	2 050	2 380 P	2 480 P
Naval Service	760	560	440	460	480	450 P	530 P
Army[2]	1 680 ‖	930	840	970	960	1 180 P	1 300 P
Royal Air Force	920	560	550	620	610	750	650 P
Other ranks: total	32 670	19 800	19 370	19 280	19 240	20 610 P	20 040 P
Naval Service	6 670	4 090	3 800	3 690	3 520	3 380 P	3 340 P
Army	19 910	12 260	12 660	13 020	12 280	13 480 P	12 930 P
Royal Air Force	6 090	3 460	2 920	2 570	3 440	3 760	3 760 P
Females as a percentage of total	7.8 ‖	10.2	9.4	8.9	8.5	8.6 P	8.8 P
Officers: total	9.7 ‖	9.9	10.6	11.0	10.7	11.0 P	12.3 P
Naval Service	5.1	10.3	7.3	9.9	8.1	9.8 P	8.3 P
Army[2]	9.9 ‖	10.1	11.6	11.6	10.7	10.8 P	13.0 P
Royal Air Force	12.8	9.3	11.4	11.0	12.6	12.0	13.8 P
Other ranks: total	7.6	10.3	9.3	8.7	8.3	8.3 P	8.4 P
Naval Service	8.7	12.0	11.8	10.6	11.2	11.6 P	11.2 P
Army	5.0	8.8	7.2	6.8	6.4	6.7 P	6.5 P
Royal Air Force	14.2	13.3	14.5	14.9	11.6	10.9	11.8 P

Source: DASA (Quad-Service)

UK Regular Forces includes all trained and untrained personnel. Gurkhas, Full Time Reserve personnel, and mobilised reservists are excluded.

Outflow from UK Regular Forces includes death and outflow to civil life including recalled reservists on release and outflow to the Home Service battalions of the Royal Irish Regiment, which was disbanded on 31 March 2008.

1. Does not include promotions to officer from other ranks or flows between Services.
2. From 1997/98, Army officer outflow figures include miscellaneous outflow.

Due to ongoing validation of data from the Joint Personnel Administration System, all Naval Service and Army flow statistics for financial year 06/07 and 07/08 and all RAF flow statistics for financial year 07/08 are provisional and subject to review.

81

CHAPTER 2 - PERSONNEL

UK ARMED FORCES

Table **2.27** Military salaries[1]: illustrative rates and indices (1990/91=100)

Indices are based on average daily rates of pay during the year. All indices are calculated using standard rank weights taken at 1 March 2008. These have been updated since the previous UKDS (2007), which used rank weights taken at 1 May 2005. Since the underlying rank weights are constant, the changes in the indices purely reflect changes in pay. The discontinuity indicated between 1990/1991 and 2003/04 actually refers specifically to a discontinuity between 2000/01 and 2001/02, and is due to the introduction of a new pay system, Pay 2000. The resulting changes to the structure of military salaries meant that individual pay rates could not be tracked over this period. Therefore, pay level weights within rank groups differ prior to 2001/02.

	1990/91		2003/04	2004/05	2005/06	2006/07	2007/08	2008/09
Military salaries Index: all ranks[2]	**100**	II	**188**	**193**	**199**	**205**	**213**	**221**
Senior officers (Major General and above)	100	II	188	194	201	208	214	221
Officers (up to Brigadier)	100	II	184	190	195	201	208	217
Other ranks (Sergeant and above)	100	II	194	200	206	212	219	227
Other ranks (up to corporal)	100	II	186	192	198	204	212	219

Illustrative rates[3] of annual military salary (in terms of Army ranks)

Pay 2000 Pay System[4]   Pounds Sterling

General	*Level 4*	..	131,980	135,675	143,673	152,728	160,625	164,159
Brigadier	*Level 5*	..	79,557	81,563	84,008	86,527	89,444	96,288
Colonel	*Level 1*	..	63,614	65,218	67,175	69,189	71,522	77,545
Lieutenant Colonel	*Level 9*	..	60,723	62,254	64,123	66,047	68,273	74,023
Major	*Level 9*	..	46,874	48,056	49,498	50,983	52,702	54,551
Captain	*Level 3*	..	32,746	33,573	34,580	35,617	36,817	38,109
Lieutenant	*Level 8*	..	25,525	26,167	26,952	27,762	28,698	29,704
2nd Lieutenant	*Level 5*	..	20,174	20,681	21,301	21,940	22,680	23,475
Warrant Officer I	*Level 7 H*	..	38,313	39,278	40,457	41,672	43,077	44,588
Warrant Officer II	*Level 9 H*	..	35,443	36,336	37,427	38,551	39,851	41,249
Staff Sergeant	*Level 7 L*	..	31,352	32,142	33,106	34,098	35,248	36,484
Sergeant	*Level 7 H*	..	30,261	31,025	31,956	32,916	34,025	35,219
Corporal	*Level 7 H*	..	27,194	27,879	28,715	29,576	30,573	31,646
Lance Corporal	*Level 9 H*	..	23,717	24,313	25,043	25,794	26,664	27,599
Private	*Level 1 L*	..	13,081	13,461	13,866	14,323	15,677	16,227

Source: DASA (Quad-Sevice)

1. Data are for UK Regular Forces which includes all trained and untrained personnel. Gurkhas, Full Time Reserve personnel, and mobilised reservists are excluded.
2. Equivalent ranks in the Naval Service and Royal Air Force are shown in **Table 2.28**.
3. The illustrative rates of annual military salary are calculated using the Pay Review Bodies' figures for the appropriate year. The rate shown for each rank is the pay level with the largest number of people at 1 March 2008.
4. In the course of 2001/02, Pay 2000 was introduced for officers and other ranks. For other ranks this involved the introduction of Higher (H) and Lower (L) incremental pay ranges to which personnel are assigned in accordance with their trade. This replaced the old spot rate system with length of service increments, where other ranks would remain on the same pay point unless, or until, they were promoted. Under the new system personnel progress annually subject to satisfactory performance.

Chart to Table 2.27 Military salaries: illustrative rates and indices

Real Growth[1] of military salaries and average earnings[2,3]

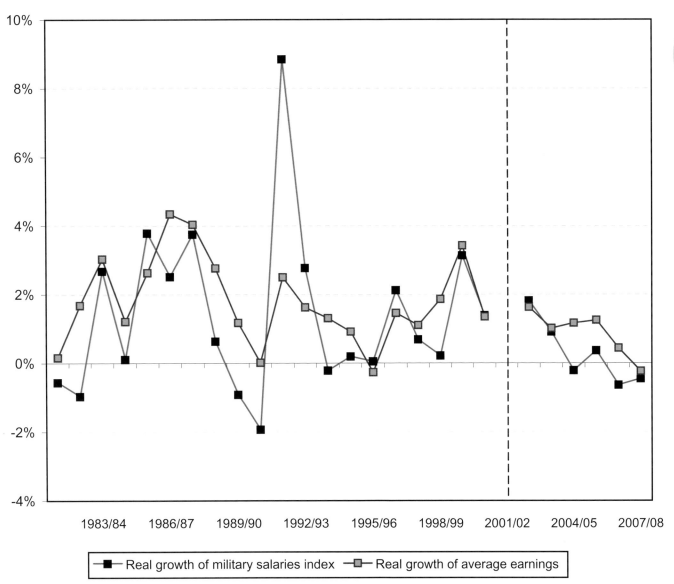

1. Real growth in salaries is growth over and above inflation. It represents the increase in purchasing power between one year and the next. For example, if salaries grew by 2%, but prices rose by 1%, real salary growth would be about 1%, because someone earning that salary could purchase around 1% more goods and services. Real pay growth can be negative if inflation is outstripping salary growth, values at 0% indicate an increase in line with inflation. The measure of inflation used here is growth in Retail Price Index (RPI).

2. When calculating the real growth of average earnings the Office for National Statistics (ONS) Average Earnings Index (LNMM: whole economy, not seasonally adjusted, including bonuses) has been employed.

3. Overall, real growth in military salaries follows a similar path to that of average earnings. However, there is a noticeable peak in 1991/92. This increase is partly a consequence of the previous year's pay award being staged but also includes increases to X Factor and a change in the pension abatement. Due to the discontinuity in the military salaries index between 2000/01 and 2001/02 it is not possible to calculate a pay increase over this period. Any increase over this period would include the effects of the introduction of Pay 2000.

Table 2.28 NATO Rank Codes and UK Service Ranks

NATO Code	Royal Navy[1]	Royal Marines[2]	Army	Royal Air Force
Officers				
OF-10	Admiral of the Fleet	-	Field Marshal	Marshal of the RAF
OF-9	Admiral	General	General	Air Chief Marshal
OF-8	Vice Admiral	Lieutenant General	Lieutenant General	Air Marshal
OF-7	Rear Admiral	Major General	Major General	Air Vice-Marshal
OF-6	Commodore	Brigadier	Brigadier	Air Commodore
OF-5	Captain	Colonel	Colonel	Group Captain
OF-4	Commander	Lieutenant Colonel	Lieutenant Colonel	Wing Commander
OF-3	Lieutenant Commander	Major	Major	Squadron Leader
OF-2	Lieutenant	Captain	Captain	Flight Lieutenant
OF-1	Sub-Lieutenant	Lieutenant/2nd Lieutenant	Lieutenant/2nd Lieutenant	Flying Officer/Pilot Officer
OF(D)	Midshipman	-	Officer Cadet	Officer Designate

NATO Code	Royal Navy	Royal Marines	Army	Royal Air Force
Other Ranks				
OR-9	Warrant Officer Class 1	Warrant Officer Class 1	Warrant Officer Class 1	Warrant Officer
OR-8	Warrant Officer Class 2	Warrant Officer Class 2	Warrant Officer Class 2	-
OR-7	Chief Petty Officer	Colour Sergeant	Staff Sergeant	Flight Sergeant/ Chief Technician
OR-6	Petty Officer	Sergeant	Sergeant	Sergeant
OR-4	Leading Rate	Corporal	Corporal	Corporal
OR-3	Lance Corporal	Lance Corporal	Lance Corporal	-
OR-2	Able Rating[3]	Marine[3]	Private (Classes 1 to 3)	Junior Technician/ Leading Aircraftman/ Senior Aircraftman
OR-1	-	-	Private (Class 4)/Junior	Aircraftman

Source: DGMO

1. The Royal Navy introduced a Warrant Officer Class 2 on 1 April 2004.
2. Royal Marine officer ranks were aligned with those of the Army on 1 July 1999.
3. The rates of Able Rating and Ordinary Seaman were merged on 1 April 1999, as were the corresponding ranks of Marine 1st class and Marine 2nd class. The ranks of Junior Rating and Junior Marine were also abolished.

Civilian equivalents to military ranks

NATO Code	Ministry of Defence civilian grade equivalent
OF-10	Permanent Under Secretary/
OF-9	2nd Permanent Under Secretary
OF-8	SCS[1] 3-star[2]
OF-7	SCS[1] 2-star[3]
OF-6	SCS[1] 1-star[4]
-	Band B1[5]
OF-5	Band B2[6]
OF-4	Band C1[7]
OF-3	Band C2[8]
OF-2	Band D[9]

Source: DGMO/MDP

1. Senior Civil Service.
2. Formerly Grade 2, Deputy Under Secretary.
3. Formerly Grade 3, Assistant Under Secretary.
4. Formerly Grades 4 and 5, Executive Director and Assistant Secretary.
5. Formerly Grade 6, Senior Principal Officer and equivalents.
6. Formerly Grade 7, Principal Officer and equivalents.
7. Formerly Senior Executive Officer and equivalents.
8. Formerly Higher Executive Officer and equivalents.
9. Formerly Executive Officer and equivalents.

CHAPTER 2 - PERSONNEL

CIVILIAN PERSONNEL

Civilian Personnel Key Points and Trends

General

- The number of Level 0 civilian personnel fell by 8,190 FTE between 1 April 2007 and 1 April 2008 from 97,690 to 89,500. This reduction comprised falls of 4,730 in the Level 1 civilian total, 850 in Trading Funds and 2,600 in locally engaged civilians.

Location

- At 1 April 2008, 63,960 FTE Level 1 civilian personnel were employed in the United Kingdom, a reduction of 4,270 personnel since 1 April 2007.

Diversity

Between 1 April 2007 and 1 April 2008 the percentage of:

- ethnic minorities (with known ethnic status) increased from 3.0 per cent to 3.1 per cent.
- disabled personnel (with known inability status) remained at 5.5 per cent.
- female personnel remained at 36 per cent (excluding Royal Fleet Auxiliary and locally engaged civilian personnel).
- personnel working part-time hours increased from 9.3 per cent to 9.5 per cent (excluding Royal Fleet Auxiliary and locally engaged civilian personnel).

At 1 April 2008 the number and percentage of:
- personnel aged 50 or above was 29,820 (38 per cent) (excluding Royal Fleet Auxiliary and locally engaged civilian personnel).

Intake / Outflow

- Inflow for 2007/08 was 5,150 FTE compared with an outflow of 10,580 FTE (excluding Royal Fleet Auxiliary and locally engaged civilian personnel) reflecting the MOD's civilian rundown.

Please note that the sickness absence table can now be found in Chapter 3.

Top Level Budgetary Structure (TLB)

At 1 April 2008 i) Land Command and Adjutant General merged to form Land Forces. ii) CinCFleet was renamed Fleet.

Trading Funds

At 1 April 2008 the Defence Aviation Repair Agency and the Army Based Repair Organisation merged to form the Defence Support Group and around 1,000 personnel transferred to the Vector Aerospace Corporation. A small number of civilians may not have been correctly allocated to the DSG when the new Trading Fund was formed and the personnel systems were integrated. This should not affect the Civilian Level 0 total but some small revisions may occur in due course.

Defence Agencies

At 1 April 2008 the Defence Analytical Services Agency and Defence Medical and Education Training Agency lost their agency status. At 1 April 2008, 26 per cent of civilian personnel were employed in Defence Agencies and Trading Funds.

CIVILIAN PERSONNEL

Table **2.29** Civilian personnel[1], at 1 April each year

Thousands: FTE

	1993		1997 [2]		2003	2004 [3]	2005	2006 [4]	2007 [4]		2008
Civilian Level 0[5]	**159.6**	||	**133.3**	||	**107.6**	**109.0**	**108.5**	**103.4** r	**97.7** r	||	**89.5**
Civilian Level 1	132.7	||	101.9		81.5	82.2	82.0	78.1	73.8		69.0
Trading Funds[5]	-	||	15.5	||	12.2	11.4	10.8	10.7	10.1	||	9.2
Locally engaged civilians	26.8	||	15.9		13.8	15.4	15.7	14.5 r	13.8 r		11.2
Civilian Level 1 - Permanent	**128.1**	||	**96.6**		**77.9**	**78.8**	**78.6**	**74.7**	**70.5**		**66.0**
Non-industrial	86.3	||	67.4		62.5	63.4	63.8	60.5	57.5		54.3
Industrial	41.8	||	29.2		15.4	15.5	14.7	14.2	13.0		11.7
Civilian Level 1 - Casual[6]	**2.4**	||	**3.1**		**1.2**	**1.0**	**1.1**	**1.1**	**0.9**		**0.8**
Non-industrial	1.4	||	2.0		0.8	0.8	0.8	0.8	0.6		0.4
Industrial	1.0	||	1.1		0.4	0.3	0.3	0.3	0.3		0.4
Civilian Level 1 - RFA	**2.2**	||	**2.2**		**2.5**	**2.3**	**2.3**	**2.3**	**2.4**		**2.3**
Trading Funds[5]	**-**	||	**15.5**	||	**12.2**	**11.4**	**10.8**	**10.7**	**10.1**	||	**9.2**
Permanent[5]	-	||	15.2	||	12.0	11.3	10.7	10.6	9.9	||	9.1
Casual[5]	-	||	0.3	|||	0.2	0.1	0.1	0.1	0.1	||	0.1
Locally engaged civilians	**26.8**	||	**15.9**		**13.8**	**15.4**	**15.7**	**14.5** r	**13.8** r		**11.2**

Source: DASA(Quad-Service)

1. Civilian Level 0 and Level 1 are defined in the Glossary.
2. From 1 April 1995 the method of counting part-time staff changed to reflect the actual hours worked (about 60 per cent of full-time hours, on average) rather than the notional 50 per cent used previously. Figures from 1996 onwards include locally employed dependents of Service personnel.
3. During 2004/05, 1,040 firefighters who were shown as non-industrial at April 2004 were reclassified to industrial.
4. LEC figures for April 2006 and 2007 have been revised due to the availability of more accurate data for those personnel based in Brunei and in the CJO TLB.
5. The following changes have affected the continuity of the civilian data: removal of GCHQ personnel from April 1994 and the contractorisation of the Atomic Weapons Establishment (6,000) in 1993. In 2001 the QinetiQ portion of the Defence Evaluation and Research Agency (8,000) was established as a private company. At 1 April 2008 the Defence Aviation Repair Agency and the Army Based Repair Organisation merged to form the Defence Support Group and around 1,000 personnel transferred to the Vector Aerospace Corporation.
6. Casual staff are usually engaged for less than 12 months.

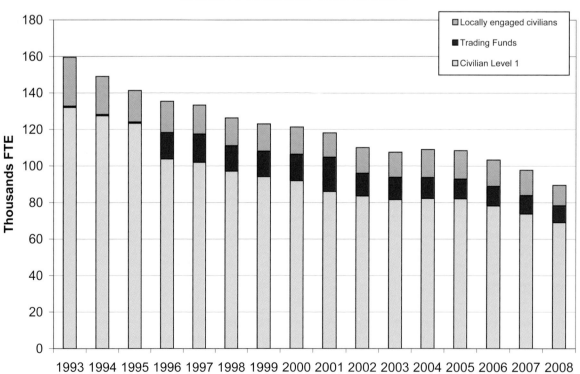

Civilian Personnel 1993 to 2008

Legend: Locally engaged civilians, Trading Funds, Civilian Level 1

CHAPTER 2 - PERSONNEL

CIVILIAN PERSONNEL

Table 2.30 Civilian personnel[1] by budgetary area and grade equivalent[2], at 1 April each year

Number: FTE

Grade[2]	1997		2003 [3]	2004	2005	2006 [4]	2007[4]	2008 [5]
Civilian Level 0	**133 330**	‖	**107 580**	**109 050**	**108 470**	**103 380** ʳ	**97 690** ʳ ‖	**89 500**
Senior Civil Service and Equivalent[6]	350		300	300	300	310	280	300
Pay Band B	2 260		2 470	2 520	2 640	2 740	2 450	2 450
Pay Band C	14 880		15 840	16 900	17 490	17 310	16 840	16 540
Pay Band D	16 280		14 140	14 480	14 470	13 500	12 170	10 990
Pay Band E	35 550		29 580	29 890	29 070	27 220	25 590	23 490
Other non-industrial[7]	70		1 010	70	700	170	790	940
Industrial	30 340		15 750	15 720	15 000	14 540	13 300	12 060
Trading Fund staff	15 530	‖	12 200	11 440	10 780	10 700	10 060 ‖	9 210
Royal Fleet Auxiliaries	2 210		2 450	2 310	2 350	2 340	2 360	2 270
Locally engaged civilians[8]	15 860		13 840	15 430	15 660	14 540 ʳ	13 840 ʳ	11 240
Royal Navy Areas	**22 310**		**5 990**	**5 990**	**5 710**	**5 290**	**5 230**	**4 600**
Pay Band C and above	3 180		620	750	690	640	580	500
Pay Band D and below	9 310		2 100	2 160	1 890	1 700	1 640	1 260
Other non-industrial[7]	20		20	-	60	-	30	30
Industrial	7 580		790	760	730	610	620	540
Royal Fleet Auxiliaries	2 210		2 450	2 310	2 350	2 340	2 360	2 270
Army Areas	**36 240**		**21 470**	**20 280**	**19 920**	**18 650**	**17 960**	**17 180**
Pay Band C and above	4 260		3 290	3 560	3 690	3 590	3 340	3 290
Pay Band D and below	18 110		12 360	11 090	10 730	9 830	8 930	8 390
Other non-industrial[7]	20		370	10	40	30	400	520
Industrial	13 850		5 440	5 620	5 450	5 200	5 300	4 970
Royal Air Force Areas	**19 290**		**11 390**	**11 710**	**11 080**	**10 770**	**8 980**	**8 710**
Pay Band C and above	2 130		1 130	1 200	1 190	1 190	1 060	1 070
Pay Band D and below	9 380		5 720	6 140	5 820	5 550	4 870	4 580
Other non-industrial[7]	30		170	-	20	10	70	80
Industrial	7 760		4 370	4 370	4 050	4 020	2 980	2 980
Defence Equipment & Support[9]	*		**24 580**	**24 730**	**24 470**	**22 490**	**20 880**	**18 010**
Pay Band C and above	*		8 240	8 760	9 150	8 970	8 710	8 430
Pay Band D and below	*		11 710	11 590	10 860	9 560	8 490	6 710
Other non-industrial[7]	*		200	50	350	40	60	70
Industrial	*		4 430	4 340	4 110	3 920	3 620	2 790
Centre	**24 100**		**18 020**	**19 400**	**20 790**	**20 720**	**20 530**	**20 260**
Pay Band C and above	7 910		5 280	5 410	5 680	5 860	5 760	5 930
Pay Band D and below	15 030		11 830	13 370	14 230	13 990	13 760	13 440
Other non-industrial[7]	-		210	10	220	80	240	230
Industrial	1 160		710	620	670	790	780	660
Other[10]	**-**		**90**	**60**	**60**	**210**	**190**	**290**
Pay Band C and above	-		40	40	30	130	110	60
Pay Band D and below	-		10	10	20	80	80	100
Other non-industrial[7]	-		40	-	-	10	-	10
Industrial	-		-	10	-	-	-	120

Source: DASA(Quad-Service)

1. Civilian Level 0 and Level 1 are defined in the Glossary.
2. Grade equivalent is shown in terms of the broader banding structure and is based on paid grade.
3. In 2001 the QinetiQ portion of the Defence Evaluation and Research Agency (8,000) was established as a private company.
4. LEC figures for April 2006 and 2007 have been revised due to the inclusion of previously unavailable data on personnel based in Brunei and in the CJO TLB.
5. At 1 April 2008 the Defence Aviation Repair Agency and the Army Based Repair Organisation merged to form the Defence Support Group and around 1,000 personnel transferred to the Vector Aerospace Corporation.
6. Includes about 50 personnel outside the Senior Civil Service but of equivalent grade.
7. Includes industrial staff on temporary promotion to non-industrial grades and staff for whom no grade information is available.
8. Locally engaged civilians and manuals cannot be split by budgetary area, so are only included in the Ministry of Defence total.
9. Defence Equipment & Support formed in 2007 by merging the Defence Logistics Organisation and Defence Procurement Agency. For consistency information in this table has been merged across the series between 2002 and 2006.
10. Staff for whom no Top Level Budget (TLB) information is available are included in this section of the table.

CIVILIAN PERSONNEL

Table 2.31 Strength of civilian personnel[1] by ethnic origin[2] and grade[3], at 1 April each year

Headcount

	1997		2003 [4]	2004	2005	2006 [5]	2007[5]	2008 [6]
Civilian Level 0[1]	135 450	II	109 850	111 080	110 480	107 300 ʳ	101 570 ʳ ‖	93 670
White	65 930	II	64 160	66 000	69 150	70 210	67 450 ‖	63 250
Senior Civil Service and equivalent[7]	300	II	250	270	260	270	240	250
Pay Band B	1 970	II	1 970	2 010	2 140	2 300	2 080	2 080
Pay Band C	12 740	II	12 390	13 090	13 750	14 180	14 020	13 790
Pay Band D	13 320	II	11 010	11 220	11 600	11 490	10 520	9 530
Pay Band E	29 600	II	22 840	22 870	23 020	23 360	22 430	20 690
Other non-industrial[8, 9]	-	II	590	40	450	110	660	770
Industrial[10]	-	II	8 880	8 420	9 390	10 010	9 620	8 940
Trading Fund staff	8 000	II	6 230	8 080	8 530	8 500	7 900 ‖	7 200
Ethnic Minorities	1 340	II	1 960	1 980	2 010	2 080	2 060 ‖	2 020
Senior Civil Service and equivalent[7]	10	II	10	10	10	10	-	-
Pay Band B	40	II	50	50	50	50	50	60
Pay Band C	160	II	300	310	350	380	400	410
Pay Band D	220	II	330	340	350	380	340	320
Pay Band E	760	II	880	880	840	890	880	850
Other non-industrial[8, 9]	-	II	20	-	20	10	30	30
Industrial[10]	-	II	240	220	200	200	180	190
Trading Fund staff	150	II	140	180	170	170	170 ‖	170
Unknown[11]	68 190	II	43 730	43 100	39 320	35 000 ʳ	32 070 ʳ ‖	28 390
Senior Civil Service and equivalent[7]	40	II	40	20	30	40	50	50
Pay Band B	260	II	480	490	500	440	400	390
Pay Band C	2 050	II	3 300	3 700	3 640	3 050	2 820	2 740
Pay Band D	2 910	II	3 040	3 140	2 750	1 900	1 570	1 380
Pay Band E	6 320	II	7 120	7 240	6 260	4 100	3 450	3 040
Other non-industrial[8, 9]	70	II	470	30	240	40	170	220
Industrial[10]	30 880	II	6 990	7 400	5 660	4 600	3 790	3 190
Royal Fleet Auxiliary (RFA)	2 210	II	2 450	2 310	2 350	2 340	2 360	2 270
Locally engaged civilians	15 860	II	13 840	15 430	15 660	16 290 ʳ	15 280 ʳ	13 080
Trading Fund staff	7 590	II	5 980	3 320	2 230	2 200	2 180 ‖	2 040

Ethnic minorities as a percentage of total excluding unknown

	1997		2003	2004	2005	2006	2007	2008
All grades	2.0	II	3.0	2.9	2.8	2.9	3.0 ‖	3.1
Senior Civil Service and equivalent[7]	3.5	II	3.1	2.2	2.2	2.5	- ʳ	-
Pay Band B	1.9	II	2.3	2.5	2.4	2.3	2.5	2.6
Pay Band C	1.2	II	2.4	2.3	2.5	2.6	2.7	2.9
Pay Band D	1.6	II	2.9	2.9	2.9	3.2	3.2	3.2
Pay Band E	2.5	II	3.7	3.7	3.5	3.7	3.8	3.9
Other non-industrial[8, 9]	-	II	2.7	- ʳ	4.4	6.6	3.8	3.5
Industrial[10]	-	II	2.6	2.5	2.1	2.0	1.9	2.0
Trading Fund staff	1.8	II	2.2	2.2	2.0	2.0	2.1 ‖	2.3

Source: DASA(Quad-Service)

1. Civilian Level 0 and Level 1 are defined in the Glossary.
2. Ethnic origin data are collected by self declaration and are thus based on self-perception.
3. Grade equivalent is shown in terms of the broader banding structure and is based on paid grade.
4. In 2001/02 a re-survey of civilian personnel was undertaken so that the new classifications used in the 2001 Census of Population could be used. In 2001 the QinetiQ portion of the Defence Evaluation and Research Agency (8,000) was established as a private company.
5. LEC figures for April 2006 and 2007 have been revised due to the inclusion of previously unavailable data on personnel based in Brunei and in the CJO TLB.
6. At 1 April 2008 the Defence Aviation Repair Agency and the Army Based Repair Organisation merged to form the Defence Support Group and around 1,000 personnel transferred to the Vector Aerospace Corporation.
7. The Senior Civil Service was formed in 1996. The totals include about 50 personnel outside the Senior Civil Service but of equivalent grade.
8. 1,040 firefighters who were shown as non-industrial in April 2004 have been reclassified to industrial grades.
9. Includes industrial staff on temporary promotion to non-industrial grades.
10. No ethnicity data are available for the industrial personnel before 2000.
11. Those for whom there is no computerised record of their ethnic origin.

CHAPTER 2 - PERSONNEL

CIVILIAN PERSONNEL

Table 2.36 Outflow of civilian personnel[1] by sex, grade[2] and whether full or part-time

Headcount

Hours, sex and grade[2]	2002/03	2003/04	2004/05	2005/06 [3]	2006/07 [3]	2007/08 [4]
Female: full time	**3 470**	**3 350**	**3 040**	**3 320**	**3 170**	**3 000**
Senior Civil Service	10	-	-	-	-	-
Pay Band B	20	30	30	30	40	30
Pay Band C	250	240	200	310	300	300
Pay Band D	320	340	280	400	390	350
Pay Band E	1 880	1 720	1 770	1 970	1 780	1 600
Other non-industrial[5]	60	40	20	20	20	70
Industrial	630	580	510	360	420	390
Trading Funds	300	380	230	230	210	250
Male: full time	**6 610**	**7 060**	**5 640**	**5 550**	**5 900**	**6 710**
Senior Civil Service	40	30	30	40	30	30
Pay Band B	150	270	120	180	180	160
Pay Band C	850	960	930	1 040	940	1 070
Pay Band D	850	790	630	750	710	860
Pay Band E	1 440	1 390	1 280	1 150	1 310	1 300
Other non-industrial[5]	90	40	110	90	10	20
Industrial	2 210	2 120	1 460	1 200	1 600	1 650
Trading Funds	980	1 470	1 090	1 100	1 120	1 600
Female: part time	**820**	**760**	**700**	**750**	**890**	**920**
Senior Civil Service	-	-	-	-	-	-
Pay Band B	-	-	-	-	10	20
Pay Band C	40	40	80	100	140	150
Pay Band D	50	70	50	70	80	80
Pay Band E	420	360	370	430	500	480
Other non-industrial[5]	20	20	-	-	10	40
Industrial	240	210	160	110	120	140
Trading Funds	40	60	30	40	40	30
Male: part time	**180**	**210**	**170**	**190**	**230**	**260**
Senior Civil Service	-	-	-	-	-	-
Pay Band B	10	10	10	-	20	10
Pay Band C	20	30	40	40	50	60
Pay Band D	10	10	10	20	10	30
Pay Band E	40	40	50	60	70	70
Other non-industrial[5]	-	-	-	-	-	10
Industrial	90	80	50	40	50	40
Trading Funds	20	30	20	30	30	30
Female outflow with unknown full time/ part time status	**530**	**370**	**210**	**100**	**60**	**40**
Male outflow with unknown full time/ part time status	**2 380**	**540**	**520**	**90**	**80**	**50**
Total Female	**4 810**	**4 480**	**3 950**	**4 170**	**4 120**	**3 970**
Total Male	**9 170**	**7 810**	**6 330**	**5 830**	**6 210**	**7 020**
Net Change of Royal Fleet Auxiliary[6]	**80**	**- 140**	**30**	**-**	**10**	**- 80**
Net Change of locally engaged civilians[6]	**- 270**	**1 590**	**230**	**630** r	**-1 000** r	**-2 200**

Source: DASA(Quad-Service)

1. Civilian Level 0 and Level 1 are defined in the Glossary.
2. Grade equivalence is shown in terms of the broader banding structure and is based on paid grade.
3. LEC figures for April 2006 have been revised due to the inclusion of previously unavailable data on personnel based in Brunei and in the CJO TLB.
4. At 1 April 2008 the Defence Aviation Repair Agency and the Army Based Repair Organisation merged to form the Defence Support Group and around 1,000 personnel transferred to the Vector Aerospace Corporation.
5. Includes industrial staff on temporary promotion to non-industrial grades and those of unknown grade.
6. Intake and Outflow for locally engaged civilians and Royal Fleet Auxiliaries are not available, therefore, only net changes in strengths of RFAs and locally engaged civilians are listed in this table.

CIVILIAN PERSONNEL

Table **2.37** Number of civilian personnel[1] by disability status[2], and grade, at 1 April 2008

Headcount

	Not disabled	Disabled	Disability status unknown	Grand Total	Disabled personnel as a percentage of total (exc unknown)
Civilian Level 0	**55 460**	**3 250**	**34 960**	**93 670**	**5.5**
Civilian Level 1	**49 060**	**3 030**	**19 080**	**71 170**	**5.8**
Senior Civil Service and equivalent[3]	260	10	30	300	5.2
Band B	1 880	70	570	2 520	3.7
Band C	12 420	720	3 790	16 940	5.5
Band D	8 070	550	2 600	11 220	6.4
Band E	17 200	1 140	6 230	24 570	6.2
Unknown	790	10	220	1 020	1.5
Industrial	8 430	520	3 370	12 320	5.8
Royal Fleet Auxiliaries[4]	-	-	2 270	2 270	..
Trading Funds	6 400	220	2 800	9 420	3.2
Locally engaged civilians[4]	-	-	13 080	13 080	..

Source: DASA (Quad-Service)

1. Civilian Level 0 and Level 1 are defined in the Glossary.
2. Disability self certification was introduced in 2001.
3. Includes about 50 personnel outside the Senior Civil Service but of equivalent grade.
4. Disability data are not currently available for Royal Fleet Auxiliaries and locally engaged civilians.

Percentage Breakdown of disability status, and grade, April 2008

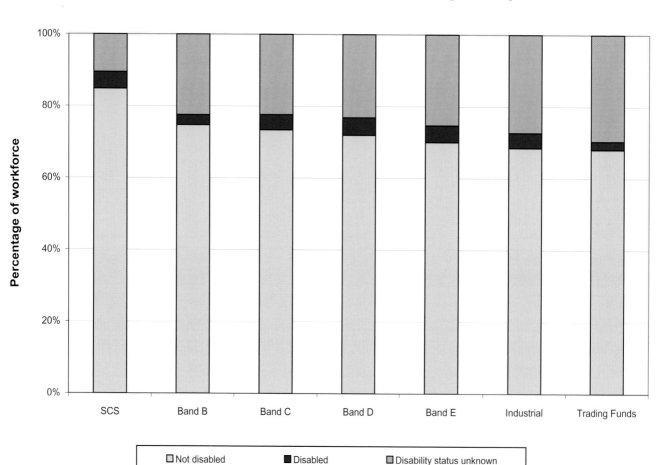

CIVILIAN PERSONNEL

Table 2.38 Age profile of civilian personnel[1] by Industrial status and sex, at 1 April 2008

Headcount

	Non-industrial		Industrial		Royal Fleet Auxiliaries[2]	Civilian Level 1[1]	Trading Funds		Locally engaged civilians[2]	Civilian Level 0[1]
	Male	Female	Male	Female			Male	Female		
16-19	60	110	140	30	-	340	90	10	-	440
20-24	820	910	320	100	-	2 160	330	120	-	2 600
25-29	1 730	1 980	400	150	-	4 260	660	300	-	5 220
30-34	1 840	2 080	410	150	-	4 470	710	360	-	5 540
35-39	3 160	3 310	850	260	-	7 590	930	330	-	8 840
40-44	5 000	4 300	1 320	420	-	11 030	1 050	320	-	12 400
45-49	5 920	4 060	1 650	420	-	12 050	1 070	300	-	13 420
50-54	5 620	3 280	1 600	390	-	10 880	990	200	-	12 070
55-59	5 200	2 680	1 670	310	-	9 870	900	170	-	10 930
60-64	3 120	1 080	1 390	200	-	5 780	480	70	-	6 330
65+	250	70	120	20	-	460	30	-	-	490
Unknowns	10	-	-	-	2 270	2 290	-	-	13 080	15 380
Total	**32 730**	**23 860**	**9 860**	**2 460**	**2 270**	**71 170**	**7 250**	**2 170**	**13 080**	**93 670**

Source: DASA(Quad-Service)

1. Civilian Level 0 and Level 1 are defined in the Glossary.
2. Age data are not available for Royal Fleet Auxiliaries, and locally engaged civilians.

Age of civilians, by sex and industrial status

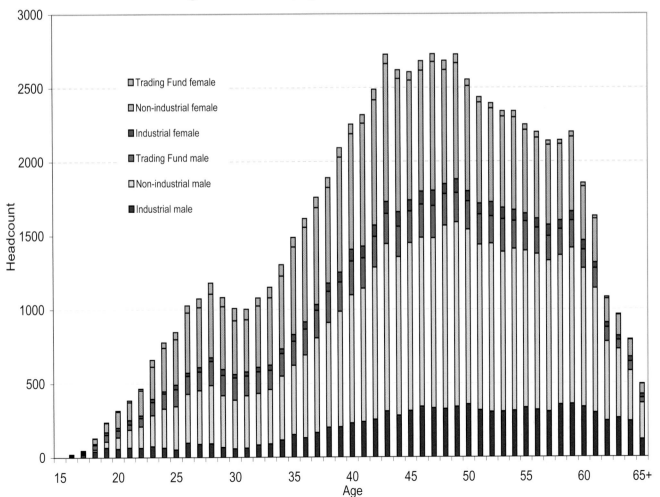

WAR PENSIONS

Table **2.39** Number of War Pensions in payment by type of pension, at 31 March each year[1]

	1995 [2]	1997	2003	2004	2005	2006 [3]	2007	2008
TOTAL IN PAYMENT	**309 840**	**324 640**	**260 730**	**247 525** ||	**235 300** ||	**223 850**	**212 535**	**201 265**
Disablement pensioners	**260 295**	**264 595**	**212 595**	**201 970** ||	**191 750** [4] ||	**182 800**	**173 850**	**165 165**
1914 war[5]	475	140	~	~	~ ||	~	-	-
Inter-war[6]	..	505	170	125	95 ||	75	60	50
1939 war onwards[7]	259 825	263 945	207 395	197 285 ||	187 465 [4] ||	178 890	170 320	161 970
Civilian	..	..	2 415	2 235	2 090 ||	1 945	1 805	1 680
Polish	..	..	1 195	1 080	980 ||	865	755	675
Mercantile marine	..	..	1 405	1 230	1 115 ||	1 005	895	785
Not known	..	..	5	15	5 ||	15	10	~
Other pensioners	**49 545**	**60 045**	**48 135**	**45 555** ||	**43 550** [4] ||	**41 035**	**38 685**	**36 100**
War widows pension[8]	48 405	59 025	47 540	44 995	42 525 ||	40 065	37 730	35 165
War widower pension[8]	..	..	30 [9]	40	55 ||	60	65	70
War orphans pension[10]	835	695	45	40	35 ||	35	30	25
War parents pension[11]	305	295	80	60	50 ||	40	35	30
Adult dependant pension	..	25	20	20	15 ||	15	10	10
Unmarried dependant pension[12]	..	~	~	~	~ ||	~	~	~
Allowance for lowered standard of occupation only[4]	..	..	..	..	460 [4] ||	435	410	420
Child allowance only[13]	..	..	410	400	405 ||	400	400	380

Source: DASA(Health Information)

1. Pensions, allowances or other payments may be awarded where disablement or death is a result of service in HM Forces, or of an injury sustained as a result of war-time service in the Naval Auxiliary Service, or the Mercantile Marine. Awards may also be made in respect of service in the Polish Forces under British command during World War Two. While most payments are made to people living in the United Kingdom, some recipients are from overseas. Pensions, allowances or other payments may also be awarded where the disablement or death of a civilian of a member of the Civil Defence Organisation is the direct result of an injury sustained as a result of enemy action in World War Two.
2. Data are not available for 1990.
3. Following the implementations of the recommendations made as part of the National Statistics Quality Review, improvements were made to the processing of current data. This resulted in some small adjustments (less than 100 total) to the figures.
4. A number of pensioners receive an Allowance for Lower Standard of Occupation, but do not receive an ongoing war pension. Some, but not all, of these were formerly classified as disablement pensioners.
5. Disabled because of service between 4 August 1914 and 30 September 1921.
6. Disabled because of service between 1 October 1921 and 2 September 1939.
7. Disabled because of service from 3 September 1939 to date.
8. Paid to the spouse of an ex-service person whose death was in service or related to disablement because of service from 4 August 1914 to date.
9. A change in the law, from 8 April 2002, governing the War Pensions Scheme means that the provisions for war widowers have been equalised to align with those available to war widows; in effect this means that claims from war widowers are no longer means tested.
10. Paid to: (i) the child of a deceased service person who has no surviving parent; (ii) a child whose mother was divorced from a serviceman at the time of death; or (iii) a child who is not in the care of the surviving parent.
11. Paid to a parent of a deceased service person.
12. Paid to a partner who lived with the ex-serviceman for at least six months before his enlistment, was maintained by him, and who has borne his child.
13. A case where a Child Allowance is in payment for a child, where one parent has died, and either the surviving parent does not qualify for a War Widows/Widowers Pension, because of remarriage or cohabitation, or the child does not live with the surviving parent.

WAR PENSIONS

Charts to Table **2.39**

Average Weekly amount of Disablement Pension (entitlement) - as at 31 March 2008

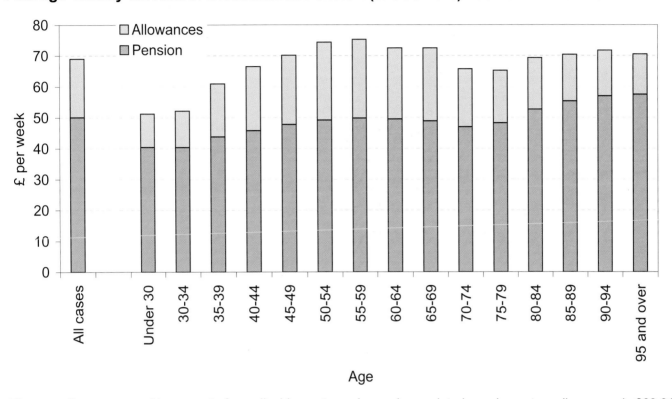

The overall average weekly amount of war disablement pension and associated supplementary allowances is £69.01.

Average amount of Widow(er)'s Pension (entitlement) - as at 31 March 2008

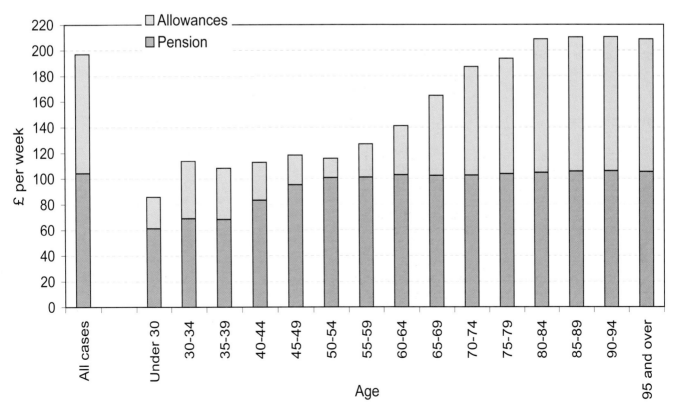

The average weekly amount received by widow(er)s is £197.01. The actual War Widow(er)s portion of the pension makes up just over half the total, with the remainder being made up of Supplementary Allowances.

97

Compensation Claims made against the Ministry of Defence

This section describes common law non-contractual compensation claims made against the Ministry of Defence. These claims are of three broad types: employer's liability for Armed Forces personnel, employer's liability for its civilian employees, and public liability claims. **Tables 2.40 and 2.41** show numbers of new claims made and numbers of claims settled, analysed by category of claim and by cause.

The Department self insures against loss. However, it employs commercial companies as claim handlers. All settlements are paid by the Department, the companies in question receiving a fee for each claim handled. Gallagher Bassett recently won the contracts in respect of third party motor claims and Service and civilian employer's liability claims for all claims received after 1 May 2007. Claims received before this date are handled by:

1982 to 2007 AXA Corporate Solutions - third party motor claims
1996 to 2007 Royal & Sun Alliance (RSA) - employer's liability claims from Armed Forces personnel
1982 to 2002 AXA Corporate Solutions - employer's liability claims from civilian personnel 2002 to 2007 Royal & Sun Alliance - Employer's liability claims from civilian personnel.
The MOD's Claims branch handles all other claims, including:
- Public liability worldwide - property damage and personal injury (except where there is an Area Claims Officer (ACO) in country)
- damage or injury caused by low flying military aircraft
- maritime claims and salvage claims
- clinical negligence
- claims made against a NATO visiting force
- high value, novel or contentious cases.

ACOs are part of the Command Secretariat and are located in Cyprus, the South Atlantic Islands, Germany (for NW Europe), Kosovo, Afghanistan and Iraq. They deal with public liability claims made against the MOD within their geographic area.

New claims

The number of new claims is the number of new cases opened by the MOD's Claims branch, ACOs and commercial claims handlers during that year; re-opened cases are not included. A new claim may be in the form of a letter from a claimant or their legal representative, or in the form of proceedings issued by a court of law. The largest number of new claims is in respect of on-duty Road Traffic Accidents involving Armed Forces personnel or MOD civilians driving a MOD-owned or MOD-hired vehicle.

Settled claims

These are claims for which a full and final settlement has been made, either by agreement between the parties, or which a court has determined. Claims are not recorded as settled until the final payment is made, which is normally the claimant's solicitor's costs and disbursements. This bill is sometimes presented some months after the compensation payment has been made, so compensation and legal costs can be paid in different financial years.

Further details may be found in the *Claims Annual Report* available from DS&C Claims.

CHAPTER 2 - PERSONNEL

COMPENSATION CLAIMS MADE AGAINST THE MOD

Table 2.40 New claims and settled claims by broad category in each year

The data in this table are outside the scope of National Statistics because they do not meet all of the high professional quality assurance standards set out in the National Statistics Code of Practice.

Number

New Claims Notified	2003/04	2004/05	2005/06	2006/07	2007/08
Total	**7 749**	**8 447**	**7 686**	**6 820**	**7 389**
Public Liability Claims	**787**	**892**	**715**	**639**	**974**
Low Flying	200	202	171	175	244
Maritime	37	18	20	24	25
Other Public Liability (inc Northern Ireland)	532	643	507	435	690
Radiation	18	29	17	5	15
Employers' Liability Claims	**1 941**	**1 983**	**1 846**	**1 404**	**1 863**
Service Employment Tribunal [1]	-	-	27	-	-
Other Service Employer's Liability	604	664	623	459	776
Asbestos Related	595	887	742	209	189
Noise Induced Hearing Loss	101	129	145	413	577
Vibration White Finger	65	37	18	58	45
Other Civilian Employer's Liability	576	266	291	265	276
Other	**5 021**	**5 572**	**5 125**	**4 777**	**4 552**
Clinical Negligence	92	86	69	67	86
Road Traffic Accidents	2 262	3 216	2 982	2 620	2 284
Area Claims Offices' Claims	2 565	2 192	2 015	2 003	2 124
Visiting Forces [2]	102	78	59	87	58

Settled Claims Notified	2003/04	2004/05	2005/06	2006/07	2007/08
Total	**6 857**	**7 757**	**8 012**	**6 980**	**6 419**
Public Liability Claims	**508**	**496**	**413**	**402**	**592**
Low Flying	130	120	124	126	141
Maritime	34	10	11	13	12
Other Public Liability (inc Northern Ireland)	343	365	278	262	438
Radiation	1	1	-	1	1
Employers' Liability Claims	**2 200**	**1 901**	**1 878**	**2 242**	**2 337**
Service Employment Tribunal[1]	12	-	4	5	57
Other Service Employer's Liability	790	706	601	800	1 063
Asbestos Related	534	613	773	607	314
Noise Induced Hearing Loss	174	116	63	355	500
Vibration White Finger	85	92	52	70	62
Other Civilian Employer's Liability	605	374	385	405	341
Other	**4 149**	**5 360**	**5 721**	**4 336**	**3 490**
Clinical Negligence	42	25	28	23	16
Road Traffic Accidents	2 334	3 706	3 717	2 986	2 103
Area Claims Offices' Claims	1 682	1 581	1 917	1 269	1 330
Visiting Forces [2]	91	48	59	58	41

Source: MOD Claims Annual Reports

1. Although generally Employment Tribunal cases are now dealt with by TLBs, the new claims in 2005/06 were Homosexual dismissal cases for which DS&C Claims agreed to retain central responsibility.
2. Claims against NATO forces visiting the UK and claims by NATO countries against UK personnel visiting those countries.

Number of settled claims by broad category in 2007/08

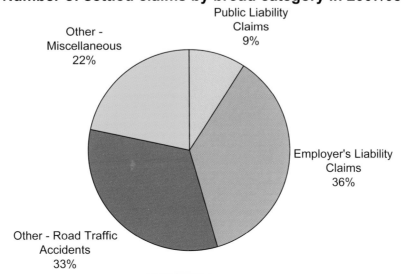

Public Liability Claims 9%

Other - Miscellaneous 22%

Employer's Liability Claims 36%

Other - Road Traffic Accidents 33%

COMPENSATION CLAIMS MADE AGAINST THE MOD

Table **2.41** New Claims and settled claims by broad cause in each year

The data in this table are outside the scope of National Statistics because they do not meet all of the high professional quality assurance standards set out in the National Statistics Code of Practice.

Number

New Claims Notified	2003/04	2004/05	2005/06	2006/07	2007/08
Total	**7 749**	**8 447**	**7 686**	**6 820**	**7 389**
Asbestos Related	614	904	809	223	190
Clinical Negligence	92	87	69	67	86
Fall	322	352	319	306	305
Handling/Sprain	87	82	51	59	53
Impact	230	254	246	178	97
Low Flying	727	614	616	506	336
Machinery/Vibration White Finger	65	37	29	58	45
Maritime	38	18	29	24	25
Noise Induced Hearing Loss	105	129	208	418	579
Other Causes	1 012	1 554	1 122	1 081	2 342
Not Known[1]	1 060	186	216	63	91
Vehicle Related	3 397	4 230	3 972	3 837	3 240

Settled Claims Notified	2003/04	2004/05	2005/06	2006/07	2007/08
Total	**6 857**	**7 757**	**8 012**	**6 980**	**6 419**
Asbestos Related	542	620	846	611	314
Clinical Negligence	42	25	28	23	16
Fall	513	318	291	395	339
Handling/Sprain	172	95	56	108	93
Impact	265	211	187	328	272
Low Flying	598	506	552	437	255
Machinery/Vibration White Finger	85	92	70	71	62
Maritime	34	10	14	13	13
Noise Induced Hearing Loss	174	116	104	357	500
Other Causes	907	840	1 021	662	1 499
Not Known[1]	122	232	242	127	162
Vehicle Related	3 403	4 692	4 601	3 848	2 894

Source: MOD Claims Annual Reports

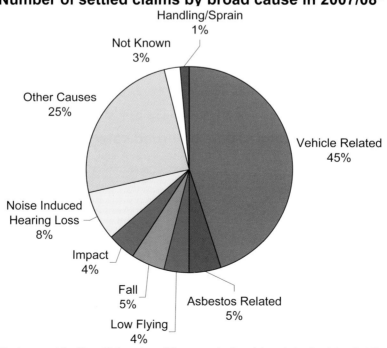

Number of settled claims by broad cause in 2007/08[2]

Handling/Sprain 1%
Not Known 3%
Other Causes 25%
Noise Induced Hearing Loss 8%
Impact 4%
Fall 5%
Low Flying 4%
Asbestos Related 5%
Vehicle Related 45%

1. The cause of a claim may not be known at the New Claims stage if for example, the claimant simply states that they have a claim but does not state exactly what it is. At settlement stage, although the cause of the claim will be recorded on the claim file, it may not always be recorded on the databases from which these data are drawn.
2. Clinical negligence, Machinery/ Vibration White Finger and Maritime are included in "other causes" as these are the causes with the smallest number of claims.

Table **2.42** Manpower holdings and ceilings by member country within the scope of the Conventional Armed Forces in Europe Treaty at 1 January 2008

The data in this table are outside the scope of National Statistics because they are provided by an organisation outside the UK Government Statistical Service.

	Holding	Ceiling
Countries not in NATO		
Armenia	43 860	60 000
Azerbaijan	64 967	70 000
Belarus	49 416	100 000
Georgia	32 307	40 000
Moldova	6 500	20 000
Russia[1]	-	1 450 000
Ukraine[2]	152 000	250 000 [3]

NATO Countries		
Belgium	40 210	70 000
Bulgaria	35 516	104 000
Canada	-	10 660
Czech Republic	38 805	93 333
Denmark	13 088	39 000
France	179 961	325 000
Germany	198 952	345 000
Greece	124 564	158 621
Hungary	20 934	100 000
Italy	144 085	315 000
Luxembourg	541	900
Netherlands	28 630	80 000
Norway	20 000	32 000
Poland	131 536	234 000
Portugal	29 811	75 000
Romania	77 697 [4]	230 000
Slovakia	17 688	46 667
Spain	106 359	300 000
Turkey	301 397	530 000
United Kingdom	**212 416**	**260 000**
United States of America	81 540	250 000

Source: Directorate for Counter-Proliferation and Arms Control

1. The Russian Federation suspended the implementation of the CFE Treaty on 12 December 2007. Consequently, Russia did not submit the annual exchange of information required by the Treaty. The given numbers of holdings are taken from the "Consolidated Information" provided by the Russian Federation on 18 December 2007 as a sign of goodwill. The information does not include the subholdings of AIFVs and HACVs, nor the holdings of Naval Infantry and Coastal Defence Forces, nor the Personnel Strength.

2. Since 1 Jan 2004 theese figures have included the TLE and the Personnel belonging to the Naval Infantry and Coastal Defence Forces (NI/CD).

3. As of 09.04.2008, according to CFE Annual Data Exchange as amended by subsequent notified corrections.

4. Numbers of ACV and Artillery holdings according to the CFE Treaty - "Correction of the Romanian Annual Data Exchange".

CHAPTER 3 - HEALTH

INTRODUCTION

This chapter provides summaries and analyses of health-related information on UK Armed Forces personnel and Health & Safety for UK Armed Forces personnel and MOD Civilians. The key findings of three of DASA Health Information's annual National Statistics publications are summarised in this chapter, along with a range of other key outputs.

A summary of the numbers and rates of deaths in the UK Armed Forces is provided in **Tables 3.1** and **3.2**. The figures cover a 10 year time series and are broken down by Service, year of death and cause. Prior to the introduction of the Health chapter in this year's edition, in UKDS 2007 and in previous years the corresponding tables appeared as **Tables 2.24** and **2.25**.

The numbers of suicides and open verdict deaths in the UK Armed Forces are broken down further in **Tables 3.3** and **3.4**. Numbers, age standardised rates and standardised mortality ratios are reported for a 24 year time series, broken down by Service, gender and age.

Table 3.5 presents the number of deaths of UK Gulf 1 veterans and for a UK Military comparison group who did not deploy to the Gulf. Figures and mortality rate ratios are presented from 1991-2007 by cause of death and are compared to mortality rates in the UK general population.

The numbers of fatalities of UK Armed Forces personnel on operations in Afghanistan and Iraq are reported in **Table 3.6**. The numbers of very seriously injured and seriously injured casualties on operations in Afghanistan, Iraq and the Balkans are presented in **Table 3.7**.

The numbers of UK Military and civilian work-related fatalities are presented for the last 10 years in **Tables 3.8** and **3.9**. Figures are provided by year and are broken down by cause.

Tables 3.10 and **3.11** report numbers and rates of major and serious injuries and illnesses for UK Military and civilian personnel. Figures are provided for the last 10 years and are broken down by Service.

Table 3.12, in this year's edition of UKDS, regarding sickness absence, corresponds to Table 2.36 in previous years' editions.

Key Points and Trends

- In 2007, a total of 201 deaths occurred among the UK Regular Armed Forces (see **Table 3.1**), of which 27 were serving in the Naval Service, 143 in the Army and 31 in the RAF.
- During the 10-year period 1998-2007, the overall Armed Forces age and gender standardised mortality rates fluctuated between a low of 66 per 100,000 in 1999 to a high of 105 per 100,000 in 2007 (see **Table 3.1**).
- For the 24-year period 1984-2007, 712 suicides occurred among UK Regular Armed Forces personnel: 694 among males (see **Table 3.3**) and 18 among females.
- Overall, male suicide rates in the UK Armed Forces were statistically significantly lower than the general UK population, with the exception of Army males aged under 20. Over the period 1984-2007 this group had a statistically significantly increased risk of approximately 50%.
- Between 1 April 1991 and 31 December 2007 there were 918 deaths among the Gulf 1 veterans and 958 deaths among the Era comparison group (see **Table 3.5**). There were no statistically significant differences in the total number of deaths or for any of the main groups of cause of death.
- Since reporting began in 2001 until the end of 2007, there have been 86 UK fatalities on Operations in Afghanistan and 174 on Operations in Iraq (see **Table 3.6**).
- Since reporting began in 2001 until the end of 2007, there have been 104 very seriously injured and seriously injured casualties on Operations in Afghanistan and 212 on Operations in Iraq (see **Table 3.7**).
- Between 1 January 1998 and 31 December 2007 there were 461 work-related fatalities of which 192 were in hostile action, 97 were on-duty road traffic accidents and 172 were work-place incidents (see **Table 3.8**).
- The number of major injuries and illnesses reported on the Central Health and Safety Project (CHASP) system increased in 2006 to 430 from 85 in 1997, an increase of 406% (see **Table 3.10**). The rate of major injury and illnesses increased over the 9 years from 26 per 100,000 MOD personnel to 153 per 100,000.

CHAPTER 3 - HEALTH

INTRODUCTION

- The number of serious injuries and illnesses recorded on the CHASP system increased in 2006 to 1,550 from 530 in 1997, an increase of 192% (see **Table 3.11**). The rate of serious injury and illnesses reported on CHASP increased over the nine years from 162 per 100,000 MOD personnel in 1997 to 550 per 100,000 in 2006.
- The increases in the rates of major and serious injuries and illnesses are thought to be due to the introduction of single Service notification cells and increasing health and safety awareness in general.
- There has been a decline in the average number of working days lost per year amongst industrial civilian personnel since 2005. For non-industrial civilian personnel, the rate is at its lowest point in the past four years (see **Table 3.12**).

Denominator Data

Annual strength data for UK Regular Armed Forces personnel were obtained for the period 1984-2005 from AFPAA. Strength data for 2006 were obtained from both the Armed Forces Personnel Administration Agency (AFPAA) and Joint Personnel Administration (JPA).

Data on the size of the UK general population and the numbers of deaths by age, gender and year were obtained for the 22 year period 1984–2005 from the ONS, GROS and NISRA. Data for 2006 were not available at the time of publication; therefore the figures from 2005 were used as an estimate for 2006 as the year on year variation in the UK population figures is unlikely to affect the findings.

Gulf Veterans Definitions

Gulf veterans consist of Service personnel deployed to any Gulf state between 1 September 1990 and 30 June 1991 and for the Navy afloat, all personnel aboard a ship east of the Suez canal during that period. The data do not include civilian personnel employed by the MOD (including the Royal Fleet Auxiliary, the NAAFI, MoD civil servants), by other Government Departments, or civilians working for Defence Contractors, the media or charitable and humanitarian organisations.

The "Era" comparison group comprises 53,143 personnel, randomly sampled from all UK Armed Forces personnel in service on 1 January 1991 and who did not deploy to the Gulf. This group is stratified according to the 53,409 Gulf veterans to reflect the socio-demographic and military composition of the Gulf cohort in terms of age, gender, Service (Naval Service, Army, Royal Air Force), officer/other rank status, regular/reservist status, and a proxy measure for fitness.

Ethical and Confidentiality Issues

The information presented in this publication does not present any ethical issues because:
- Information relating to deaths is publicly available.
- No medical information is presented detailing the injuries sustained.
- As only aggregated data are presented, individuals cannot be identified.

Links To Websites

Further information on deaths in the UK Armed Forces, including cause of death breakdowns for each Service, can be found in the latest National Statistic Publication published in March 2008: http://www.dasa.mod.uk/natstats/deaths/pdfs/deaths01mar08.pdf

Further information on suicides in the UK Armed Forces is provided in the March 2008 National Statistic publication: http://www.dasa.mod.uk/publications/pdfs/suicide/suicideMar08.pdf

The March 2008 publication of the Gulf 1 Veterans Mortality National Statistic gives further information on the methodology used and provides a breakdown of deaths due to neoplasms (cancers): http://www.dasa.mod.uk/natstats/gulf/pdfs/gulf0108.pdf

The operational casualty and fatality tables are available on the MOD website, where further information on field hospital admissions and aero-medical evacuations is also available for operations in Afghanistan and Iraq:

http://www.mod.uk/DefenceInternet/FactSheets/OperationsFactsheets/OperationsInIraqBritishCasualties.htm

http://www.mod.uk/DefenceInternet/FactSheets/OperationsFactsheets/OperationsInAfghanistanBritishCasualties.htm

http://www.mod.uk/DefenceInternet/AboutDefence/CorporatePublications/DoctrineOperationsandDiplomacyPublications/OperationsinTheBalkans/TheBalkanCasualtyTable.htm

Further information on coding of deaths to ICD10, including a full breakdown of codes, can be found on the World Health Organisation website:

http://www.who.int/classifications/apps/icd/icd10online

CHAPTER 3 - HEALTH

DEATHS IN THE UK ARMED FORCES

Table **3.1** Deaths in the UK Regular Armed Forces, year of occurrence by Service, numbers and rates[1]

In order to make meaningful comparisons of the numbers of deaths between the Services and take their different strengths into account, rates were calculated and standardised for age and gender, using the 2006 Armed Forces strength as the standard population.

During the 10-year period 1998-2007, the overall Armed Forces age and gender standardised mortality rates fluctuated between a low of 66 per 100,000 in 1999 and a high of 105 per 100,000 in 2007.

In 2003 and 2004 there were increases in the number of deaths in the Naval Service due to 3 helicopter incidents involving multiple deaths during operations in the Middle East. In 2006 there was one incident involving multiple fatalities when two Royal Marines died, however, another 6 Royal Marines and one member of Navy personnel died on operations in separate incidents.

The increase in the RAF mortality rate from 61 per 100,000 in 2004 to 71 per 100,000 in 2005 was accounted for by a Hercules crash in Iraq in January 2005 which claimed the lives of 9 RAF personnel. The similar increase from 71 to 84 per 100,000 in 2006 was accounted for by the loss of 12 RAF personnel in a Nimrod crash in Afghanistan in September 2006.

The increase in Army fatality rates from 94 per 100,000 in 2006 to 128 per 100,000 in 2007 was mainly accounted for by operations in Iraq and Afghanistan which resulted in 86 lives lost in 2007 (71 as a result of hostile action), compared to 67 lives lost (47 as a result of hostile action) in 2006.

Numbers of deaths	1998	1999	2000	2001	2002	2003	2004	2005	2006 [2]	2007
Total	**165**	**141**	**147**	**142**	**147**	**173**	**169**	**158**	**190**	**201**
Naval Service	26	26	25	33	26	37	37	27	33	27
Army	97	83	88	80	94	97	95	91	110 r	143
Royal Air Force	42	32	34	29	27	39	37	40	47 r	31

Death rates[3,4] per 100,000 strength

Total	**78**	**66**	**71**	**69**	**72**	**82**	**80**	**78**	**96** [2]	**105**
Naval Service	62	60	63	80	67	90	91	69	85 r	69
Army	87	73	79	71	83	79	77	81	94 r	128
Royal Air Force	66	49	62	49	52	73	61	71	84 r	66

Source: DASA (Health Information)

1. The information on deaths presented here is for the UK Regular Armed Forces (including Gurkhas) and includes all trained and untrained personnel. The data exclude the Home Service of the Royal Irish Regiment, mobilised reservists, full time reservists, Territorial Army and Naval activated reservists as DASA do not receive routine notification of all deaths amongst reservists and non-regulars, unless they are deployed on active service.
2. Numbers and rates of deaths in 2006 have been revised since the last UKDS publication. The number of Army deaths has increased by one due to a missing member of personnel being declared dead. One RAF death was removed from the figures due to reclassification as a member of reservist personnel.
3. Rates have been age and gender standardised to the 2006 Armed Forces population and are expressed per 100,000 strength.
4. Changes in rates of deaths are due to the use of 2006 Armed Forces strengths denominator data, and also reflect the changes to numbers of deaths described above.

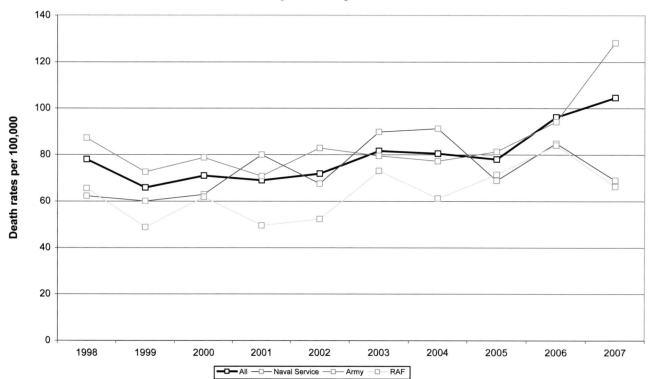

Mortality rates by Service 1998-2007

DEATHS IN THE UK ARMED FORCES

Table 3.2 Deaths in the Regular Armed Forces, causes, numbers and rates 1998-2007[1,2]

Over the 10 years 1998 to 2007 there has been little change in the rate of disease-related conditions. Similarly for deaths due to accidents there has been little change over the course of the last ten years.

However, deaths as a result of hostile action (killed in action and died of wounds) have increased, reflecting the deployments in Iraq and Afghanistan, and the changing tempo of operations.

	1998	1999	2000	2001	2002	2003	2004	2005	2006	2007
Total	**165**	**141**	**147**	**142**	**147**	**173**	**169**	**158**	**190**	**201**
Disease-related conditions	**52**	**40**	**35**	**41**	**40**	**40**	**43**	**45**	**40**	**37**
of which										
Cancers	32	25	16	24	19	18	22	23	25	27
Diseases of the circulatory system	13	12	16	9	18	14	18	16	14	6
Other	7	3	3	8	3	8	3	6	1	4
External causes of injury and poisoning	**112**	**99**	**111**	**100**	**107**	**133**	**125**	**113**	**147**	**160**
Deaths due to accidents	**91**	**70**	**71**	**80**	**89**	**69**	**90**	**71**	**88**	**80**
Land transport accident	62	43	45	50	65	49	61	53	61	50
Other	29	27	26	30	24	20	29	18	27	30
Deaths due to Violence	**2**	**2**	**4**	**5**	**3**	**39**	**16**	**22**	**49**	**73**
Killed in Action[3]	1	1	1	2	-	37	10	21	41	59
Died of Wounds[3]	-	-	-	-	-	1	-	-	6	12
Other	1	1	3	3	3	1	6	1	2	2
Suicide and Open verdicts	**19**	**27**	**36**	**15**	**15**	**25**	**19**	**20**	**10**	**7**
Cause not currently available	**1**	**2**	**1**	**1**	**-**	**-**	**1**	**-**	**3**	**4**

Rate per 100,000 strength	1998	1999	2000	2001	2002	2003	2004	2005	2006	2007
Total	**78**	**66**	**71**	**69**	**72**	**82**	**80**	**78**	**96**	**105**
Disease-related conditions	**26**	**20**	**17**	**21**	**21**	**19**	**22**	**22**	**20**	**19**
of which										
Cancers	16	12	8	12	10	8	11	11	13	14
Diseases of the circulatory system	6	6	8	5	10	7	9	8	7	3
Other	4	2	1	4	2	4	2	3	1	2
External causes of injury and poisoning	**52**	**45**	**53**	**48**	**50**	**63**	**58**	**56**	**74**	**84**
Deaths due to accidents	**42**	**31**	**34**	**39**	**42**	**33**	**42**	**35**	**45**	**42**
Land transport accident	30	19	21	24	30	23	28	26	31	26
Other	13	12	12	15	12	10	14	9	14	16
Deaths due to Violence	**1**	**1**	**2**	**2**	**1**	**18**	**8**	**11**	**25**	**38**
Killed in Action[3]	-	1	-	1	-	17	5	10	21	31
Died of Wounds[3]	-	-	-	-	-	-	-	-	3	6
Other	-	-	1	1	1	-	3	-	1	1
Suicide and Open verdicts	**9**	**13**	**17**	**7**	**7**	**12**	**9**	**10**	**5**	**4**
Cause not currently available	**-**	**1**	**1**	**-**	**-**	**-**	**-**	**-**	**2**	**2**

Source: DASA (Health Information)

1. Rates have been age and gender standardised to the 2006 Armed Forces population and are expressed per 100,000 strength.

2. DASA code all cause of death information to the World Health Organisation's International Statistical Classification of Diseases and Health-related Problems 10th revision (ICD-10).

3. DASA have included the Joint Casualty Compassionate Cell categories of killed in action and died of wounds which together provide information on the number of Service personnel who have died on operations as a result of hostile action. The term 'killed in action' is used when a battle casualty has died outright or as a result of injuries before reaching a medical facility, whilst 'died of wounds' refers to battle casualties who died of wounds or other injuries after reaching a medical treatment facility.

105

DEATHS IN THE UK ARMED FORCES

Charts to Table 3.2 Deaths in the Regular Armed Forces, causes, numbers and rates 1998-2007

Cause of death for all Regular UK Armed Forces personnel, 1998-2007, rate per 100,000

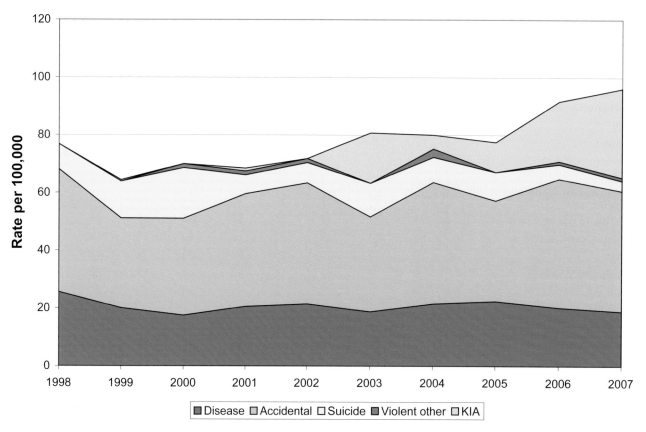

Disease ☐ Accidental ☐ Suicide ■ Violent other ☐ KIA

Cause of death for all Regular UK Armed Forces personnel, 2007

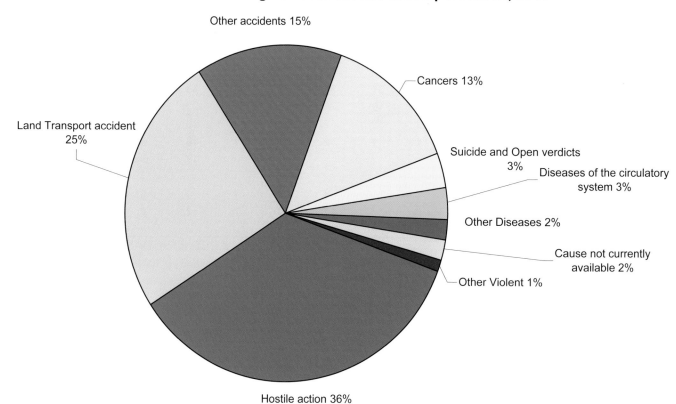

Other accidents 15%

Cancers 13%

Land Transport accident 25%

Suicide and Open verdicts 3%

Diseases of the circulatory system 3%

Other Diseases 2%

Cause not currently available 2%

Other Violent 1%

Hostile action 36%

CHAPTER 3 - HEALTH

SUICIDES IN THE UK ARMED FORCES

Service-specific age-standardised rates were calculated using the 2006 Regular Armed Forces male population only to make comparisons across the Services. Owing to the age composition of the UK Armed Forces, these analyses cover personnel aged 16-59 only. These rates estimate the rate of suicides among males for each Service, as if each Service had the same age distribution as the 2006 male Regular Armed Forces population.

Due to the small numbers involved when further breaking down annual numbers of suicides, the data for graphs have been aggregated to give 3 year moving averages. This eliminates some of the random variation that can occur from year to year and provides a clearer picture of possible trends.

The analyses made here are based on relatively small numbers. This presents a particular challenge for complex and detailed statistical analysis. As this section presents several sub-group analyses in which some categories may only involve a handful of cases, there is a risk of misinterpreting a chance association for a real finding. We strongly recommend caution in reading too much into past trends and assuming that they still apply today or will continue to do so in the future. In particular, they cannot take into account a large number of policy initiatives that have been introduced in the past few years.

The data presented includes both coroner-confirmed suicides and open verdict deaths. In accordance with ONS practice, the term 'suicide' should be understood to include all suicide and open verdict deaths. There are 21 deaths in the "awaiting verdict" category involving a wide range of external accidental or violent causes. These have been referred to a coroner (or, for Scotland, the Procurator Fiscal) and some may be returned as suicides or open verdicts. Due to the low numbers of cases among female Service personnel (18 deaths), most of the analyses have been restricted to males only (aged 16-59 years).

Table 3.3 Number of suicide and open verdict and awaiting verdict deaths by Service and gender, 1984-2007

	Verdict	Total	Male	Female
All Services	Suicide	**544**	531	13
	Open	**168**	163	5
	Awaiting	**21**	21	-
Naval Service	Suicide	**83**	81	2
	Open	**37**	36	1
	Awaiting	**1**	1	-
Army	Suicide	**335**	329	6
	Open	**96**	92	4
	Awaiting	**20**	20	-
Royal Air Force	Suicide	**126**	121	5
	Open	**35**	35	-
	Awaiting	**-**	-	-

Source: DASA (Health Information)

Age standardised rates of suicides, by Service, males, 1984-2007[1,2,3]

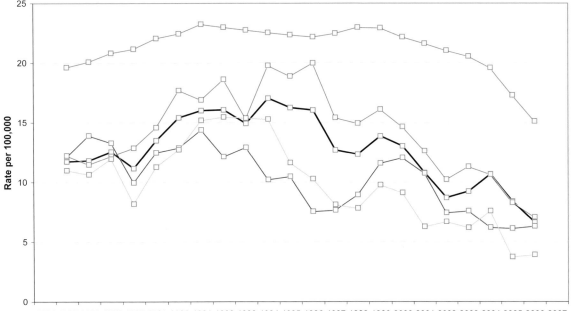

3 year moving average mid-point

Legend: — All — Naval Service — Army — RAF — UK

1. Data points for 2002-2004, 2003-2005, 2004-2006 and 2005-2007, may change when information on waiting verdicts is received.
2. Each year shown is the mid point of a 3 year period, e.g. 1985 refers to 1984-1986.
3. Standardised to the 2006 regular Armed Forces strengths.

SUICIDES IN THE UK ARMED FORCES

Table **3.4** Number of Suicides, Standardised Mortality Ratios and Age Specific Mortality Ratios 1984-2007, males only

To enable comparisons with the number of suicides in the UK population, Standardised Mortality Ratios (SMR), adjusted for age and year, have been calculated. An SMR is defined as the ratio of the number of deaths observed in the study population (UK Armed Forces) to the number of deaths expected if the study population had the same age group and year specific rates as the standard (UK general population). An SMR over (or under) 100 indicates a higher (or lower) number of observed deaths than expected (based on standard population rates). An SMR of 100 implies that there is no difference in rates when comparing the UK Regular Armed Forces population with the UK population.

95% confidence intervals (95% CI) were calculated based on the Normal approximation, except where the number of observed events was less than 30, when they were derived directly from the Poisson distribution. If independent samples of the same size are repeatedly drawn from a population, with a 95% confidence interval calculated from each sample, then 95% of these intervals should contain the population mean. The width of the confidence interval gives us some idea of how uncertain we should be about the unknown parameter. Smaller samples result in wider confidence intervals, whereas larger and more representative samples will give narrower confidence intervals (providing greater accuracy).

The mortality rate is scaled for the standard population to be 100 (here the standard population is the UK population). The same scaling is used when measuring the mortality rate for the population being considered.
If the mortality rate for this population is the same as for the UK population the underlying (true) mortality rate would be 100. The calculation of the rate based on data for a sample of the population over a restricted time period gives an estimate of the true rate.
The observed mortality rate can be used to test the null hypothesis that the true mortality rate for this sample = 100 (the same as for the UK population) against the alternative hypothesis that it is not equal to 100 (differs from the UK population), using a 5% significance level.

When calculating a 95% confidence interval for the mortality rate, the lower and upper end-points of the interval are calculated from the observed value, giving 95% confidence that the true value lies within this interval. There is an exact relationship between the test and confidence interval. If there are very few deaths in the time period used to estimate the mortality rates, the estimate for the mortality rate will not be accurate (its standard deviation will not be small).

For each Service, and for the UK Regular Armed Forces as a whole, the overall SMR was statistically significantly lower than expected on the basis of rates in the UK general population. For the Naval Service the SMR was 47 (95% CI=39-56) compared to the UK standard of 100, for the Army the SMR was 70 (95% CI=64-77) and for the RAF the SMR was 46 (95% CI=39-54).

For each Service and for the UK Regular Armed Forces as a whole, the age-specific mortality ratios for each age group were also lower than expected on the basis of rates among the UK general population, with the exception of young Army males aged under 20 years. These young Army males have experienced 50% more suicides over the period 1984-2007 than their UK general population counterparts, a finding which is statistically significant.

Age in years

	Total	<20	20-24	25-29	30-34	35-39	40+
Total	**694**	**81**	**214**	**147**	**104**	**87**	**61**
Standardised Mortality Ratio	**58**	124	71	52	49	50	41
95% Confidence Interval	**(54-63)**	(100-155)	(62-81)	(44-61)	(40-59)	(40-61)	(32-53)
Naval Service	**117**	7	29	23	22	24	12
Standardised Mortality Ratio	**47**	63	48	39	46	57	38
95% Confidence Interval	**(39-56)**	(25-129)	(32-70)	(25-59)	(29-69)	(37-85)	(20-67)
Army	**421**	68	153	83	50	43	24
Standardised Mortality Ratio	**70**	150	87	57	49	55	47
95% Confidence Interval	**(64-77)**	(118-190)	(75-102)	(46-70)	(37-65)	(40-74)	(30-70)
Royal Air Force	**156**	6	32	41	32	20	25
Standardised Mortality Ratio	**46**	69	47	52	50	37	40
95% Confidence Interval	**(39-54)**	(25-150)	(34-67)	(38-70)	(35-70)	(22-56)	(26-59)

Source: DASA (Health Information)

UK GULF VETERANS MORTALITY

Table 3.5 Deaths among UK Gulf 1 veterans[1]: 1 April 1991 - 31 December 2007

This section provides summary statistics on the causes of deaths that occurred among the UK veterans of the 1990/91 Gulf Conflict between 1 April 1991 and 31 December 2007. The mortality rates were analysed alongside those of a comparison group, the Era cohort, who were not deployed to the Gulf.

Mortality rate ratios were calculated to compare deaths in the Gulf and Era cohorts. The rate ratios provided here were calculated using as denominator the total person-years at risk (the length of time each person has been in study), taking into account deaths and emigrations from the UK. People who had left the Services and subsequently emigrated were deemed to be lost to follow up because we had no means of knowing if and when they may have died. The mortality rate ratios given here differ marginally from the crude deaths ratio owing to some small differences in the number of person years at risk between the Gulf and Era comparison groups.

The single year age distribution among those aged 40 and over has been found to show differences, with those in this age-group deployed to the Gulf generally younger than those in the Era group. Therefore, age adjusted estimates for the Era comparison group have been created by calculating the mortality rate for each single year of age at 1 January 1991 in each calendar year since 1991. This rate was applied to the equivalent numbers in each single year of age at 1 January 1991 and year of death in the Gulf population, from which deaths and emigrations from the UK were subtracted, to calculate the estimated total for each calendar year. These estimated numbers by calendar year were divided by the Gulf population, from which deaths and emigrations from the UK were subtracted, to produce adjusted rates.

ICD Chapter[2]	Cause of death	Number			Crude Mortality Rate Ratio	Adjusted[3] Mortality Rate Ratio	Adjusted[3] 95% Confidence Interval		
		Gulf	Era	Adjusted[3] Era					
	All deaths	**918**	**958**	**936**	**0.95**	**0.98**	**(0.89**	**-**	**1.07)**
	All cause coded deaths	**905**	**951**	**931**	**0.94**	**0.97**	**(0.89**	**-**	**1.07)**
I - XVIII	**Disease-related causes**	**463**	**550**	**528**	**0.83**	**0.88**	**(0.78**	**-**	**1.00)**
I	Certain infectious and parasitic diseases	7	3	3	2.31	2.51	(0.60	-	10.56)
II	Neoplasms	212	232	219	0.90	0.97	(0.80	-	1.17)
V	Mental and behavioural disorders	14	24	22	0.58	0.65	(0.33	-	1.27)
VI	Diseases of the nervous system	15	22	23	0.67	0.70	(0.37	-	1.33)
IX	Diseases of the circulatory system	154	183	179	0.83	0.87	(0.70	-	1.07)
X	Diseases of the respiratory system	13	12	12	1.07	1.06	(0.47	-	2.39)
XI	Diseases of the digestive system	34	49	48	0.69	0.71	(0.46	-	1.11)
III, IV, XII, XVIII	All other disease related causes[4]	14	25	22	0.55	0.63	(0.31	-	1.25)
XX	**External causes of mortality**	**442**	**401**	**403**	**1.09**	**1.09**	**(0.95**	**-**	**1.25)**
	Transport accidents:	190	159	162	1.18	1.17	(0.94	-	1.45)
	Land transport accident:	157	134	136	1.16	1.14	(0.91	-	1.45)
	Pedestrian	17	7	8	2.40	2.26	(0.93	-	5.47)
	Motorcycle rider	47	40	40	1.16	1.16	(0.76	-	1.78)
	Car occupant	46	37	38	1.23	1.21	(0.78	-	1.87)
	Other[5]	47	50	50	0.93	0.92	(0.61	-	1.38)
	Water transport	5	2	2	2.47	2.43	(0.46	-	12.78)
	Air and space transport	28	23	24	1.20	1.20	(0.69	-	2.08)
	Other external causes of accidental injury:	71	68	67	1.03	1.04	(0.74	-	1.45)
	Falls	9	11	11	0.81	0.87	(0.37	-	2.06)
	Exposure to inanimate mechanical forces	14	18	19	0.77	0.70	(0.34	-	1.43)
	Accidental drowning and submersion and other accidental threats to breathing	10	8	8	1.24	1.16	(0.45	-	3.03)
	Accidental poisoning by and exposure to noxious substances	15	13	11	1.14	1.23	(0.56	-	2.69)
	Accidental exposure to other and unspecified factors	17	11	11	1.53	1.54	(0.72	-	3.31)
	Other	6	7	6	0.85	0.90	(0.29	-	2.78)
	Intentional self-harm and events of undetermined intent[6]	162	144	144	1.11	1.12	(0.89	-	1.40)
	Assault	5	10	10	0.49	0.46	(0.15	-	1.37)
	Legal intervention and operations of war	6	10	11	0.59	0.63	(0.23	-	1.72)
	Sequelae of external causes of morbidity and mortality	-	2	1	-	-	*		*
	Deaths where the inquest has been adjourned	8	8	*	*	*	*		*
	Other deaths for which cause data are not yet available	**1**	**2**	*	*	*	*		*
	Overseas deaths for which cause data are not available	**12**	**5**	*	*	*	*		*

Source: DASA (Health Information)

1. Service and Ex-Service personnel only.
2. Causes have been coded to the World Health Organisation's International Statistical Classification of Diseases and Related Health Problems, 10th revision (ICD-10), 1992.
3. Adjusted for the single years of age structure of the Gulf cohort at 1 January 1991. The numbers may not add up to the totals shown due to rounding.
4. Includes cases with insufficient information on the death certificate to provide a known cause of death.
5. Under ICD-10 coding if the death certificate does not specifically mention the type of vehicle that was involved in the accident, the death is coded to "motor- or non-motor vehicle accident, type of vehicle unspecified". There were 37 of these deaths among Gulf veterans compared to 35 in the Era group.
6. Includes both coroner-confirmed suicides and open verdict deaths in line with the definition used by the Office for National Statistics (ONS).

The main sources of deaths information are the NHS Information Centre's Central Register, the General Register Office for Scotland and the Northern Ireland Statistics and Research Agency.

CHAPTER 3 - HEALTH

UK GULF VETERANS MORTALITY

Charts to Table **3.5** Deaths among UK Gulf 1 veterans[1]: 1 April 1991 - 31 December 2007

Estimated mortality rates for a similar sized cohort of the general UK population with the same age and gender profile are calculated using mortality and population information provided by the ONS. These are applied to the Gulf and Era populations to produce comparable mortality rates.

Mortality rates for disease-related causes for both Gulf veterans and the age-adjusted Era comparison group have gradually increased between 1991 and 2007. These follow the trends in rates for disease-related causes among the UK general population cohort. This suggests that the increase in disease-related deaths among Gulf veterans over time reflects the natural aging of the cohort. However, the mortality rates due to disease-related causes for both Gulf veterans and the age-adjusted Era group are statistically significantly lower than for the UK general population cohort.

Mortality rates for external causes for both the Gulf veterans and the age-adjusted Era comparison group have decreased between 1991 and 2007. However the estimated mortality rates for the UK general population cohort have stayed reasonably constant during this period.

Gulf and era[3] mortality rates for disease-related causes

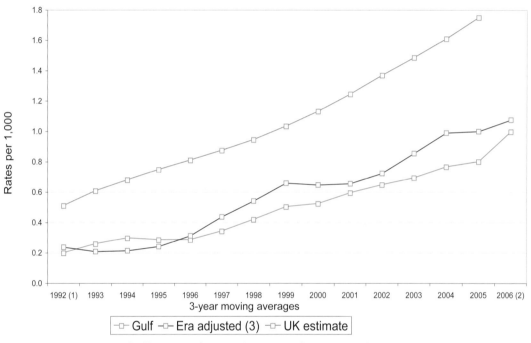

Gulf and era[3] mortality rates for external causes

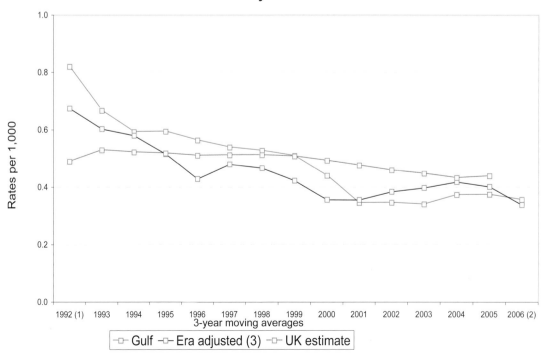

1. Data for 1 April 1991 - 31 December 1991 have been adjusted to a full year.
2. 2007 cause data for the UK general population are not currently available.
3. Adjusted for the single years of age structure of the Gulf cohort at 1 January 1991.

110

CHAPTER 3 - HEALTH

OPERATIONAL FATALITIES AND CASUALTIES

This section provides the numbers of fatalities and casualties involving personnel deployed on operations. The casualty data include the Naval Service, Army, RAF, Royal Fleet Auxiliary (RFA) personnel, and MOD Civilians. The figures provided below exclude those individuals categorised as VSI or SI whose condition was identified to be caused by illness. In agreement with Under Secretary of State for Defence, DASA are responsible for reporting on all medium scale operations since 2001. Data on operations smaller than medium-scale are not centrally compiled. The operations reported on below reflect those operations for which data have been published on the MOD website. The tables present the numbers of fatalities and casualties since reporting began in 2001 up until end of 2007.

Although there are no known data quality issues, the data in these tables are outside the scope of National Statistics because they do not currently meet all of the high professional assurance standards set out in the National Statistics Code of Practice, with regards to guidance on release practice procedure.

Table **3.6** Number of UK Operational Fatalities[1,2,3,4]

		2001	2002	2003	2004	2005	2006	2007
Afghanistan	Total	-	3	-	1	1	39	42
	Killed in Action	-	-	-	1	1	20	36
	Died of Wounds	-	-	-	-	-	1	1
	Other	-	3	-	-	-	18	5
Iraq	Total	-	-	53	22	23	29	47
	Killed in Action	-	-	39	10	18	18	24
	Died of Wounds	-	-	1	-	2	9	13
	Other	-	-	13	12	3	2	10

Source: DASA (Health Information)

1. Figures include UK Regular and Reservist Armed Forces Personnel.
2. 2001 data for Afghanistan starts 7 October.
3. Some deaths may not have clearly defined cause information and could be subject to change depending on the outcome of the Boards of Inquiry and/or Coroners' Inquest.
4. These data include all deaths occurring as a result of accidental or violent causes while deployed and deaths due to disease related causes during the deployment.

111

Table **3.7** Number of UK Operational Casualties[1,2,3,4,5]

Notification of Casualty (or "NOTICAS") is the name for the formalised system of reporting casualties within the UK Armed Forces. The NOTICAS reports raised for casualties contain information on how serious medical staff in theatre judge their condition to be. They are not strictly medical categories but are designed to give an indication of the severity of the illness to inform what the individual's next of kin are told. Very seriously injured and seriously injured are the two most serious categories into which personnel can be classified:
Very Seriously Ill/Injured/Wounded or VSI – The illness or injury is of such severity that life is imminently endangered.
Seriously Ill/Injured/Wounded or SI – The patient's condition is of such severity that there is cause for immediate concern, but there is no imminent danger to life.
The VSI and SI categories are defined by Joint Casualty & Compassionate Policy & Procedures. The figures provided below exclude those individuals categorised as VSI or SI whose condition was identified to be caused by illness. The data include Naval Service, Army, RAF, MOD Civilians and Royal Fleet Auxiliary (RFA) personnel. Validated NOTICAS data for casualties in Afghanistan, Iraq and Kosovo are held from January 2001 onwards. In agreement with the Under Secretary of State for Defence, operational casualty data prior to 2001 have not been examined.

		2001 [1]	2002	2003	2004	2005	2006 [2]	2007
Afghanistan	Total	-	1	1	6	2	31	63
	Very Seriously Injured or Wounded (VSI)[3,4]	-	1	-	3	2	18	23
	Seriously Injured or Wounded (SI)[3,4]	-	-	1	3	-	13	40
Iraq	Total	-	-	46	45	20	32	69
	Very Seriously Injured or Wounded[3,4]	-	-	14	14	5	11	24
	Seriously Injured or Wounded[3,4]	-	-	32	31	15	21	45
Balkans[5]	Total	6	2	3	2	-	2	2
	Very Seriously Injured or Wounded[3,4]	2	2	-	-	-	-	-
	Seriously Injured or Wounded[3,4]	4	-	3	2	-	2	2

Source: DASA (Health Information)

1. 2001 data starts at 7 October for Afghanistan.
2. Civilians are not included in the figures prior to 01/01/2006.
3. The VSI and SI injury data includes records classified as 'Other Causes'. This classification is used when there is insufficient information to attribute a casualty to injury or natural cause.
4. The casualty figures provided exclude those individuals categorised as VSI or SI whose condition was identified to be caused by illness.
5. The Balkans covers operational casualties in Slovenia, Croatia, Bosnia-Herzegovina, Serbia, Kosovo, Montenegro and Macedonia.

CHAPTER 3 - HEALTH

HEALTH AND SAFETY

The information provided here covers a range of health and safety incidents as set out by the HSE Reporting of Injuries, Diseases and Dangerous Occurrences regulations 1995 (RIDDOR). Cases include both MOD and non-MOD personnel: regular Service personnel, members of the volunteer and regular reserves if they have been mobilised, MOD civilian staff, and any other civilians on MOD property or injured in or by MOD vehicles. Civilians are required to notify the HSE when they are involved in an incident. For Service personnel, there is no current legal requirement, set out by the RIDDOR, for their injuries to be notified to the HSE. However, all these incidents should be recorded on the MOD's Central Health and Safety Project system (CHASP). The CHASP system was introduced in 1997 to enable the MOD to monitor and analyse accident trends throughout the Department and ensure compliance with current health and safety legislation.

A MOD reporting form should be raised for recording any of the following events:
- deaths resulting from work activity;
- injuries or ill health to MOD employees resulting from their work activity, which in normal circumstances would cause more than one hour loss of work time;
- deaths, injuries or illness to any other person where the cause might be attributable to MOD activities or where it has occurred on MOD land or property, which can be linked to a failure in responsibility by the MOD with regard to land or property;
- including those involving hostile activity during peacekeeping (excluding war);
- an event which would normally have resulted in one of the above outcomes but no person was affected (near hit, maritime hazardous incident or an event deemed worthy of reporting such as fire or property damage).

Although there are no known data quality issues, the data in these tables are outside the scope of National Statistics because they do not currently meet all of the high professional quality assurance standards set out in the National Statistics Code of Practice, with regards to the guidelines on release practice procedures

Table 3.8 Work related fatalities by type of incident, UK Service personnel and Civilians

'Work-related fatalities' have been defined as injury related deaths occurring on-duty or on MOD property after excluding suicides. 'Hostile action' is the combination of the JCCC reporting categories killed in action and died of wounds for operational deaths that are a result of hostile fire. Between 1997 and 2006 the UK Regular Armed Forces have been deployed to Northern Ireland, Sierra Leone, the Balkans, Afghanistan and Iraq. Road traffic accidents are those which occur on public highways whilst the Service personnel are on duty. A 'work place incident' is the result of a fatality for whom the MOD is responsible, that is they are deemed to be 'within the wire', thus work place incidents will include any vehicle incidents that occur on MOD property.

Type of Incident	1998	1999	2000	2001	2002	2003	2004	2005	2006	2007
Total	**43**	**28**	**18**	**30**	**25**	**57**	**43**	**39**	**77**	**101**
Hostile action	1	1	1	2	-	38	10	21	47	71
Road traffic accident - on duty	22	10	4	10	8	7	10	7	8	11
Work place incident	20	17	13	18	17	12	23	11	22	19

Source: DASA (Health Information)

Table 3.9 On-duty work place incidents resulting in injury-related deaths by cause, UK Service personnel and Civilians

Work Place Incidents	1998	1999	2000	2001	2002	2003	2004	2005	2006	2007
Total	**20**	**17**	**13**	**18**	**17**	**12**	**23**	**11**	**22**	**19**
Adventure training	1	-	1	3	1	-	1	3	-	1
Diving	-	-	-	2	1	-	-	-	-	-
Drowning	2	1	-	-	-	1	1	-	-	1
Electrocution	-	-	1	1	1	-	-	-	-	-
Explosive device	-	2	-	1	2	1	-	1	-	-
Fall	1	-	3	1	-	1	1	-	1	-
Fixed wing aircraft	4	5	-	1	1	1	2	-	14	-
Gunshot wound	1	-	1	1	1	2	2	3	1	2
Heat Injury	1	-	-	-	-	1	-	1	1	-
Parachute failure	-	-	2	1	2	-	-	2	-	1
Sport	-	-	-	-	1	-	-	1	-	-
Rotary blade aircraft	4	3	1	4	2	2	11	-	1	7
RTA - MOD property	2	1	1	-	1	1	-	-	-	1
Land transport accident	4	2	1	2	1	2	3	-	3	2
Other	-	3	2	1	3	-	2	-	1	4

Source: DASA (Health Information)

CHAPTER 3 - HEALTH

HEALTH AND SAFETY

The CHASP system was introduced in 1997 for the reporting of all work related incidents. In April 2000 a second version of CHASP was launched, introducing improvements to the system and clarification of the data types required for analysis and reporting. This new version was widely publicised and promoted, leading to a noticeable improvement in reporting adverse health and safety incidents on the CHASP system. During 2004/05, the Army trialled a new system for reporting health and safety incidents, allowing Army personnel to report health and safety incidents to a dedicated 24 hour call centre (Army Incident Notification Cell, AINC). Following the success of the Army system both the Navy (Naval Service Incident Notification Cell, NSINC) and Defence Equipment and Support (Defence Equipment and Support Incident Notification Cell, DINC) have rolled out similar systems for collating health and safety incidents. These initiatives have resulted in improvements in the number of events reported on the system, as can be seen in Tables 3.10 and 3.11 below.

The number of major injuries and illnesses reported on the Central Health and Safety Project (CHASP) system increased in 2006 to 430 from 85 in 1997, an increase of 406% (see Table 3.10). The rate of major injury and illnesses increased over the 9 years from 26 per 100,000 MOD personnel in to 153 per 100,000.

The number of serious injuries and illnesses recorded on the CHASP system increased in 2006 to 1,550 from 530 in 1997, an increase of 192% (see Table 3.11 below). The rate of serious injury and illnesses reported on CHASP increased over the nine years from 162 per 100,000 MOD personnel in 1997 to 550 per 100,000 in 2006.

The increases in the rates of major and serious injuries and illnesses are thought to be due to the introduction of single Service notification cells and increasing health and safety awareness in general.

The data in these tables are outside the scope of National Statistics because they do not meet all of the high professional quality assurance standards set out in the National Statistics Code of Practice.

Table 3.10 Major injuries and illnesses UK Service personnel and Civilians, by financial year, numbers and rates per 100,000[1,2,3,4]

Major injuries and illnesses are defined by the HSE as work-related cases which:
- could result in death or in hospitalisation (or being confined to bed, if at sea) for more than 24 hours
- could result in a person not in MOD employment and who was not at work to be taken from a MOD site to a hospital for treatment as a result of MOD work activity or site infrastructure.

Numbers	1997	1998	1999	2000	2001	2002	2003	2004	2005	2006
Total	**85**	**215**	**215**	**210**	**200**	**200**	**205**	**280**	**295**	**430**
Naval Service	30	50	25	40	25	30	20	20	40	90
Army	15	80	105	80	105	95	75	145	155	245
Royal Air Force	20	25	30	40	25	30	40	50	40	30
Civilian	20	60	55	55	45	45	70	60	60	65

Rate (per 100,000 strength)	1997	1998	1999	2000	2001	2002	2003	2004	2005	2006
Total	**26**	**67**	**67**	**68**	**66**	**67**	**69**	**93**	**101**	**153**
Naval Service	65	111	55	94	62	75	51	52	106	230
Army	14	73	95	73	95	86	69	132	143	227
Royal Air Force	37	41	56	70	49	53	75	93	76	65
Civilian	17	55	50	51	44	49	73	66	64	75

Source: DASA (Health Information)

Table 3.11 Serious injuries and illnesses UK Service personnel and Civilians by financial year, numbers and rates per 100,000[1,2,3,4]

Serious injuries and illnesses are those that are not defined as "major" according to the HSE criteria, but which could result in a person being unable to perform their normal duties for more than three days.

Numbers	1997	1998	1999	2000	2001	2002	2003	2004	2005	2006
Total	**530**	**1 370**	**1 365**	**1 370**	**1 235**	**990**	**1 010**	**1 190**	**1 300**	**1 550**
Naval Service	60	180	125	130	115	60	60	75	75	120
Army	45	325	370	360	430	415	430	630	765	980
Royal Air Force	90	235	200	245	180	155	180	185	165	110
Civilian	340	630	675	635	515	360	335	300	295	340

Rate (per 100,000 strength)	1997	1998	1999	2000	2001	2002	2003	2004	2005	2006
Total	**162**	**428**	**432**	**438**	**405**	**330**	**337**	**398**	**447**	**550**
Naval Service	132	408	285	305	269	145	148	185	194	306
Army	39	296	335	328	392	376	385	563	704	914
Royal Air Force	156	419	365	446	337	293	339	345	327	230
Civilian	294	572	623	600	515	379	361	324	320	388

Source: DASA (Health Information)

1. The numbers provided in the table include both regular and reservist personnel, MOD civilian staff, and any other civilians injured on MOD property or in/by MOD vehicles.
2. Figures exclude Health & Safety related fatalities
3. Rates calculated using Armed Forces strengths as the denominator
4. The numbers of injuries have been rounded to the nearest 5, and therefore may not always add up to the totals provided.

CHAPTER 3 - HEALTH

HEALTH AND SAFETY

Chart to Table 3.10 Major injuries and illnesses UK Service personnel and Civilians, rates [1,2,3] per 100,000, by financial year

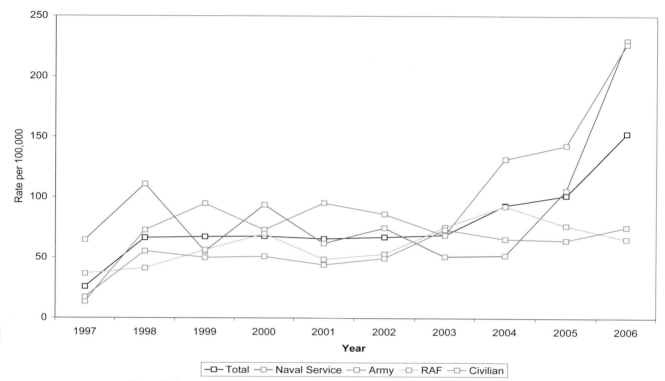

Chart to Table 3.11 Serious injuries and illnesses UK Service personnel and Civilians, rates [1,2,3] per 100,000, by financial year

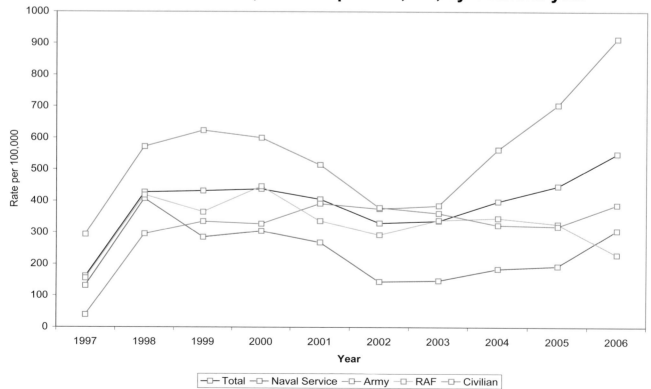

1. Figures exclude Health & Safety related fatalities.
2. Rates calculated using Armed Forces strengths as the denominator.
3. The numbers presented in the graphs include both regular and reservist personnel, MOD civilian staff, and any other civilians injured on MOD property or in/by MOD vehicles.

CHAPTER 3 - HEALTH

CIVILIAN PERSONNEL SICKNESS ABSENCE

Table **3.12** Number of working days lost per year due to sickness of civilian personnel[1], by ICD Code and industrial/ non-industrial marker

			Working days (thousands)		
		Year ending 31 December			Year ending 31 March
		2005	2006	2007	2007/08
	Non-industrial total	**548.4**	**486.8**	**471.7**	**453.0**
	ICD category[2]				
IPO	Certain infectious and parasitic diseases	33.9	41.0	41.1	39.9
NGB	Neoplasms	13.6	14.4	14.7	14.7
PSD	Mental and behavioural disorders	106.8	104.2	99.6	97.7
NSS	Diseases of the nervous system	16.0	17.3	16.9	16.9
CIR	Diseases of the circulatory system	21.6	16.9	18.3	18.2
DRS	Diseases of the respiratory system	85.2	63.6	64.0	56.9
DDS	Diseases of the digestive system	35.8	37.4	35.4	34.8
ACI	Injury, poisoning and certain other consequences of external causes	37.1	36.2	37.1	36.2
BFO	Diseases of the blood forming organs and certain disorders	2.4	4.2	2.7	2.7
DEM	Diseases of the ear and mastoid process	5.7	5.3	4.6	4.7
DEY	Diseases of the eye and adnexa	4.6	5.0	4.6	4.7
DGY	Diseases of the genito-urinary system	15.0	17.8	16.4	15.6
EMN	Endocrine, nutritional and metabolic diseases	3.5	3.5	3.4	3.5
MSD	Diseases of the musculoskeletal system and connective tissue	66.6	62.0	64.1	62.1
OPP	Factors influencing health status and contact with health service	44.9	32.6	31.1	29.5
PCP	Pregnancy, childbirth and the peurperium	6.0	7.4	6.7	6.7
SCO	Diseases of the skin and subcutaneous tissue	4.0	3.9	3.4	3.4
SID	Cause of absence not yet known	45.6	14.1	7.5	4.7
	Industrial total	**186.4**	**172.8** r	**154.8**	**147.5**

Source: DASA (Quad-Service)

Sickness rates[3] - number of days divided by the average strength (FTE) for that period.

	Year ending 31 December			Year ending 31 March
	2005	2006	2007	2007/08
Non-industrial total	**8.55**	**8.04**	**8.22**	**8.01**
Industrial total	**12.54**	**12.14** r	**11.85**	**11.54**

Source: DASA (Quad-Service)

1. This excludes Royal Fleet Auxiliary, Trading Fund and locally engaged personnel.
2. International Statistical Classification of Diseases and Related Health Problems, Version 10.
3. Rates are based on absence days and are FTE working days lost. For example, if a part-time employee working 50% of full-time hours is sick for 7 calendar days, this is 5 x 50% = 2.5 FTE working days lost.

CHAPTER 4 - FORMATIONS, VESSELS, AIRCRAFT AND VEHICLES OF THE ARMED FORCES
INTRODUCTION

Formations of the Naval Service, Army and Royal Air Force at 1 April each year

Due to the inclusion of the preceding Health chapter in this year's publication, all tables in Chapter 4 of UKDS 2008 correspond, in the same order, to the tables found in Chapter 3 of previous editions of UKDS.

Table 4.1 shows the number of submarines and ships in the Royal Navy and Royal Fleet Auxiliary, Royal Marine Commando units, squadrons of helicopters and fixed-wing aircraft in the Fleet Air Arm, and Reserve Units.

More information about:
- Royal Navy ships can be found at: http://www.royalnavy.mod.uk/server/show/nav.1244
- Royal Navy submarines can be found at: http://www.royalnavy.mod.uk/server/show/nav.2419
- Royal Fleet Auxiliary can be found at: http://www.rfa.mod.uk/
- Royal Marines can be found at: http://www.royalnavy.mod.uk/server/show/nav.2566
- Naval Air Squadrons can be found at: http://www.royal-navy.mod.uk/server/show/nav.2236
- Royal Navy Reserve can be found at:
  http://www.royalnavy.mod.uk/server/show/conWebDoc.1572/changeNav/3533
- Royal Marine Reserve can be found at: http://www.royalnavy.mod.uk/server/show/nav.2974

Table 4.2 shows the numbers of Regiments and Infantry battalions in the Regular and Territorial Army; and Corps, Divisional and Brigade headquarters.

More information about:
- Regiments and Battalions is at: http://www.army.mod.uk/structure/corps/default.aspx
- Divisions and Brigades is at: http://www.army.mod.uk/structure/divisions/default.aspx
- The Territorial Army can be found at: http://www.army.mod.uk/structure/ta/default.aspx
- The Royal Armoured Corps can be found at: http://www.army.mod.uk/armoured/armoured.aspx
- The Infantry can be found at: http://www.army.mod.uk/infantry/infantry.aspx
- The Army Air Corps can be found at: http://www.army.mod.uk/air/air.aspx
- The Royal Artillery can be found at: http://www.army.mod.uk/artillery/artillery.aspx
- The Royal Engineers can be found at: http://www.army.mod.uk/royalengineers/engineers.aspx
- The Royal Corps of Signals can be found at: http://www.army.mod.uk/signals/signals.aspx
- The Royal Electrical & Mechanical Engineers is at: http://www.army.mod.uk/reme/reme.aspx
- The Army Medical Services can be found at: http://www.army.mod.uk/join/career-paths/1099.aspx

Table 4.3 shows the number of squadrons in the Royal Air Force (RAF) and the Royal Auxiliary Air Force (RAuxAF), and units in the RAF Regiment.

More information about:
- RAF squadrons can be found at: http://www.raf.mod.uk/organisation/squadrons.cfm
- Royal Auxiliary Air Force Units can be found at: http://www.raf.mod.uk/rafreserves/
- RAF Regiment can be found at: http://www.raf.mod.uk/rafregiment/

Table 4.4 shows the number of regiments and squadrons in the Special Forces, Joint Helicopter Command and Joint Force Harrier.

Royal Navy and Royal Fleet Auxiliary operational ships and submarines

Table 4.5 shows the numbers of Royal Navy and Royal Fleet Auxiliary ships and submarines by class and base port, categorized by those that were operational and those undergoing refit at 1 April 2008.

Militarily useful British-registered merchant vessels at 31 December each year

Militarily useful British-registered merchant vessels are vessels that could be requisitioned in the appropriate circumstances in support of the armed forces. Other types of ship might also be used in certain cases. Foreign-flagged, but British-owned ships could also be requisitioned in certain circumstances.

Table 4.6 shows the number of passenger and dry cargo merchant vessels by principal categories and sizes.

Table 4.7 shows the number of merchant tankers, specialist and fishing vessels by principal categories and sizes.

CHAPTER 4 - FORMATIONS, VESSELS, AIRCRAFT AND VEHICLES OF THE ARMED FORCES

INTRODUCTION

Aircraft Fleets by type of aircraft at 1 April each year

Forward Available Fleet (FAF) is a way of managing aircraft resources which aims to enable the optimal level of availability, which has been used since 2006. FAF is defined as the number of aircraft required to undertake the mandated task; including aircrew and ground crew training, 'in-work' rectification and operational / tactical trials.

Table 4.8 shows the aircraft fleets for the Royal Navy Fleet Air Arm.

Table 4.9 shows the aircraft fleets for the Royal Air Force Air Command including Operational Conversion Units and Training Aircraft. The RAF no longer identified separate Required Operating Fleets for Operational Conversion Units with effect from 1 April 2005. This table now incorporates Operational Conversion Units which, prior to UKDS 2005, were in the table corresponding to that which is now **Table 4.10**.

Table 4.10 shows the aircraft fleets by type in the Joint Helicopter Command and Joint Force Harrier.

More information about:
- Fleet Air Arm aircraft can be found at: http://www.royalnavy.mod.uk/server/show/nav.2232
- Army aircraft can be found at: http://www.army.mod.uk/equipment/aircraft/default.aspx
- RAF aircraft can be found at: http://www.raf.mod.uk/equipment/aircraft.cfm

Equipment holdings within the scope of the Treaty on Conventional Armed Forces in Europe

The equipment numbers shown in **Tables 4.11, 4.12** and **4.13** cover holdings in the UK, Germany, Cyprus and Gibraltar.

Table 4.11 shows the surveyed holdings of Tanks and Artillery by type of equipment, and indicates which types of equipment are obsolete and non-operational at 1 January each year.

Table 4.12 shows the surveyed holdings of Armoured Combat Vehicles and Armoured Combat Vehicle Look-alikes by type of equipment, and indicates which types of equipment are obsolete and non-operational at 1 January each year.

Table 4.13 shows the surveyed holdings of Attack helicopters and Combat aircraft by type of equipment, and indicates which types of equipment are obsolete and non-operational at 1 January each year.

Table 4.14 shows the declared Holdings and Ceilings of Tanks, Armoured Combat Vehicles and Artillery by country within the scope of the Conventional Armed Forces in Europe Treaty at 1 January 2008.

Table 4.15 shows the declared Holdings and Ceilings of Attack helicopters and Combat aircraft by country within the scope of the Conventional Armed Forces in Europe Treaty at 1 January 2008.

Key Points

- There are 13 submarines, and 74 ships in the Royal Navy. There are 22 vessels in the Royal Fleet Auxiliary Service (see **Table 4.1**) at 1 April 2008.
- There are 46 Regular Army and 18 Territorial Army combat arms regiments, and respectively 37 and 23 combat support regiments (see **Table 4.2**) at 1 April 2008.
- The UK has 354 battle tanks and 347artillery held within the scope of the CFE Treaty (see **Table 4.11**) at 1 April 2008.
- There are 108 Tornado GR and 43 Tornado F3 aircraft, and 34 Typhoons in the Royal Air Force Air Command (see **Table 4.9**) at 1 April 2008.
- The UK has 1728 Armoured Combat Vehicles and 958 Armoured Combat Vehicle look-alikes held within the scope of the CFE Treaty (see **Table 4.11**) at 1 April 2008.
- The UK has 269 attack helicopters and 452 combat aircraft held within the scope of the CFE Treaty (see **Table 4.15**) at 1 April 2008.

FORMATIONS

Table **4.1** Number of vessels in the Royal Navy and Royal Fleet Auxiliary, and squadrons in the Fleet Air Arm, at 1 April each year

Royal Navy submarines		1990	1997	2002	2003	2004	2005	2006	2007	2008
Total	**Vessels**	**33** ||	**15** [1]	**16**	**16**	**15**	**15**	**14**	**13**	**13**
Trident / Polaris	Vessels	4 ||	3 [1]	4	4	4	4	4	4	4
Fleet	Vessels	29 ||	12 [1]	12	12	11	11	10 [2]	9 [3]	9 [4]

Royal Navy ships		1990	1997	2002	2003	2004	2005	2006	2007	2008
Aircraft Carriers	Vessels	3 ||	3 [1]	3	3	3	3	2 [5]	2	2
Landing Platform Docks / Helicopter	Vessels	2 ||	2 [1]	1	1	2	3	3	3	3
Destroyers	Vessels	14 ||	12 [1]	11	11	11	9	8 [6]	8	8
Frigates	Vessels	35 ||	23 [1]	21	20	20	19	17 [7]	17	17
Mine countermeasures vessels	Vessels	41 ||	19 [1]	22	22	19	16	16	16	16
Patrol ships and craft	Vessels	34 ||	34 [1]	23	22	26	26	22 [8]	22	22 [9]
Support ships	Vessels	8 ||	1 [1]	-	-	-	-	-	-	-
Survey ships	Vessels	8 ||	6 [1]	3	3	5	5	5	5	5
Ice patrol ships	Vessels	1 ||	1 [1]	1	1	1	1	1	1	1

Royal Fleet Auxiliary Service		1990	1997	2002	2003	2004	2005	2006	2007	2008
Tankers	Vessels	13	9	7	7	7	11 [10]	10 [11]	10	8 [12]
Fleet replenishment ships	Vessels	4	5	4	4	6	2 [10]	2	2	2
Aviation training ship	Vessels	-	1	1	1	1	1	1	1	1
Landing ships	Vessels	5	5	5	5	4	3	3 [13]	4 [14]	4 [15]
Forward repair ships	Vessels	1	1	1	1	1	1	1	1	1
Roll-on Roll-off vessels	Vessels	*	*	2	7	6	6	6	6	6

Royal Marines		1990	1997	2002	2003	2004	2005	2006	2007	2008
RM Commando	Commandos	3	3	3	3	3	3	3	3	3
Command Support Group	Commandos	1	1	1	1	1	1	1	1	1
Infantry Battalion	Battalion	-	-	-	-	-	-	-	-	1 [16]
Logistic unit	Regiments	1	1	1	1	1	1	1	1	1
Artillery unit	Regiments	1	1	1	1	1	1	1	1	1
Engineer unit	Squadrons	1	1	1	1	1	1	1	1	1
Nuclear Guarding and Fleet Security	Squadrons	..	..	3	3	3	3	3	3	3
Assault (landing craft)	Squadrons	..	..	4	4	4	4	4	4	4

Naval Aircraft		1990	1997	2002	2003	2004	2005	2006	2007	2008
Fixed Wing Aircraft[17]	Squadrons	3	3 ||	1	1	1	1	1	1	1
Helicopters[18,19]	Squadrons	17	15 ||	8	8 ||	5	6	6	7	7

Reserve Units		1990	1997	2002	2003	2004	2005	2006	2007	2008
Royal Navy Reserve Units	Units	..	..	16	16	16	16	14	14	14
Royal Marine Reserve Units	Units	..	..	5	5	5	5	5	5	5

Source: MOD Resources and Plans

1. All Royal Naval vessels are counted in 1990. Only active vessels are counted from 1997.
2. HMS Spartan was withdrawn from service during the year.
3. HMS Sovereign was withdrawn from service during the year.
4. HMS Superb due to leave service during year.
5. HMS Invincible was placed into a state of very low readiness in late 2005.
6. HMS Cardiff was withdrawn from service during the year.
7. HMS Marlborough and HMS Grafton were withdrawn from service during the year.
8. HMS Leeds Castle and the NI Squadron, consisting of HMS Brecon, HMS Cottesmore and HMS Dulverton, were withdrawn from service during the year.
9. HMS Clyde entered service during the year. HMS Dumbarton Castle was withdrawn from service.
10. Four Fleet replacement ships were re-categorised as Tankers to reflect their primary role.
11. RFA Grey Rover was withdrawn from service during the year.
12. RFA Brambleleaf and RFA Oakleaf were withdrawn from service during the year.
13. RFA Mounts Bay enterered service during the year. RFA Sir Tristram was withdrawn from service.
14. RFA Largs Bay and RFA Cardigan Bay entered service during the year. RFA Sir Galahad was withdrawn from service.
15. RFA Lyme Bay entered service during the year. RFA Sir Bedivere was withdrawn from service.
16. 1 Rifles became part of 3 Commando Brigade on 1 April 2008.
17. Excludes Joint Force Harrier squadrons from 1 April 2000 and 727 Sqn (ex Grading Flight).
18. Excludes Joint Helicopter Command squadrons from 1 October 1999.
19. OCUs/ OEUs excluded from 2005 onwards.

118

CHAPTER 4 - FORMATIONS, VESSELS, AIRCRAFT AND VEHICLES OF THE ARMED FORCES

FORMATIONS

Table 4.2 Number of Regiments, Infantry battalions & Major Headquarters, in the Regular & Territorial Army, at 1 April each year

Combat arms			1990	1997	2002	2003	2004	2005	2006 [1]	2007	2008
Armour											
	Regular Army	Regiments	19	11	10	10	10	10	10	10	10
	Territorial Army	Regiments	5	6	4	4	4	4	4	4	4
Infantry											
	Regular Army	Battalions	55	40	40	40	40	40	36	36	36
	Territorial Army	Battalions	41	33	15	15	15	15	15	14	14
	Home Service Forces	Battalions	11	7	4	4	4	4	-	-	-
Special Forces											
	Regular Army	Regiments	1	1	*[2]	*	*	*	*	*	*
	Territorial Army	Regiments	2	2	*[2]	*	*	*	*	*	*
Aviation											
	Regular Army	Regiments	4	5	*[3]	*	*	*	*	*	*
	Territorial Army	Regiments	..	1	*[3]	*	*	*	*	*	*

Combat support			1990	1997	2002	2003	2004	2005	2006 [1]	2007	2008
Artillery											
	Regular Army[4]	Regiments	22	15	15	15	14	14	14	14	14
	Territorial Army[5]	Regiments	7	6	7	7	7	7	7	7	7
Engineers											
	Regular Army	Regiments	13	10	11	11	11	11	11	11	11
	Territorial Army	Regiments	8	9	5	5	5	5	5	5	5
Signals											
	Regular Army	Regiments	13	11	11	12	11	11	11	12	12
	Territorial Army	Regiments	11	11	11	11	11	11	11	11	11

Combat service support			1990	1997	2002	2003	2004	2005	2006 [1]	2007	2008
Equipment support											
	Regular Army	Battalions	..	6	7	7	7	7	7	7	7
	Territorial Army	Battalions	..	5	4	4	4	4	4	4	2 [6]
Logistics											
	Regular Army	Regiments	..	24	20	21	21	22	17	17	17
	Territorial Army	Regiments	..	19	17	17	17	17	15	17	17
Medical Regiments / Field Hospitals[7]											
	Regular Army	Number	16	12	8	8	8	8	11	8	8
	Territorial Army	Number	17	18	15	15	15	15	13	13	13

Corps, Division & Brigade HQ[8]		1990	1997	2002	2003	2004	2005	2006 [1]	2007	2008
NATO Corps HQ		..	..	1	1	1	1	1	1	1
Division / District HQ:	deployable	..	..	2	2	2	2	2	2	2
	non-deployable	..	..	5	5	5	5	5	5	5
Brigade HQ:	deployable	..	..	8	9	9	9	8	8	7
	non-deployable	..	..	13	13	13	13	10	9	9

Source: MOD Resources and Plans

1. The numbers for 2006 reflect the Army's implementation of the Future Army Structure (FAS), announced on 16 December 2004.
2. From 1 April 2000 these units form part of Direct Special Forces. See **Table 4.4**.
3. From 1 April 2000 these units form part of the Joint Helicopter Command. See **Table 4.4**.
4. Excludes 14th Regiment Royal Artillery.
5. Includes the Honourable Artillery Company.
6. Restructuring of Royal Electrical and Mechanical Engineers was announced in 2008.
7. Field Ambulance structures have been subsumed into the Medical Regiment concept as part of structural changes across the Medical Services. Field Ambulances still exist in the Territorial Army.
8. Does not include temporary structures such as 6 Division HQ or 11 Light Brigade.

FORMATIONS

Table 4.3 Number of squadrons in the Royal Air Force and the Royal Auxiliary Air Force, at 1 April each year

Excludes Operational Conversion Units which train qualified aircrew for different aircraft types

120

Regular Air Force		1990	1997	2002	2003	2004	2005	2006	2007	2008
Strike / attack	Squadrons	11	6	5	5	5	5			
Offensive support	Squadrons	5	5	2 ¹	2	2	1	13 r,2	13 r	11 ³
Reconnaissance	Squadrons	3	5	5	5	5	5			
Air defence	Squadrons	9	6	5	4	4	4			
Maritime patrol	Squadrons	4	3	3	3	3	3	3	2	2
Airborne Early Warning	Squadrons	1	2	2	2	2	2	- r	- r	-
ISTAR (inc Airborne Early Warning)	Squadrons	-	-	-	-	-	-	3 r	3 r	4 ⁴
Air transport / Air Refuelling	Squadrons	15	13	9 ⁵	9	9	9	8	8	8
Search and Rescue	Squadrons	2	2	2	2	2	2	2	2	2
RAF FP Wg	HQs	..	..	4	4	4	4	6	6	7
RAF Ground based air defence⁶	Squadrons	*	*	4	4	4	4	3	2	-
RAF Regiment Field	Squadrons	*	*	6	6	6	6	6	6	7 ⁷
RAF Regt (Jt CBRN)	Squadrons	-	-	-	-	-	-	-	1	1
Tactical Provost Wg	HQ	*	-	-	-	-	-	1	1	1
Tactical Provost	Squadrons	*	-	-	-	-	-	2	1	1
Specialist Policing Wg⁸	HQ	*	-	-	-	-	-	1	1	1
Specialist Policing Sqns⁸	Squadrons	*	-	-	-	-	-	3	3	3

Auxiliary Air Force		1990	1997	2002	2003	2004	2005	2006	2007	2008
Air Movements	Squadrons	1	1	1	1	1	1	1	1	1
Aeromedical⁹	Squadrons	1	2	2	2	2	2	2	2	2
HQ Augmentation	Squadrons	3	3	1	1	1	1	1	1	1
Intelligence	Squadrons	2	2	2	2	2	2	2	2	2
Photographic Interpretation	Squadrons	1	1	1	1	1	1	1	1	1
Public Relations	Squadrons	-	-	1	1	1	1	1	1	1
Meteorological	Squadrons	1	1	1	1	1	1	1	1	1
RAuxAF Regt Field	Squadrons	6	5	4	4	4	4	4	3	3
FP Operations Support	Squadrons	-	1	4	4	4	4	4	4	4
Tactical Provost	Squadrons	-	-	1	1	1	1	1	1	1
RAuxAF Regt Chemical, Biological, Radiological and Nuclear	Squadrons	-	-	-	-	-	-	1	1	1

Source: MOD Resources and Plans

There have been changes in the format of this table due to restructuring in 2006. As a result it has been necessary to revise figures published in previous editions of UKDS.

1. Excludes Joint Force Harrier squadrons from 1 April 2000. See **Table 4.4** - Joint units.
2. From 2006, 4 Air Defence squadrons amalgamated with Strike/Attack, Offensive support and Reconnaisance to form multi-roled squadrons. One squadron moved from reconnaissance to ISTAR, one squadron was disbanded.
3. 6 Sqn (Jag) was disbanded on 30 April 07, 25 Sqn was disbanded 1 April 08. 43 Sqn also cover the role of the OCU since the disbandment of 56 Sqn, however this is not their only role.
4. 39 Sqn was re-formed on 23 January 2008.
5. Excludes Support Helicopter squadrons in the Joint Helicopter Command from October 1999. See **Table 4.4** - Joint units.
6. Delivery of Ground based air defence is now vested with the Army. The remaining 2 squadrons were reroled on 1 Apr 08 to increase the numbers of FP Wgs and Field Regts.
7. In UKDS editions 2003 and 2004, Ground Based Air Defence and Field Squadrons for years 2001 to 2004 were also included under Regular Air Force.
8. Project DARWIN1 and Project BEAGLE re-brigaded Specialist Policing assets under Specialist Policing Wg in 2006.
9. Includes Air Transportable Surgical.

CHAPTER 4 - FORMATIONS, VESSELS, AIRCRAFT AND VEHICLES OF THE ARMED FORCES

AIRCRAFT

Table 4.8 Aircraft Fleets by type of aircraft for the Royal Navy Fleet Air Arm, at 1 April each year

From 2006 onwards the term Required Operating Fleet is no longer used and has been replaced by Forward Available Fleet as defined in the introduction to Chapter 4. The Required Operating Fleet was the total number of aircraft needed to undertake the defined military task.

Aircraft type	Aircraft role	Required Operating Fleet				FAF[1]		
		2002	2003	2004	2005	2006	2007	2008
Merlin Mk 1	Anti-Submarine	21	27	33	33	27	30	30
Lynx Mk 3	Anti-Submarine / Anti-Ship	31	29	29	29	23	21	21
Lynx Mk 8	Anti-Submarine / Anti-Ship	26	26	26	26	23	20	20
Sea King Mk 2 AEW [2]	Airborne Early Warning	5	-	-	-	-	-	-
Sea King Mk 5	Anti-Submarine and Search & Rescue	10	12	12	12	11	11	11
Sea King MK 6	Anti-Submarine	15	8	3	2	-	-	-
Sea King Mk 7 ASAC [2]	Airborne Surveillance and Area Control	5	10	10	10	9	9	10
Hawk	Fleet Training Support	15	15	15	14	14	12	12
Jetstream T2	Aircrew Training	8	8	8	8	8	8	8
Jetstream T3[3]	Aircrew Training and Support	3	3	3	3	3	2	2 [3]

Source: MOD Resources and Plans

1. Forward Available Fleet - see Introduction to Chapter 4
2. The Sea King Mk 7 replaced the Sea King Mk 2 in the Airborne Surveillance role.
3. The RN Comms Flight is due to become non-operational during 2008.

Table 4.9 Aircraft Fleets by type of aircraft for the Royal Air Force Air Command including Operational Conversion Units and Training Aircraft, at 1 April each year

The RAF no longer identified separate Required Operating Fleets for Operational Conversion Units with effect from 1 April 2005. Operational Conversion Units train qualified aircrew for different aircraft types. As at 1 Apr 07 STC and PTC amalgamated into Air Command which now controls all RAF flying assets.

Aircraft Role	Aircraft type	1990	1997	Required Operating Fleet 2002	2003	2004	2005	FAF[1] 2006	2007	2008
Air - Combat	Tornado GR	166	128	110	110	110 ||	101 [1] ||	106	106	108
	Jaguar GR1/A/3/3A	40	40	38	38	38	32 ||	13	13	- [2]
	Jaguar T2A/T4	7	7	7	7	7	5 ||	3	-	-
	Harrier GR3/5/7[3]	63	51	*	*	*	* ||	*	*	*
	Harrier T4/10[3]	14	9	*	*	*	* ||	*	*	*
	Tornado F3	99	104	90	90	90	83 ||	72	59	47 [4]
	Typhoon	-	-	-	-	-	- ||	25	32	34
C4 and ISTAR	Nimrod R1	3	3	3	3	3	3 ||	3	3	3
	Canberra PR9	3	4	4	4	4	4 ||	3	- [5]	-
	Canberra T4	6	1	1	1	1	1 ||	-	- [5]	-
	Sentry AEW	-	6	6	6	6	6 ||	6	6	6
Maritime	Nimrod MR2	32	24	20	20	20	14 ||	14	14	14 [6]
Air Support	VC10 C1K	10	10	10	10	10	10 ||	10	10	10
	VC10 K3	4	4	4	4	4	4 ||	4	4	4
	VC10 K4	-	5	5	4	4	2 ||	2	2	1
	Sea King HAR3/3A [7]	16	19	19	21	21	23 ||	23	23	23
	Tristar K1	1	1	1	1	1	1 ||	1	1	1
	Tristar KC1	4	4	4	4	4	4 ||	4	4	4
	Tristar C2	2	3	3	3	3	3 ||	3	3	3
	Hawk (100 Sqn)	*	*	*	*	* ||	16 [8] ||	16	14	16
Logistics	BAe 125 CC3	10	7	5	5	5	5 ||	5	5	5
	BAe 146 CC2	2	3	2	2	2	2 ||	2	2	2
	C-17	-	-	4	4	4	4 ||	4	4	5
	Hercules C1/C3/C4/C5	59	50	50	51	51	50 ||	50	44	44
Support Helicopters[9]	Chinook	28	27 ||	*	*	*	* ||	*	*	*
	Puma	35	33 ||	*	*	*	* ||	*	*	*
	Wessex	46	17 ||	*	*	*	* ||	*	*	*

Training Aircraft

Aircraft Role	Aircraft type	1990	1997	2002	2003	2004	2005	2006	2007	2008
Elementary Training[10]	Viking	. .	82	82	82	87	72 ||	72	82	82
	Vigilant	. .	53	55	61	61	61 ||	61	63	63
Basic Training[10]	Tucano	. .	66	76	73	73	44 [11] ||	44	52	52
	Jetstream T1	. .	10	9	9	9	11 ||	-	-	-
	Dominie T1	. .	8	9	9	7	9 ||	9	8	8
Advanced Training[10]	Hawk T1/T1A/T1W	. .	62	69	72	65 ||	61 ||	61	55	49
RAF Aerobatic Team (Red Arrows)	Hawk T1/T1A	. .	10	10	10	10	13 ||	13	13	13

Source: MOD Resources and Plans

1. Forward Available Fleet - see **Introduction to Chapter 4**.
2. Jaguar GR1A/3/3A were declared non-operational with effect from 30 April 07.
3. Harrier aircraft were transferred to the Joint Force Harrier on 1 April 2000. See **Table 4.10**.
4. Tornado F3 are reducing and due to be disbanded.
5. Canberra was declared non-operational with effect from July 2006.
6. The Nimrod MR2 are to be replaced by the Nimrod MRA4.
7. Excludes two Sea King aircraft attached to 78 Sqn (based in the Falkland Islands).
8. Prior to 2005, 100 Sqn were included under Personnel and Training Command, and not STC. Up to 1 Apr 2007 the data shown in the table are for STC only.
9. Support helicopters were transferred to the Joint Helicopter Command on 1 October 1999. See **Table 4.10**.
10. Air Command also use Beechking Air 200, Tutor, Firefly, Squirrel and Griffin aircraft owned by a private contractor in training roles.
11. Reduction in Tucano ROF reflected maturing Resources and Management programmes.

CHAPTER 4 - FORMATIONS, VESSELS, AIRCRAFT AND VEHICLES OF THE ARMED FORCES

AIRCRAFT

Table 4.10 Aircraft Fleets by type of aircraft in the Joint Helicopter Command and Joint Force Harrier, at 1 April each year

The Joint Helicopter Command was formed on 1 October 1999.
The Joint Force Harrier was formed on 1 April 2000. See **Table 4.9** for earlier data on RAF aircraft.

Joint Helicopter Command	Aircraft type	Required Operating Fleet					2006	2007	FAF[1] 2008
		2002	2003	2004	2005		2006	2007	2008
Royal Navy Helicopters	Sea King HC4 [2]	33	33	33	33		29	26	26
	Sea King HC6[3]	-	-	-	-		-	3	3
	Lynx AH7 [4]	6	6	6	6		6	6	6
	Gazelle [4]	9	8	8	-		-	-	-
Army Aviation Helicopters	Lynx	117	116	116	98 [5]		74	68	59
	Gazelle	117	113	113	91 [5]		57	45	42
	Apache	..	..	..	.. [5]		38	42	51
	Islander	6	6	6	6 [5]		5	5	5
	Defender 4000[6]	-	-	-	3 [5]		3	3	3
RAF Helicopters	Chinook HC2	31	31	31	31		27	27	29
	Puma HC1	37	37	37	37		26	24	23
	Merlin Mk 3	-	18 [7]	18	18		15	15	15
	Merlin MK3a[8]								3
	Wessex HC1	8	- [7]	-	-		-	-	-

Joint Force Harrier	Aircraft type	2002	2003	2004	2005		2006	2007	2008
Royal Navy Aircraft	Sea Harrier FA2[2]	26	26	17	8		- [9]	-	-
	Harrier T4 / T8	4	4	4	2		- [9]	-	-
RAF Aircraft (including OCUs[10])	Harrier GR	48	48	48	45		45	45	45
	Harrier T10 / T12	9	8	8	7		7	7	6

Source: MOD Resources and Plans

1. Forward Available Fleet - see **Introduction to chapter 4**.
2. Prior to 2006 the Required Operational Fleet was the Aircraft Establishment plus the Air Engineering Pool (AEP). Sea King HC4 had an AEP of 4, and Sea Harrier FA2 an AEP of 2.
3. Sea King HC 6 was brought into service from 1 April 2006 to replace Sea King HC4 undergoing modification.
4. Operated by the Royal Navy, but owned by the Army and included in the Army Aviation Helicopter figures.
5. Reduction due to restructuring under medium term strategy plans and moving personnel to Attack Helicopters.
6. The In Service Date for the Defender 4000 was 24 December 2004.
7. Merlin replaced Wessex in 2002.
8. Procured under UOR to support current operations.
9. The Sea Harrier and Harrier T8 were decommisioned prior to 1 April 2006.
10. Operational Conversion Units train qualified aircrew for different aircraft types. In editions of UKDS prior to 2006 these were shown separately. The RAF no longer identifies ROFs for OCUs separately from front line aircraft.

Treaty on Conventional Armed Forces in Europe (CFE)

Conventional armaments and equipment limited by the Treaty are battle tanks, armoured combat vehicles, artillery, combat aircraft and attack helicopters subject to the numerical limitations set forth in Articles IV, V, VII, the Protocol on National Ceilings and the Protocol on Territorial Ceilings.

Conventional armaments and equipment subject to the Treaty means battle tanks, armoured combat vehicles, artillery, combat aircraft, primary trainer aircraft, unarmed trainer aircraft, combat helicopters, unarmed transport helicopters, armoured vehicle launched bridges, armoured personnel carrier look-alikes and armoured infantry fighting vehicle look-alikes subject to information exchange in accordance with the Protocol on Information Exchange.

The following criteria are adumbrated from Article III of the CFE Treaty.

All battle tanks, armoured combat vehicles, artillery, combat aircraft and attack helicopters, as defined in Article II, within the area of application shall be subject to the numerical limitations and other provisions set forth in Articles IV, V, VII, the Protocol on National Ceilings and the Protocol on Territorial Ceilings, with the exception of those which in a manner consistent with a State Party's normal practices:

128

(A)   Are in the process of manufacture, including manufacturing-related testing;

(B)   Are used exclusively for the purposes of research and development;

(C)   Belong to historical collections;

(D)   Are awaiting disposal, having been decommissioned from service in accordance with Article IX;

(E)   Are awaiting, or being refurbished for, export or re-export and are temporarily retained within the area of application. Such battle tanks, armoured combat vehicles, artillery, combat aircraft and attack helicopters shall be located elsewhere than at sites declared under the terms of Section V of the Protocol on Information Exchange or at no more than 10 such declared sites which shall have been notified in the previous year's annual information exchange. In the latter case, they shall be separately distinguishable from conventional armaments and equipment limited by the Treaty;

(F)   Are, in the case of armoured personnel carriers, armoured infantry fighting vehicles (AIFVs), heavy armament combat vehicles (HACVs) or multi-purpose attack helicopters, held by organisations designed and structured to perform in peacetime internal security functions; or

(G)   Are in transit through the area of application between an origin and final destination both outside the area of application, and are in the area of application for no longer than a total of seven days.

The term "**area of application**" means the entire land territory of the States Parties in Europe from the Atlantic Ocean to the Ural Mountains, which includes all the European island territories of the States Parties, including the Faroe Islands of the Kingdom of Denmark, Svalbard including Bear Island of the Kingdom of Norway, the islands of Azores and Madeira of the Portuguese Republic, the Canary Islands of the Kingdom of Spain and Franz Josef Land and Novaya Zemlya of the Russian Federation.

In the case of the Republic of Kazakhstan and the Russian Federation, the area of application includes all territory lying west of the Ural River and the Caspian Sea.

In the case of the Republic of Turkey, the area of application includes the territory of the Republic of Turkey north and west of a line extending from the point of intersection of the Turkish border with the 39th parallel to Muradiye, Patnos, Karayazi, Tekman, Kemaliye, Feke, Ceyhan, Dogankent, Gözne and thence to the sea.

Descriptions of equipments

The following descriptions are adumbrated from Article II of the CFE Treaty.

"**Battle tank**": a self-propelled armoured fighting vehicle, capable of heavy firepower, primarily of a high muzzle velocity direct fire main gun necessary to engage armoured and other targets, with high cross-country mobility and a high level of self-protection, not designed and equipped primarily to transport combat troops. Such vehicles serve as the principal weapon system of ground-force tank and other armoured formations.
Battle tanks are tracked armoured fighting vehicles which weigh at least 16.5 metric tons unladen weight and which are armed with a 360-degree traverse gun of at least 75 millimetres calibre. Also, any wheeled armoured fighting vehicles entering into service which meet all the other criteria stated above shall also be deemed battle tanks.

"**Artillery**": large calibre systems capable of engaging ground targets by delivering primarily indirect fire. Such artillery systems provide the essential indirect fire support to combined arms formations. Large calibre artillery systems are guns, howitzers and artillery pieces combining their characteristics; mortars and multiple launch rocket systems with a calibre of 100 millimetres and above. In addition, any future large calibre direct fire system with a secondary effective indirect fire capability shall be counted against the artillery ceilings.

129

"**Armoured combat vehicle**": a self-propelled vehicle with armoured protection and cross-country capability. These include armoured personnel carriers, armoured infantry fighting vehicles and heavy armament combat vehicles.

"**Armoured personnel carrier**": an armoured combat vehicle designed and equipped to transport a combat infantry squad and, as a rule, armed with an integral or organic weapon of less than 20 millimetres calibre.

"**Armoured infantry fighting vehicle**": an armoured combat vehicle designed and equipped primarily to transport a combat infantry squad, normally providing the capability for the troops to deliver fire from inside the vehicle under armoured protection, and armed with an integral or organic cannon of at least 20 millimetres calibre and sometimes an antitank missile launcher. These vehicles serve as the principal weapon system of armoured infantry or mechanised infantry or motorised infantry formations and units of ground forces.

"**Heavy armament combat vehicle**": an armoured combat vehicle with an integral or organic direct fire gun of at least 75 millimetres calibre, weighing at least 6.0 metric tonnes unladen weight, that does not fall within the definitions of an armoured personnel carrier, or an armoured infantry fighting vehicle or a battle tank.

"**Armoured personnel carrier look-alike**" and "**armoured infantry fighting vehicle look-alike**": an armoured vehicle based on the same chassis as, and externally similar to, an armoured personnel carrier or armoured infantry fighting vehicle, respectively, which does not have a cannon or gun of 20 millimetres calibre or greater and has been constructed or modified in such a way as not to permit the transportation of a combat infantry squad. Taking into account the provisions of the Geneva Convention "For the Amelioration of the Conditions of the Wounded and Sick in Armed Forces in the Field" of 12 August 1949 that confer a special status on ambulances, armoured personnel carrier ambulances shall not be deemed armoured combat vehicles or armoured personnel carrier look-alikes.

"**Armoured vehicle launched bridge**": a self-propelled armoured transporter-launcher vehicle capable of carrying and, through built-in mechanisms, of emplacing and retrieving a bridge structure. Such a vehicle with a bridge structure operates as an integrated system.

"**Combat helicopter**": a rotary wing aircraft armed and equipped to engage targets or equipped to perform other military functions.

"**Attack helicopter**": a combat helicopter equipped to employ anti-armour, air-to-ground, or air-to-air guided weapons and equipped with an integrated fire control and aiming system for these weapons. The term "attack helicopter" comprises specialised attack helicopters and multi-purpose attack helicopters.

"**Specialised attack helicopter**": an attack helicopter designed primarily to employ guided weapons.

"**Multi-purpose attack helicopter**": means an attack helicopter designed to perform multiple military functions and equipped to employ guided weapons.

CHAPTER 4 - FORMATIONS, VESSELS, AIRCRAFT AND VEHICLES OF THE ARMED FORCES
CFE VEHICLES & AIRCRAFT

"**Combat aircraft**": means a fixed-wing or variable-geometry wing aircraft armed and equipped to engage targets by employing guided missiles, unguided rockets, bombs, guns, cannons, or other weapons of destruction, as well as any model or version of such an aircraft which performs other military functions such as reconnaissance or electronic warfare. The term "combat aircraft" does not include primary trainer aircraft.

"**Primary trainer aircraft**": are designed and constructed for primary flying training and means aircraft which may possess only limited armament capability necessary for basic training in weapon delivery techniques.

"**Combat support helicopters**": means a combat helicopter which does not fulfil the requirements to qualify as an attack helicopter and which may be equipped with a variety of self-defence and area suppression weapons, such as guns, cannons and unguided rockets, bombs or cluster bombs, or which may be equipped to perform other military functions.

"**Unarmed transport helicopters**": are not equipped for the employment of weapons.

Table **4.11** Tanks and Artillery Holdings in the UK, Germany, Cyprus and Gibraltar within the scope of the Conventional Armed Forces in Europe Treaty, at 1 January each year

	1997	2002	2003	2004	2005	2006	2007	2008
Battle Tanks [1]	**521**	**608** [2]	**560**	**421**	**402**	**373**	**392**	**354**
Challenger 1	396	248	178	46	14	14	12	10
Challenger 2	19	329	341	331	342	313	337	306
Chieftain [3]	98	22 [2]	30	32	32	32	30	30
Centurion [3]	8	9 [2]	11	12	14	14	13	8

	1997	2002	2003	2004	2005	2006	2007	2008
Artillery [1]	**436**	**459** [2]	**441**	**416**	**406**	**413**	**355**	**347**
Multiple Launch Rocket System	63	64	62	62	60	48	47	42
105 mm Light Gun	149	149	133	146	146	147	132	132
AS90 155mm gun	164	165	152	149	139	156	119	134
FH70 155m towed howitzer	48	48	47	11	12	12	11	8
105 mm Pack Howitzer [3]	3	15 [2]	24	25	25	26	23	14
5.5" Towed Howitzer [3]	3	8 [2]	12	12	13	13	13	9
Abbot 105mm self-propelled gun [3]	4	5 [2]	5	5	5	5	5	3
M110 8" self-propelled howitzer [3]	1	3 [2]	4	4	4	4	3	3
Tampella Mortar [3]	1	2 [2]	2	2	2	2	2	2

Source: Directorate for Counter-Proliferation and Arms Control

1. See descriptions of equipment on previous pages.
2. Obsolete equipment used for static display, training aids & targetry are included in the reported figures from 2002.
3. Obsolete non-operational equipment used as training aids, gate guardians and museum pieces on CFE declared sites.

Table 4.12 Armoured Combat Vehicle Holdings in the UK, Germany, Cyprus and Gibraltar within the scope of the Conventional Armed Forces in Europe Treaty, at 1 January each year

Armoured Combat Vehicles	1997	2002	2003	2004	2005	2006	2007	2008
Armoured Combat Vehicles	**2 411**	**2 344**	**2 361**	**2 403**	**2 114**	**2 117**	**2 054**	**1 728**
Warrior	523	530	484	482	454	404	450	352
AFV 432 Rarden	11	11	7	4	2	-	1	-
AFV 432	892	786	790	811	661	724	631	484
Saxon	424	469	465	482	435	445	362	265
Spartan	495	509	573	557	462	440	453	451
Stormer	-	10	13	13	9	11	21	33
Viking	*	*	* ‖	18 [1]	53	60	102	98
Mastiff	-	-	-	-	-	-	-	18
Humber [2]	1	-	1	2	2	2	2	5
Saracen [2]	4	2	2	3	4	3	3	3
Saladin [2]	2	7	8	8	9	8	8	6
Scorpion [2]	59	20	18	23	23	20	21	13

Armoured Combat Vehicle Look-alikes	1997	2002	2003	2004	2005	2006	2007	2008
Armoured Combat Vehicle Look-alikes	**1 016**	**1 695**	**1 515**	**1 486**	**1 472**	**1 349**	**1 243**	**958**
Warrior RA	68	74	63	59	70	67	61	49
Warrior Rep	90	97	92	89	92	80	85	75
Warrior Rec	36	39	34	37	31	29	33	23
AFV 434	*	167	157	157	171	167	138	118
AFV 432 81mm Mortar	75	88	83	73	59	61	43	34
AFV 432 CP/RA	104	117	111	113	124	113	113	103
AFV 432 Cymbeline	23	17	8	13	-	-	-	-
AFV 432 EW	5	17	13	18	19	25	25	19
AFV 436	231	234	236	234	275	227	230	200
AFV 439	44	48	45	44	52	43	43	43
Samson	82	78	74	71	46	55	43	36
Saracen CP [2]	-	1	-	-	-	-	-	-
Saxon AD	28	25	19	9	9	10	10	8
Saxon CP	30	67	45	43	40	35	5	-
Saxon FCC	20	31	33	41	42	45	41	19
Saxon Maintenance	31	37	36	30	33	31	33	18
Shielder	*	28	26	25	29	28	25	20
Spartan Milan	10	9	10	9	9	3	9	1
Spartan Javelin	72	52	-	-	-	-	-	-
Stormer HVM	*	132	118	113	118	85	55	92
Striker	56	59	58	54	50	51	47	7
Sultan	*	267	243	243	192	183	187	76
Fuchs NBC	11	11	11	11	11	11	11	12
Viking Rep/Rec	-	-	-	-	-	-	6	5

Armoured Vehicle Launcher Bridge	1997	2002	2003	2004	2005	2006	2007	2008
Armoured Vehicle Launcher Bridge	**49**	**53**	**46**	**45**	**43**	**45**	**44**	**39**
Chieftain	49	53	46	45	43	45	38	25
Titan	-	-	-	-	-	-	6	14

Source: Directorate for Counter-Proliferation and Arms Control

1. These Armoured Combat Vehicles are included in the reported figures from 2004, in accordance with the CFE treaty.
2. Obsolete non-operational equipment used as training aids, gate guardians and museum pieces on CFE declared sites.

Table **4.13** Aircraft Holdings in the UK, Germany, Cyprus and Gibraltar within the scope of the Conventional Armed Forces in Europe Treaty, at 1 January each year

	1997	2002	2003	2004	2005	2006	2007	2008
Attack helicopters [1]	**289**	**267**	**254**	**272**	**263**	**276**	**278**	**269**
Lynx	116	108	95	98	87	84	81	65
Gazelle	154	133	120	117	111	116	124	127
Apache	-	11	25	43	49	61	58	64
Wessex HC5C	1	-	-	-	-	-	-	-
Scout [2]	18	15 [3]	14	14	16	15	15	13

	1997	2002	2003	2004	2005	2006	2007	2008
Combat aircraft [1]	**624**	**511**	**502**	**504**	**503**	**501**	**471**	**452**
Canberra	13	11	11	10	11	8	1	1
Harrier	117	96	96	97	88	84	95	96
Jaguar	132	117	117	114	112	106	73	68
Tornado	324	277	269	275	283	275	259	240
EuroFighter2000[4]	-	-	-	-	-	19	34	40
Buccaneer [2]	6	1	1	1	1	1	1	-
F4 Phantom [2]	26	7	6	5	6	6	6	5
Hunter [2]	6	2	1	1	1	1	1	1
Lightning [2]	-	-	1	1	1	1	1	1

	1997	2002	2003	2004	2005	2006	2007	2008
Primary Trainers [5]	**183**	**166**	**166**	**173**	**176**	**176**	**164**	**154**
Hawk	140	124	122	129	128	127	130	127
Jet Provost	43	42	44	44	48	49	34	27

	1997	2002	2003	2004	2005	2006	2007	2008
Combat Support Helicopters [5]	**155**	**114**	**126**	**123**	**121**	**124**	**124**	**128**
Chinook	33	46	41	42	43	43	43	43
Puma	42	39	43	42	44	45	45	45
Wessex	56	26	16	13	8	9	9	7
Gazelle (RAF)	24	3	5	4	4	5	5	5
Merlin	-	-	21	22	22	22	22	28

	1997	2002	2003	2004	2005	2006	2007	2008
Unarmed Transport Helicopter [5]	**20**	**23**	**28**	**28**	**28**	**29**	**28**	**28**
Sea King	20	23	28	28	28	29	28	28

Source: Directorate for Counter-Proliferation and Arms Control

133

1. See descriptions of equipment on previous pages.
2. Obsolete non-operational equipment used as training aids, gate guardians and museum pieces on CFE declared sites.
3. Obsolete equipment used for static display, training aids & targetry are included in the reported figures from 2002.
4. Eurofighter 2000 also known as 'Typhoon'.
5. Figures for these vehicle types have been added as they are declared under the CFE treaty, although there is no ceiling on their numbers under the treaty.

Table 4.14 Declared Tanks, Armoured Combat Vehicles and Artillery Holdings and Ceilings by country within the scope of the Conventional Armed Forces in Europe Treaty, at 1 January 2008

Includes Treaty Limited Equipment with land-based maritime sources such as Marines and Naval Infantry.

Countries not in NATO	Tanks Holdings	Tanks Ceiling	Armoured Combat Vehicles Holdings	Armoured Combat Vehicles Ceiling	Artillery Holdings	Artillery Ceiling
Armenia	110	220	140	220	239	285
Azerbaijan	319	220	181	220	349	285
Belarus	1 499	1 800	2 339	2 600	1 419	1 615
Georgia	183	220	134	220	238	285
Moldova	-	210	210	210	148	250
Russia [1,2]	4 865	6 350	9 149	11 280	5 696	6 315
Ukraine [3]	2 875	3 200	4 127	5 050	3 245	3 600

Countries in NATO	Tanks Holdings	Tanks Ceiling	Armoured Combat Vehicles Holdings	Armoured Combat Vehicles Ceiling	Artillery Holdings	Artillery Ceiling
Belgium	135	334	542	1 005	133	320
Bulgaria [4]	615	1 475	1 036	2 000	1 279	1 750
Canada	-	77	-	263	-	32
Czech Republic [5]	179	957	515	1 367	317	767
Denmark	174	353	296	336	57	503
France	992	1 306	2 840	3 820	773	1 292
Germany	1 607	4 069	2 369	3 281	1 237	2 445
Greece	1 566	1 735	2 188	2 498	1 783	1 920
Hungary [5]	159	835	1 140	1 700	459	840
Italy	1 200	1 348	3 258	3 339	1 461	1 955
Netherlands	290	743	644	1 040	243	607
Norway	141	170	230	275	68	491
Poland [5]	958	1 730	1 414	2 150	1 080	1 610
Portugal	187	300	362	430	381	450
Romania [4]	1 245	1 375	1 755	2 100	1 318	1 475
Slovakia [4]	245	478	515	683	338	383
Spain	520	891	1 003	2 047	886	1 370
Turkey	2 312	2 795	2 902	3 120	3 156	3 523
United Kingdom	**354**	**1 015**	**1 728** [6]	**3 176**	**347**	**636**
United States of America	91	4 006	613	5 152	218	2 742

Source: Directorate for Counter-Proliferation and Arms Control

1. The Russian Federation suspended the implementation of the CFE Treaty on 12 December 2007. Consequently, Russia did not submit the annual exchange of information required by the Treaty. The given numbers of holdings are taken from the "Consolidated Information" provided by the Russian Federation on 18 December 2007 as a sign of goodwill.
2. Manpower and Treaty Limited Equipment is only for that in the Atlantic to the Urals zone
3. Including Conventional Armaments and Equipment limited by the Treaty belonging to the Naval Infantry and Coastal Defence Forces of Ukraine: 39 Battle Tanks, 187 Armoured Combat Vehicles (incl. 84 Armoured Infantry Fighting Vehicles) and 65 pieces of artillery.
4. These countries joined NATO on 29 March 2004.
5. Czech Republic, Hungary and Poland became NATO members on 12 March 1999.
6. UK ACV holdings: The UK notified 97 saxon and 147 AFV432 as going out of service during 2007. The AFV432s are now filtering back into service from a major refit program as AFV432 Mk3 "Bulldog" vehicles.

The ceiling figures given above differ from the figures in editions of UKDS from 2006 and earlier. This is because the figures were previously reproduced from the Military Balance publication, which used an unratified version of the Adapted CFE Treaty, and we are now using ceiling figures from the ratified version of the CFE Treaty.

Table 4.15 Declared Attack Helicopters and Combat Aircraft Holdings and Ceilings by country within the scope of the Conventional Armed Forces in Europe Treaty, at 1 January 2008

Countries not in NATO	Attack helicopters		Combat aircraft [1]	
	Holdings	Ceiling	Holdings	Ceiling
Armenia	8	50	16	100
Azerbaijan	15	50	67	100
Belarus	22	80	176	294
Georgia	9	50	9	100
Moldova	-	50	-	50
Russia [2,3]	413	855	1 919	3 416
Ukraine	170	250	526	800

Countries in NATO	Holdings	Ceiling	Holdings	Ceiling
Belgium	43	46	93	232
Bulgaria[4]	19	67	113	235
Canada	-	13	-	90
Czech Republic[5]	38	50	42	230
Denmark	8	18	62	106
France	254	374	433	800
Germany	168	280	347	900
Greece	32	65	566	650
Hungary[5]	45	108	90	180
Italy	127	142	447	650
Netherlands	16	50	106	230
Norway	-	24	57	100
Poland[5]	93	130	118	460
Portugal	-	26	106	160
Romania[4]	31	120	84	430
Slovakia[4]	16	40	46	100
Spain	31	80	168	310
Turkey	32	130	319	750
United Kingdom	**269**	**356**	**452**	**900**
United States of America	48	396	207	784

Source: Directorate for Counter-Proliferation and Arms Control

1. Does not include land-based maritime aircraft for which a separate limit has been set.
2. The Russian Federation suspended the implementation of the CFE Treaty on 12 December 2007. Consequently, Russia did not submit the annual exchange of information required by the Treaty. The given numbers of holdings are taken from the "Consolidated Information" provided by the Russian Federation on 18 December 2007 as a sign of goodwill.
3. Manpower and Treaty Limited Equipment is only for that in the Atlantic to the Urals zone.
4. These countries joined NATO on 29 March 2004.
5. Czech Republic, Hungary and Poland became NATO members on 12 March 1999.

The ceiling figures given above differ from the figures in editions of UKDS from 2006 and earlier. This is because the figures were previously reproduced from the Military Balance publication, which used an unratified version of the Adapted CFE Treaty, and we are now using ceiling figures from the ratified version of the CFE Treaty.

CHAPTER 5 - MILITARY SEARCH AND RESCUE

INTRODUCTION

The Military Search and Rescue Service

The Military Search and Rescue (SAR) Service exists primarily to assist military and civilian aircrew in difficulty, although a large proportion of its work involves assisting shipping or people in distress, both on land and at sea. SAR cover for the United Kingdom and a large area of the surrounding sea is provided 24 hours a day and 365 days a year by the Royal Air Force and the Royal Navy.

The SAR force currently consists of RAF and RN SAR Sea King helicopters operating from 8 locations around the UK, specially equipped RAF Nimrod aircraft based in RAF Kinloss in Scotland and 4 RAF Mountain Rescue Teams. Two RAF SAR helicopter units operate in Cyprus and the Falklands.

Incidents can include long range medical evacuation from ships at sea, assistance to vessels in distress, cliff fallers, swimmers, divers and surfers. On land many callouts are to search for missing persons or to rescue injured climbers, walkers, riders or those involved in road traffic accidents. SAR units are also often called upon to provide hospital-to-hospital transfers. Missions can include the rescue of foreign mariners, assistance to foreign flagged vessels or to other countries such as France.

Additional aeronautical Search and Rescue services are provided by 4 Maritime and Coastguard Agency helicopter units. Details of their activity are not included.

The RAF Aeronautical Rescue Co-ordination Centre (ARCC) at RAF Kinloss controls all military aerial resources. It watches over an area extending from the Faeroes in the North, the English Channel in the South, about halfway across the Atlantic Ocean and halfway across the North Sea. It has direct data and voice links with rescue assets in the UK and Europe. Detailed maps and charts are combined with an intimate knowledge of UK topography to enable controllers to match resources to tasks quickly and co-ordinate the rescue operation.

More information about Royal Navy and RAF SAR can be found at:
http://www.royal-navy.mod.uk/server/show/conWebDoc.293/changeNav/3533 and
http://www.raf.mod.uk/careers/abouttheraf/searchandrescue.cfm

Data Information

The UK SAR data source is a weekly download from the ARCC database at RAF Kinloss. Every incident recorded by ARCC is included in these tables. Incident data from Cyprus and the Falklands is received by email on an ad-hoc basis and may be incomplete. All data is validated and checked by DASA on receipt.

Table 5.1 shows the numbers of incidents, callouts and people moved from 1997 to 2007.

Table 5.2 shows the number of callouts and people moved by UK Military Search and Rescue units from 1997 to 2007.

Table 5.3 shows the numbers of callouts and people moved by UK Military Search and Rescue units by type of assistance from 1997 to 2007.

Table 5.4 shows the numbers of callouts and people moved in each region around the UK from 1997 to 2007.

Table 5.5 shows the locations of UK Military Search and Rescue callouts in 2007.

Key Points

- In 2007, there were 1,877 UK and overseas incidents resulting in 2,065 callouts of Royal Navy and RAF Helicopters, Nimrod aircraft and Mountain Rescue Teams. A total of 1,817 people were moved (**Table 5.1**).

- Incidents and callouts both rose 6% compared with 2006, while the number of people moved rose by 18%. Incidents and callouts are both at their highest level since 1996 (**Table 5.1**).

- 96% of UK callouts in 2007 were to civilian incidents (**Table 5.2**).

- 48% of UK callouts in 2007 were to Scotland, the South West region or Wales. A further 32% of callouts were to incidents at sea (**Table 5.4**).

CHAPTER 5 - MILITARY SEARCH AND RESCUE

Table 5.1 Military Search and Rescue incidents, callouts and people moved: 1997 - 2007

Incidents are emergencies attended by Royal Navy or Royal Air Force units whose primary task is Search and Rescue, plus other military aircraft and ships that are available to Aeronautical Rescue Co-ordination Centres.

Each Search and Rescue unit attending an incident is described as a callout. An incident may result in one or more callouts. An example is two callouts to a mountain incident, with a helicopter and a Mountain Rescue Team working together to assist a casualty. Callouts are for Royal Navy and RAF units whose primary task is Search and Rescue, plus other military aircraft and ships that attended incidents because they were available to Aeronautical Rescue Co-ordination Centres.

People moved involves moving people from a hostile environment to a safe environment or to a medical facility to receive urgent medical attention and between medical facilities at the request of the NHS.

UK SAR units are co-ordinated by the Aeronautical Rescue Co-ordination Centre at Kinloss (Scotland). Plymouth and Aldergrove (N. Ireland) closed in 1997 and 2002 respectively. The overseas SAR units are based at RAF Akrotiri in Cyprus and Mount Pleasant in the Falkland Islands.

	Incidents			Callouts			People moved		
	All	UK	Overseas	All	UK	Overseas	All	UK	Overseas
1997	1 831	1 750	81	2 024	1 941	83	1 304	1 226	78
1998	1 776	1 697	79	1 980	1 898	82	1 309	1 243	66
1999	1 787	1 714	73	1 988	1 912	76	1 269	1 204	65
2000	1 827	1 781	46	1 990	1 941	49	1 356	1 316	40
2001	1 645	1 608	37	1 800	1 763	37	1 207	1 182	25
2002	1 577	1 544	33	1 718	1 684	34	1 251	1 224	27
2003	1 677	1 600	77	1 809	1 714	95	1 333	1 273	60
2004	1 564	1 504	60	1 711	1 638	73	1 449	1 412	37
2005	1 641	1 584	57	1 766	1 702	64	1 431	1 384	47
2006	1 767	1 703	64	1 948	1 875	73	1 538	1 463	75
2007	1 877	1 803	74	2 065	1 973	92	1 817	1 767	50

Source: DASA(Equipment & Personnel Analysis)

Military Search and Rescue incidents, callouts and people moved

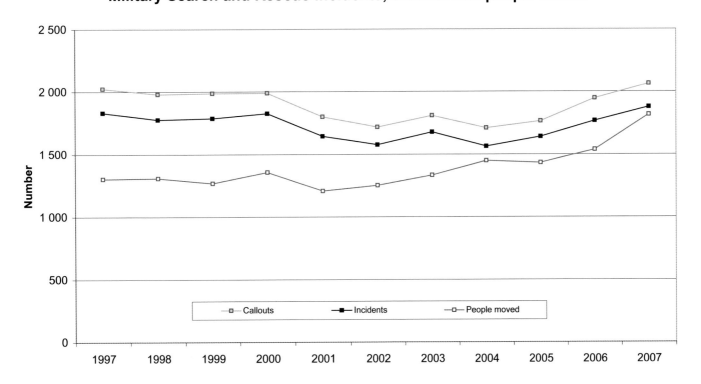

CHAPTER 5 - MILITARY SEARCH AND RESCUE

Table 5.2 Callouts and people moved by UK Military Search and Rescue units: 1997 - 2007

The primary role of Search & Rescue units is to recover military aircrew from crashed aircraft. However the vast majority of callouts are to assist the general public.

Royal Navy Search and Rescue helicopters: The Royal Navy's SAR units are 771 Squadron based at the Royal Naval Air Station Culdrose (HMS Seahawk) in Cornwall and the HMS Gannet SAR Flight located at Glasgow Prestwick International Airport.

Royal Air Force Search and Rescue helicopters: RAF Sea King rescue helicopters of Nos. 22 and 202 Squadrons operate from six locations - RAF Boulmer, RAF Valley, RAF Lossiemouth, RAF Leconfield, RAF Chivenor and RAF Wattisham.

Other helicopters: 'Other' types of helicopters are primarily Sea King helicopters operated by contractors.

RAF Mountain Rescue Service: The Mountain Rescue Service HQ is based at RAF Valley and coordinates the RAF's four Mountain Rescue Teams (MRT) based at: RAF Kinloss, RAF Leuchars, RAF Leeming & RAF Valley.

RAF Nimrod: Specially equipped Nimrod maritime patrol aircraft, based at RAF Kinloss in Scotland, are always on standby and can be at the scene of an emergency quickly to act as "Top Cover" - an on-scene coordinator for helicopters or ships involved in the rescue operation.

Callouts	UK Total	Helicopters			MRT	Fixed wing aircraft		Ships		Civilian	Military
		RN	RAF	Other		Nimrod	Other				
1997	**1 941**	495	1 258	16	88	79	2	3		1 833	108
1998	**1 898**	463	1 257	20	82	71	2	3		1 777	121
1999	**1 912**	499	1 235	-	113	65	-	-		1 786	126
2000	**1 941**	499	1 278	-	92	71	1	-		1 819	122
2001	**1 763**	502	1 115	-	91	54	1	-		1 660	103
2002	**1 684**	436	1 122	-	79	46	1	-		1 586	98
2003	**1 714**	424	1 173	-	80	37	-	-		1 618	96
2004	**1 638**	453	1 079	-	67	37	2	-		1 538	100
2005	**1 702**	478	1 114	-	73	37	-	-		1 610	92
2006	**1 875**	497	1 258	1	86	32	1	-		1 785	90
2007	**1 973**	592	1 258	-	102	21	-	-		1 892	81

People moved	UK Total	Helicopters			MRT	Fixed wing aircraft		Ships		Civilian	Military
		RN	RAF	Other		Nimrod	Other				
1997	**1 226**	328	877	6	15	-	-	-		1 166	60
1998	**1 243**	283	937	11	12	-	-	-		1 138	105
1999	**1 204**	355	832	-	17	-	-	-		1 150	54
2000	**1 316**	360	934	-	22	-	-	-		1 267	49
2001	**1 182**	386	781	-	15	-	-	-		1 139	43
2002	**1 224**	314	900	-	10	-	-	-		1 181	43
2003	**1 273**	320	922	-	31	-	-	-		1 206	67
2004	**1 412**	416	978	-	17	-	1	-		1 355	57
2005	**1 384**	380	907	-	97	-	-	-		1 315	69
2006	**1 463**	479	968	-	16	-	-	-		1 409	54
2007	**1 767**	507	1 219	-	41	-	-	-		1 710	57

Source: DASA(Equipment & Personnel Analysis)

CHAPTER 5 - MILITARY SEARCH AND RESCUE

Table 5.3 Callouts and people moved by UK Military Search and Rescue units by type of assistance: 1997 - 2007

2 definitions have been renamed (see below).

The types of assistance that involve moving people are:
Medrescue: Moving an injured casualty from a hostile environment to a medical facility.
Rescue: Moving an uninjured person from a hostile to a benign environment.
Recovery: Moving people declared dead on scene or confirmed dead on arrival by a qualified doctor.
Medtransfer (formerly Medevac): Moving a sick person between medical facilities such as a hospital, or occasionally to move transplant organs.
Transfer (formerly Airlift): Moving military personnel, or their families, on compassionate grounds.

The types of assistance that do not involve moving people are:
Search: Search for craft, people, etc which does not result in a recovery or rescue.
Not Required: Arrived at the scene of an incident but no action needed.
Recalled: Recalled from an incident whilst en route.
Assist: Transporting personnel or equipment to the scene of an incident, or providing on-scene assistance.
Top Cover: On-scene assistance, e.g. communications, that does not result in further intervention.
Other: Includes False Alarm, Hoax, Precaution, Aborted and Civil Aid.

Callouts

	UK total	Type of Assistance involving moving people					Other Types of Assistance					
		Med-rescue	Rescue	Med-transfer	Recovery	Transfer	Search	Not Req	Recall	Assist	Top cover	Other
1997	**1 941**	590	98	220	50	5	351	187	172	92	90	86
1998	**1 898**	539	109	201	40	7	393	166	164	105	88	86
1999	**1 912**	563	132	210	31	7	371	136	154	132	78	98
2000	**1 941**	607	135	230	24	16	366	173	131	95	87	77
2001	**1 763**	562	121	218	35	7	316	116	173	91	75	49
2002	**1 684**	583	112	198	21	5	311	101	171	61	65	56
2003	**1 714**	669	123	174	25	14	280	94	180	48	55	52
2004	**1 638**	593	122	186	29	15	271	60	192	58	64	48
2005	**1 702**	670	119	141	31	22	283	105	188	39	65	39
2006	**1 875**	736	102	175	37	23	328	89	238	49	48	50
2007	**1 973**	724	138	197	20	15	312	123	225	87	52	80

People moved

	UK total	Med-rescue	Rescue	Med-transfer	Recovery	Transfer
1997	**1 226**	721	219	224	54	8
1998	**1 243**	667	317	209	43	7
1999	**1 204**	640	307	216	32	9
2000	**1 316**	713	276	241	29	57
2001	**1 182**	629	281	228	36	8
2002	**1 224**	654	343	201	21	5
2003	**1 273**	779	280	174	25	15
2004	**1 412**	672	494	195	33	18
2005	**1 384**	778	408	143	31	24
2006	**1 463**	830	384	175	43	31
2007	**1 767**	872	658	198	22	17

Callouts by type of assistance: 2007

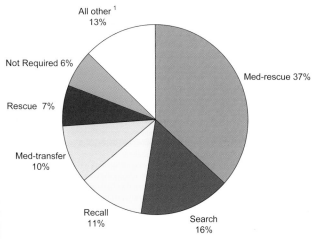

- All other [1] 13%
- Med-rescue 37%
- Not Required 6%
- Rescue 7%
- Med-transfer 10%
- Recall 11%
- Search 16%

1 All other includes Top Cover, Other, Assist, Recovery and Transfer

Source: DASA(Equipment & Personnel Analysis)

CHAPTER 5 - MILITARY SEARCH AND RESCUE

Table 5.4 Callouts and people moved by UK Military Search and Rescue units in each region: 1997 - 2007

The statistical regions of the United Kingdom are the Government Office Regions for England, Wales, Scotland and Northern Ireland. Callouts are allocated to regions using coordinates provided by the Search and Rescue Units. The regions on this table are calculated using Microsoft MapPoint 2004 software. The At Sea figures are dependent on the algorithm used in MapPoint to define the coastline. Further information on the UK Government Office Regions can be found at :- http://www.statistics.gov.uk/geography/gor.asp.

Callouts

	UK total	North East	North West	Yorkshire & Humber	East Midlands	West Midlands	East of England	London	South East	South West	Wales	Scotland	Northern Ireland	At Sea
1997	1 941	26	82	51	36	13	62	5	36	216	239	437	22	716
1998	1 898	41	94	49	29	10	59	3	27	219	237	383	28	719
1999	1 912	43	84	50	44	6	55	7	28	175	214	447	18	741
2000	1 941	60	102	46	40	9	65	2	33	185	206	473	15	705
2001	1 763	30	62	54	32	11	55	4	39	253	197	438	16	572
2002	1 684	48	88	61	27	13	52	2	19	209	213	375	14	563
2003	1 714	54	82	61	25	9	76	5	30	182	243	397	11	539
2004	1 638	60	96	35	22	8	62	10	29	196	207	371	11	531
2005	1 702	48	96	62	20	8	57	7	13	234	221	383	15	538
2006	1 875	50	109	48	34	6	78	15	19	259	253	433	8	563
2007	1 973	49	84	103	46	21	57	11	25	227	239	475	9	627

People moved

	UK total	North East	North West	Yorkshire & Humber	East Midlands	West Midlands	East of England	London	South East	South West	Wales	Scotland	Northern Ireland	At Sea
1997	1 226	18	49	35	14	5	16	4	12	156	206	345	14	352
1998	1 243	25	81	22	15	13	28	1	12	161	191	284	22	388
1999	1 204	26	67	27	19	4	26	5	13	143	161	312	13	388
2000	1 316	44	86	22	23	1	26	2	15	158	162	311	4	462
2001	1 182	22	49	41	18	6	22	3	48	159	149	276	10	379
2002	1 224	32	71	28	10	4	22	2	9	146	172	235	15	478
2003	1 273	29	72	35	12	3	48	2	9	163	223	314	6	357
2004	1 412	39	124	34	15	3	24	9	15	179	180	318	8	464
2005	1 384	39	128	61	10	6	36	6	6	183	193	366	12	338
2006	1 463	46	63	33	25	3	47	11	14	204	204	404	3	406
2007	1 767	41	81	155	15	97	24	11	9	283	205	348	6	492

Source: DASA(Equipment & Personnel Analysis)

CHAPTER 5 - MILITARY SEARCH AND RESCUE

Table 5.5 Map of UK Military Search and Rescue callouts: 2007

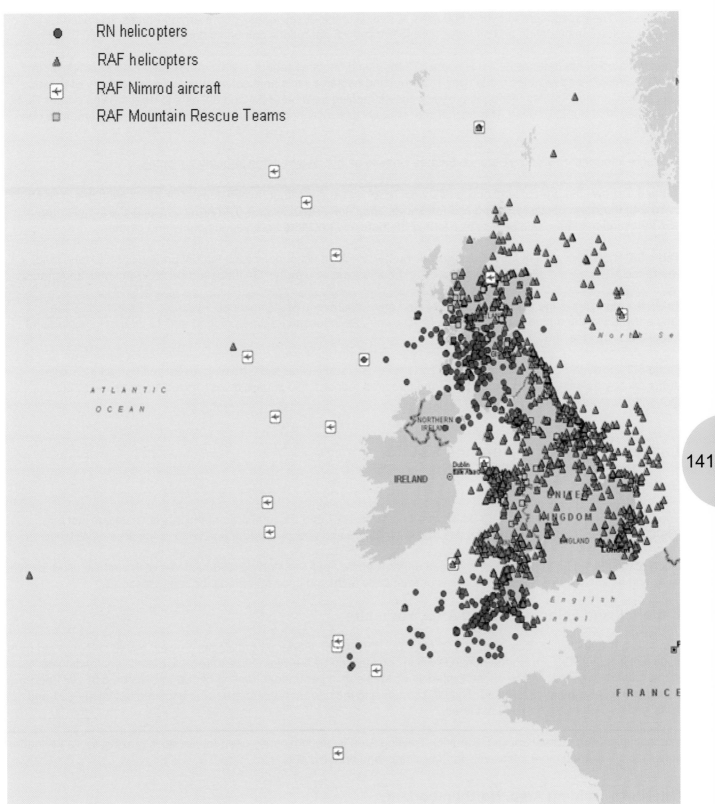

Source: DASA(Equipment & Personnel Analysis)

CHAPTER 6 - LAND HOLDINGS AND BUILDINGS

INTRODUCTION

Land holratings – tables 6.1, 6.2 & 6.3

1,000 hectares = 3.86 sq miles

The Ministry of Defence is one of the largest landowners in the country, with an estate equal to about 1% of the UK land mass. The estate, spread over 4,000 sites, is critical to the effectiveness of the Armed Forces. It is used for training and accommodation and provides a base from which operations can be instigated.

The total area of the defence estate is some 373 thousand hectares (about 1,440 square miles), an area similar in size to Cornwall, and includes rights over 133 thousand hectares. It is held solely to support the delivery of defence capability. Defence Estates manages property assets ranging from barracks and airfields to rural training areas. These are valued at about £20 billion. The annual cost of new construction, maintenance and property management is over £2 billion.

For more information, visit the Defence Estates website at: http://www.defence-estates.mod.uk/

Table 6.1 shows the area of land occupied by each Service and whether owned, leased or with legal rights. The MOD owns 240 thousand hectares of land and foreshore, about the size of Dorset. The Army occupies the largest area at 157 thousand hectares, with access to a further 88 thousand hectares from various rights and grants.

Table 6.2 shows the area of MOD holdings by country. England accounts for the largest portion of MOD land holdings, where the MOD owns 190 thousand hectares and has access to a further 34 thousand hectares in rights and grants.

Table 6.2 also shows the respective areas of land and foreshore in MOD holdings, by country. Foreshore is the land between low and high tide marks. The MOD owns 222 thousand hectares of land and 19 thousand hectares of foreshore within the UK.

Table 6.3 shows the area of MOD holdings by type of use, such as airfields, training areas and barracks. Training areas occupy the largest area at 292 thousand hectares (about 1,130 square miles), including rights over 128 thousand hectares.

Larger areas of the Defence Estate

Salisbury Plain, Wiltshire

The Army has been connected with Salisbury Plain since 1897 and the total area of the current estate is just over 38,000 hectares. It is 25 miles by 10 miles (40km by 16km) and occupies about one ninth of the area of Wiltshire.

Much of the land is let to farmers or is grazed under license. Approximately 12,150 hectares of the land is used for live firing and as impact areas. Public access is permanently restricted in certain areas for safety reasons.

Catterick and Feldom Training Area, Yorkshire

The area's military history dates from as far back as 1798. Later, General Lord Baden-Powell, based in Richmond from 1908 to 1910, as GOC the Northumbrian Division, was tasked by the War Office to establish a military training centre in the north of England, and he chose Catterick. Its status as a permanent training centre was secured in 1921 and a period of intensive building followed. The land comprising the current training area was acquired between 1921 and 1985 and its current size is 7870 hectares.

In conjunction with military training, Catterick Training Area is predominantly used for livestock grazing, while the better in-bye land is farmed more intensively for hay, silage and arable crops.

Otterburn Training Area, Northumberland

A military presence, in the form of Roman legions, existed in the Otterburn area as long ago as the first and second centuries AD. In 1911, the War Office bought 7,690 hectares of land and the artillery ranges were extended during the Second World War.

CHAPTER 6 - LAND HOLDINGS AND BUILDINGS

INTRODUCTION

The training area now consists of some 22,900 hectares of land, all owned by the MOD, and is the largest single impact area range in the UK. It is partitioned into three separate Danger Areas: Redesdale Range, Otterburn Range, Bellshiels Demolition Area and has three Outside Gun Areas. Some 45,000 soldiers use the area each year. The Cheviot Dry Training Area is to the north of these areas.   Otterburn Training Area also includes 2 ranges at Ponteland near Newcastle and at Whitburn on the coast between Newcastle and Sunderland.   In 2007 DTE Otterburn expanded to include Ballykinler and Magilligan training areas in Northern Ireland.

Dartmoor Training Area, Devon

Military training has taken place on Dartmoor since the early 1800s, being used intensively for tactical exercises with live ammunition during the Second World War. Today the MOD uses (by freehold, lease or license) approximately 12,760 hectares of the National Park's 94,400 hectares. The Dartmoor Training Area is used for light forces' exercises, mostly for Royal Marines and other units based in the southwest.

There are three Range Danger Areas: Okehampton, Merrivale and Willsworthy, which when this land is not in use for live firing, provide for dry training with blank ammunition. There are smaller training areas at Cramber and Ringmoor.

RAF Spadeadam, Cumbria

Located on the edge of the Wark Forest between Hadrian's Wall and the Scottish Borders. The site now occupied by the RAF used to be known as the Spadeadam Wastes, mostly remote and uninhabited, until 1957 when the Intermediate Range Ballistic Missile Test Centre was built.

RAF Spadeadam is home to the Electronic Warfare Tactics Range, one of two such facilities in Europe, offering a unique facility for the training of aircrews in a hostile Electronic Warfare environment. The Range is contained within Low Flying Area 13, which extends from Hawick in Scotland, South to Alston in England, and from Langholm in the West to Hexham in the East.

RAF Spadeadam provides realistic Electronic Warfare training for aircrew, primarily for the RAF, but other NATO Air Forces use the range as well.

The land area is about 3642 hectares, making it the largest RAF Station in the UK. The majority of this land is sub-let for timber production to the Forestry Commission.

Service Family Accommodation – tables 6.4 & 6.5

The Defence Housing Executive (DHE) took over responsibility for housing services from the Armed Services on 1 April 1996. In November 1996 most of the MOD's housing stock in England and Wales was sold to a private company, Annington Homes Limited (AHL). The homes required for Service families were leased back, with the condition that the MOD release a minimum number of properties over 25 years for disposal by AHL.

On 1 April 2004 the DHE ceased to be a separate Agency and became part of Defence Estates. This organisation is now called the Defence Estates' Directorate of Operations Housing. DE Ops Housing retains responsibility for managing all the Service Family Accommodation (SFA) for the Royal Navy and Marines, the Army and the Royal Air Force in the UK. It operates through a network of seven Housing Information Centres (HICs), in three regions, which report to the Directorate Head Office located at RAF Brampton in Cambridgeshire. The Director of Operations Housing reports to the Director General of Operations, Defence Estates.

Table 6.4 shows the numbers of Service Family Accommodation properties in the UK and the numbers and proportion vacant. There are around 51,000 properties in the UK, of which around 10,500 are currently vacant. There are around 40,000 occupants in England, Wales and Scotland, and around 1000 in Northern Ireland

Table 6.5 shows the surveyed condition of Service Family Accommodation properties within Great Britain. Around 94% of properties are assessed as Standard 1 or 2 (good condition, or requiring minor improvements) as of 31st March..

CHAPTER 6 - LAND HOLDINGS AND BUILDINGS

LAND HOLDINGS

Table 6.1 Land holdings by parent service area and whether owned, leased or with legal rights, at 1 April each year in thousand hectares

	1990	1997	2002	2003	2004	2005	2006	2007	2008
Total land & foreshore holdings and rights held [1]	**344.0**	**364.1**	**366.1**	**371.1**	**371.0**	**365.7**	**365.6**	**365.6**	**373.4**
Land and foreshore holdings	**240.6**	**239.6**	**241.1**	**240.0**	**239.9**	**240.7**	**240.7**	**240.7**	**240.3**
Freehold	225.1	223.9	220.7	219.6	219.5	220.4	220.4	220.4	220.0
Leasehold	15.5	15.7	20.4	20.4	20.4	20.4	20.3	20.3	20.3
Rights held [1]	**103.4**	**124.5**	**124.9**	**131.1**	**131.1**	**124.9**	**124.9**	**124.9**	**133.1**
of which:									
Royal Navy	**39.7**	**39.4**	**43.9**	**43.8**	**43.8**	**43.9**	**43.9**	**43.9**	**43.6**
Land and foreshore holdings	**13.2**	**13.3**	**17.7**	**17.6**	**17.6**	**17.7**	**17.7**	**17.7**	**17.4**
Freehold	10.8	10.9	15.2	15.1	15.1	15.2	15.2	15.2	14.9
Leasehold	2.4	2.4	2.5	2.5	2.5	2.5	2.5	2.5	2.5
Rights held [1]	**26.5**	**26.1**	**26.2**	**26.2**	**26.2**	**26.2**	**26.2**	**26.2**	**26.2**
Army	**221.0**	**243.7**	**245.1**	**251.0**	**251.0**	**245.1**	**245.1**	**245.1**	**245.2**
Land and foreshore holdings	**154.3**	**155.9**	**157.0**	**156.7**	**156.7**	**157.0**	**157.0**	**157.0**	**157.1**
Freehold	150.3	151.9	151.4	151.2	151.2	151.4	151.4	151.4	151.4
Leasehold	4.0	4.0	5.7	5.5	5.5	5.7	5.7	5.7	5.7
Rights held [1]	**66.7**	**87.8**	**88.1**	**94.3**	**94.3**	**88.1**	**88.1**	**88.1**	**88.1**
Royal Air Force	**54.3**	**52.2**	**46.7**	**46.7**	**46.7**	**46.6**	**46.6**	**46.6**	**46.6**
Land and foreshore holdings	**45.3**	**42.9**	**37.4**	**37.3**	**37.3**	**37.3**	**37.3**	**37.3**	**37.3**
Freehold	37.4	34.8	29.0	28.9	28.9	29.0	29.0	29.0	29.0
Leasehold	7.9	8.1	8.3	8.4	8.4	8.3	8.3	8.3	8.3
Rights held [1]	**9.0**	**9.3**	**9.3**	**9.4**	**9.4**	**9.3**	**9.3**	**9.3**	**9.3**
The Centre [2]	**29.0**	**27.5**	**26.5**	**25.9**	**25.9**	**26.3**	**26.3**	**26.3**	**34.5**
Land and foreshore holdings	**27.8**	**26.2**	**25.2**	**24.7**	**24.7**	**25.0**	**25.0**	**25.0**	**25.0**
Freehold	26.6	25.2	24.2	23.7	23.7	24.0	24.0	24.0	24.0
Leasehold	1.2	1.0	1.0	1.0	1.0	1.0	1.0	1.0	1.0
Rights held [1]	**1.2**	**1.3**	**1.3**	**1.2**	**1.2**	**1.3**	**1.3**	**1.3**	**9.5**
Other [3]	*	**1.2**	**3.8**	**3.7**	**3.7**	**3.8**	**3.8**	**3.8**	**3.8**
Land and foreshore holdings	*	**1.2**	**3.8**	**3.7**	**3.7**	**3.8**	**3.8**	**3.8**	**3.8**
Freehold	*	1.1	0.8	0.7	0.7	0.8	0.8	0.8	0.8
Leasehold	*	0.1	3.0	3.0	3.0	3.0	3.0	3.0	3.0
Rights held [1]	*	-	-	-	-	-	-	-	-

Source: MOD Defence Estates

These holdings include land declared as surplus to defence requirements.
A thousand hectares is 3.86 square miles.

1. Rights held are Land and foreshore that are not owned by, or leased to MOD, but over which the Department has limited rights under grants and rights.
2. The Centre includes Defence Equipment & Supply and Central Staff.
3. Includes former Service married quarters leased by the Defence Housing Executive from Annington Property Ltd.

Statistics show that the estate size has not moved significantly in recent years. Disposals and acquisitions have occurred, but the overall impact on the overall estate size is not significant. The basis of measurement will be reviewed during the next year to ensure it reflects changes and improvements in technology.

CHAPTER 6 - LAND HOLDINGS AND BUILDINGS

LAND HOLDINGS

Table 6.2 Land holdings by country and whether owned, leased or with legal rights, at 1 April each year in thousand hectares

	1990	1997	2002	2003	2004	2005	2006	2007	2008
Land & foreshore holdings and Rights held [1]	344.0	364.1	366.1	371.1	371.0	365.7	365.6	365.6	373.4
Land and foreshore holdings	240.6	239.6	241.1	240.0	239.9	240.7	240.7	240.7	240.3
Freehold	225.1	223.9	220.7	219.6	219.5	220.4	220.4	220.4	220.0
Leasehold	15.5	15.7	20.4	20.4	20.4	20.4	20.3	20.3	20.3
Rights held [1]	103.4	124.5	124.9	131.1	131.1	124.9	124.9	124.9	133.1
England	226.0	226.9	224.6	229.8	229.7	224.2	224.2	224.2	223.9
Land and foreshore holdings	195.4	192.6	190.2	189.1	189.0	189.8	189.8	189.8	189.5
Freehold	182.9	179.8	172.8	171.7	171.6	172.5	172.5	172.5	172.2
Leasehold	12.5	12.8	17.4	17.4	17.4	17.3	17.3	17.3	17.3
Rights held [1]	30.6	34.3	34.4	40.7	40.7	34.4	34.4	34.4	34.4
Wales	23.4	23.0	22.9	22.9	22.9	22.9	22.9	22.9	22.9
Land and foreshore holdings	21.0	20.9	20.7	20.7	20.7	20.7	20.7	20.7	20.7
Freehold	20.9	20.8	20.5	20.5	20.5	20.5	20.5	20.5	20.5
Leasehold	0.1	0.1	0.2	0.2	0.2	0.2	0.2	0.2	0.2
Rights held [1]	2.4	2.1	2.2	2.2	2.2	2.2	2.2	2.2	2.2
Scotland	91.2	110.9	115.2	115.2	115.2	115.3	115.3	115.3	123.4
Land and foreshore holdings	20.8	22.9	27.1	27.1	27.1	27.2	27.2	27.2	27.1
Freehold	18.3	20.4	24.6	24.6	24.6	24.6	24.6	24.6	24.6
Leasehold	2.5	2.5	2.6	2.5	2.5	2.6	2.6	2.6	2.6
Rights held [1]	70.4	88.0	88.1	88.1	88.1	88.1	88.1	88.1	96.3
Northern Ireland	3.4	3.3	3.2	3.2	3.2	3.2	3.2	3.2	3.2
Land and foreshore holdings	3.4	3.2	3.1	3.1	3.1	3.1	3.1	3.1	3.1
Freehold	3.0	2.9	2.8	2.8	2.8	2.8	2.8	2.8	2.8
Leasehold	0.4	0.3	0.3	0.3	0.3	0.3	0.3	0.3	0.3
Rights held [1]	-	0.1	0.1	0.1	0.1	0.1	0.1	0.1	0.1

	1990	1997	2002	2003	2004	2005	2006	2007	2008
Land and foreshore holdings	240.6	239.6	241.1	240.0	239.9	240.7	240.7	240.7	240.3
Land	222.6	221.0	222.5	221.4	221.3	222.1	222.0	222.0	221.7
England	180.3	177.3	174.9	173.8	173.7	174.5	174.5	174.5	174.2
Wales	20.0	19.8	19.7	19.7	19.7	19.7	19.7	19.7	19.7
Scotland	19.2	20.8	25.0	25.0	25.0	25.0	25.0	25.0	24.9
Northern Ireland	3.1	3.1	2.9	2.9	2.9	2.9	2.9	2.9	2.9
Foreshore	18.0	18.6	18.6	18.6	18.6	18.6	18.6	18.6	18.6
England	15.1	15.3	15.3	15.3	15.3	15.3	15.3	15.3	15.3
Wales	1.0	1.0	1.0	1.0	1.0	1.0	1.0	1.0	1.0
Scotland	1.6	2.1	2.1	2.1	2.1	2.1	2.1	2.1	2.1
Northern Ireland	0.3	0.2	0.2	0.2	0.2	0.2	0.2	0.2	0.2

Source: MOD Defence Estates

These holdings include land declared as surplus to defence requirements.
A thousand hectares is 3.86 square miles.

1. Rights held are Land and foreshore that are not owned by, or leased to MOD, but over which the Department has limited rights under grants and rights.

Statistics show that the estate size has not moved significantly in recent years. Disposals and acquisitions have occurred, but the overall impact on the overall estate size is not significant. The basis of measurement will be reviewed during the next year to ensure it reflects changes and improvements in technology.

LAND HOLDINGS

Table 6.3 Land holdings by type of use and whether owned, leased or with legal rights, at 1 April each year in thousand hectares

	1990	1997	2002	2003	2004	2005	2006	2007	2008
Airfields	**28.3**	**28.9**	**26.5**	**26.7**	**26.7**	**26.4**	**26.4**	**26.4**	**26.2**
Freehold	26.9	27.2	24.8	25.0	25.0	24.7	24.7	24.7	24.5
Leasehold	0.1	0.1	0.2	0.2	0.2	0.2	0.2	0.2	0.2
Rights [1]	1.3	1.6	1.5	1.5	1.5	1.5	1.5	1.5	1.5
Naval bases	**1.3**	**1.4**	**1.2**	**1.1**	**1.1**	**1.2**	**1.2**	**1.2**	**1.2**
Freehold	1.3	1.3	1.1	1.0	1.0	1.1	1.1	1.1	1.1
Leasehold	-	0.1	0.1	0.1	0.1	0.1	0.1	0.1	0.1
Rights [1]	-	-	-	-	-	-	-	-	-
Training areas, ranges	**254.8**	**278.4**	**283.5**	**283.9**	**283.9**	**283.5**	**283.5**	**283.5**	**291.6**
Freehold	142.6	145.7	148.8	149.1	149.1	148.8	148.8	148.8	148.7
Leasehold	13.1	13.3	15.2	15.2	15.2	15.2	15.2	15.2	15.2
Rights [1]	99.1	119.4	119.5	119.6	119.6	119.5	119.5	119.5	127.7
Barracks, camps	**11.3**	**10.9**	**11.4**	**17.9**	**17.9**	**11.4**	**11.4**	**11.4**	**11.4**
Freehold	10.2	10.2	10.6	10.7	10.7	10.6	10.6	10.6	10.6
Leasehold	0.3	0.3	0.3	0.5	0.5	0.3	0.3	0.3	0.3
Rights [1]	0.9	0.4	0.5	6.7	6.7	0.5	0.5	0.5	0.5
Storage, supply depots	**9.6**	**11.1**	**11.8**	**9.7**	**9.7**	**11.7**	**11.7**	**11.7**	**11.7**
Freehold	9.5	10.6	11.3	9.2	9.2	11.2	11.2	11.2	11.2
Leasehold	0.1	0.1	0.1	0.1	0.1	0.1	0.1	0.1	0.1
Rights [1]	-	0.4	0.4	0.4	0.4	0.4	0.4	0.4	0.4
Research and Development	**28.4**	**21.8**	**18.4**	**18.9**	**18.9**	**18.4**	**18.4**	**18.4**	**18.4**
Freehold	26.5	20.3	16.8	17.4	17.4	16.8	16.8	16.8	16.8
Leasehold	1.2	0.9	1.0	1.0	1.0	1.0	1.0	1.0	1.0
Rights [1]	0.7	0.6	0.6	0.5	0.5	0.6	0.6	0.6	0.6
Radio & W/T stations	**6.4**	**7.3**	**6.4**	**6.3**	**6.3**	**6.4**	**6.4**	**6.4**	**6.4**
Freehold	5.6	5.8	5.1	5.0	5.0	5.1	5.1	5.1	5.1
Leasehold	0.4	0.5	0.6	0.6	0.6	0.6	0.6	0.6	0.6
Rights [1]	0.4	1.0	0.7	0.7	0.7	0.7	0.7	0.7	0.7
Miscellaneous	**3.8**	**4.3**	**6.8**	**6.6**	**6.6**	**6.7**	**6.7**	**6.7**	**6.6**
Freehold	2.5	2.8	2.2	2.2	2.2	2.2	2.2	2.2	2.1
Leasehold	0.3	0.3	2.9	2.7	2.7	2.8	2.8	2.8	2.8
Rights [1]	1.0	1.2	1.7	1.7	1.7	1.7	1.7	1.7	1.7

	1990	1997	2002	2003	2004	2005	2006	2007	2008
Defence land used for agricultural purposes [2]	**110.8**	**96.2**	**91.8**	**103.0**	**100.5**	**106.3**	.. [3]	.. [3]	.. [3]
Grazing only	61.2	51.9	60.0	70.2	68.3	71.0	..	..	..
Full agricultural use	49.6	44.3	31.8	32.8	32.2	35.3	..	..	..

Source: MOD Defence Estates

These holdings include land declared as surplus to defence requirements.
A thousand hectares is 3.86 square miles.

1. Rights held are Land and foreshore that are not owned by, or leased to MOD, but over which the Department has limited rights under grants and rights.
2. Values are included within the usage totals above.
3. Following changes in the tenancies of agricultural land, these data are no longer available.

Statistics show that the estate size has not moved significantly in recent years. Disposals and acquisitions have occurred, but the overall impact on the overall estate size is not significant. The basis of measurement will be reviewed during the next year to ensure it reflects changes and improvements in technology.

CHAPTER 6 - LAND HOLDINGS AND BUILDINGS

LAND HOLDINGS

Charts to tables 6.1, 6.2, 6.3 Analysis of land holdings, at 1 April 2008

Parent Service area

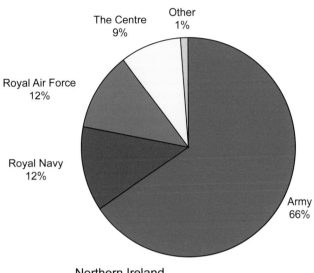

The Centre 9%
Other 1%
Royal Air Force 12%
Royal Navy 12%
Army 66%

Country

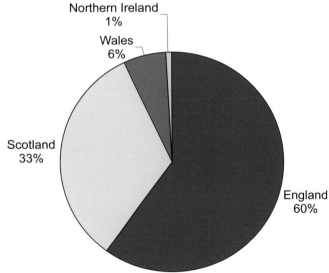

Northern Ireland 1%
Wales 6%
Scotland 33%
England 60%

Type of Use

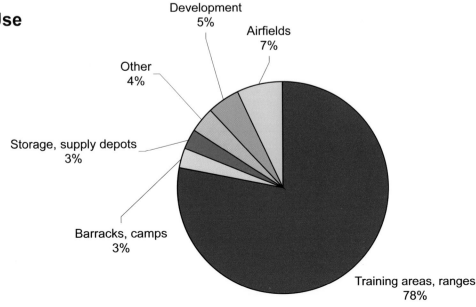

Research and Development 5%
Airfields 7%
Other 4%
Storage, supply depots 3%
Barracks, camps 3%
Training areas, ranges 78%

CHAPTER 6 - LAND HOLDINGS AND BUILDINGS

BUILDINGS

Table 6.4 Service family accommodation in the United Kingdom, at 31 March each year in thousands of dwellings

Defence Estates' Directorate of Operations Housing is responsible for Service Family Accommodation (SFA) in England, Wales and Scotland. At 31st March 2008 it managed some 48,800 properties, and assumed responsibility for Northern Ireland from 1 April 2008.

Vacant properties

There are about 9000 vacant properties in England, Wales and Scotland. Around 2500 of these are either awaiting incoming deployments, modernisation or disposal, whilst the remainder are available to let or are already under offer to Service families.

Number of Occupants

DE Ops Housing provides SFA for entitled Service personnel in accordance with Tri-Service Accommodation Regulations, as well as for other entitled/eligible personnel, and for core welfare purposes. SFA is temporarily utilised for other defence purposes such as single living accommodation.

DE Ops Housing also reports on the number of Substitute Service Family Accommodation (SSFA) properties occupied by entitled Service personnel, i.e. those who would otherwise occupy SFA were it available when and where required. SSFA is private property, is not part of DE Ops Housing stock, and is provided under contract. At 2 April 2008 there were over 39,000 entitled and eligible occupants in England, Wales and Scotland, including 1,175 in SSFA. 1000 entitled and eligible personnel occupy SFA in Northern Ireland and this will increase to approx 1340 by September 2008 as 3 major Unit Moves complete.

Permanent holdings

	1990	1997	2002	2003	2004	2005	2006	2007	2008
United Kingdom	**75.0**	**68.6**	**55.8**	**53.8**	**52.8**	**51.9**	**51.8**	**51.1**	**51.2**
England & Wales	*	*	48.1	46.3	45.8	45.3	45.1	44.9	45.2
Scotland	*	*	4.5	4.3	4.1	3.8	3.8	3.5	3.6
Northern Ireland	*	*	3.2	3.2	2.9	2.8	2.9	2.7	2.4

Vacant accommodation

	1990	1997	2002	2003	2004	2005	2006	2007	2008
United Kingdom	**11.8**	**13.2**	**9.4**	**8.8**	**8.2**	**7.9**	**9.5**	**10.1**	**10.5**
England & Wales	*	*	8.1	7.4	7.0	6.7	7.9	8.2	8.1
Scotland	*	*	0.7	0.8	0.7	0.7	0.8	0.8	0.9
Northern Ireland	*	*	0.6	0.6	0.5	0.5	0.8	1.1	1.5

Vacant properties as a percentage of all dwellings

Percentage

	1990	1997	2002	2003	2004	2005	2006	2007	2008
United Kingdom	**16**	**19**	**17**	**16**	**16**	**15**	**18**	**20**	**21**
England & Wales	*	*	17	16	15	15	18	18	18
Scotland	*	*	16	19	17	18	21	23	25
Northern Ireland	*	*	19	19	17	18	28	41	63

Source: Housing Directorate of Defence Estates

CHAPTER 6 - LAND HOLDINGS AND BUILDINGS

BUILDINGS

Table 6.5 Surveyed condition of Service family accommodation in Great Britain at 31 March each year in thousands of dwellings

Defence Estates Directorate of Operations Housing is committed to upgrading all of its core properties to Standard 1 for Condition, and this is reflected in the Defence Estates Corporate Plan. Core properties are those that are expected to be required in the long term. Not all of the existing stock will be upgraded as some will be handed back to Annington Homes Ltd or disposed of by Defence Estates.

At 31 March 2008, 94% of properties were at either Standard 1 for Condition or Standard 2 for Condition, with the remainder at Standard 3 or 4. Defence Estates Directorate Operations Housing will assume responsibilty for properties in Northern Ireland from 1 April 2008. Standard for Condition data for SFA in Northern Ireland is not held.

Standard for Condition categories:

All SFA in Great Britain is rated by Standard for Condition on a scale of 1 to 4, with 1 being the highest. This rating is achieved by assessing a property against 102 different attributes organised under 8 categories; Building Fabric, Health and Safety, Electrical, Security, Sanitary, Kitchen, Bedroom, and Energy Efficiency. All 8 categories must score at standard 1 for the overall Standard for Condition to be 1.

Examples of required improvements for a Standard 2 property are: a thermostatic shower, new kitchen, or an upgrade to loft insulation.

A Standard 3 property may require: a complete re-wire and consumer unit, new kitchen, bathroom, and an upgrade to insulation of lofts and plumbing.

Standard 4 properties will typically require a new bathroom, electrical system, kitchen, insulation upgrade, and health & safety review.

Surveyed holdings by standards for Condition	Total stock	Core stock[1]						Total stock[2]
	2000	2002	2003	2004	2005	2006	2007	2008
Total (Great Britain)	**57.4** [3]	**37.0**	**41.7**	**41.7**	**42.9**	**43.0**	**44.4**	**48.8**
Standard 1 for Condition	12.8	19.0	20.9	22.8	24.0	25.1	26.6	28.4
Standard 2 for Condition	28.4	14.8	18.3	16.4	17.9	15.8	15.7	17.4
Standard 3 for Condition	15.7	2.9	2.4	2.4	0.9	2.0	2.0	2.0
Standard 4 for Condition	0.6	0.2	0.1	0.1	0.1	0.1	0.1	0.1
Not Recorded	*	*	*	*	*	*	*	0.8

Source: Housing Directorate of Defence Estates

149

1. Core stock are those properties that are expected to be required in the long term.
2. For the period 2002-07 condition of holdings was reported against core stock. From 2008, for consistency with other reporting this was changed to report against total stock.
3. Over 90% of permanent holdings had been surveyed by 2002.

Chapter 7 - Northern Ireland, Military Aid to the Civil Authorities and Conflict Prevention

Two of the military tasks under the Defence mission Standing Home Commitments are: Military Aid to the Civil Power in Northern Ireland and Military Aid to the Civil Authorities. Chapter 7 is divided into two sections: Northern Ireland, and Military Aid to the Civil Authorities and Conflict Prevention.

Military Task 2.2: Military Aid to the Civil Power in Northern Ireland

Military Aid to the Civil Power in Northern Ireland supports the police in the defeat of terrorism and in the maintenance of public order in order to assist HM Government's objective of returning to normality.
In fulfilling this objective, troop numbers have continued to decrease, with the Royal Irish Regiment being disbanded. After 2008, it is likely that Northern Ireland statistics will no longer be included in UKDS.

Table 7.1 shows the numbers of Service personnel committed to Northern Ireland under the command of the General Officer Commanding Northern Ireland, and the numbers of personnel in the Royal Irish Regiment (Home Service) included in this figure. Also shown are the numbers of regular Army units at 1 April each year. The numbers of Service personnel committed to Northern Ireland continued to reduce.
As of 1 April 2007, the General Officer Commanding Northern Ireland TLB became an Intermediate Higher Level Budget (IHLB) under the Land Command TLB.

Table 7.2 shows the numbers of Service personnel committed to and deployed in Northern Ireland, and the numbers of Service personnel committed to Northern Ireland but deployed elsewhere.

Table 7.3 shows the numbers of Service personnel deaths and injuries, the numbers of persons charged with terrorist and serious public order offences, the weight of explosives, numbers of weapons, and amounts of explosives and ammunition found each financial year.

Table 7.4 shows the numbers of Army personnel deployed to Northern Ireland at 1 April in each year from 1969 to 2008. Numbers in the Royal Irish Regiment (Home Service) are also shown, although this regiment was disbanded on 1 August 2007. The table also shows the numbers of Service personnel deaths and injuries since 1969.

More information on the Security Situation in Northern Ireland can be found at the Police Service of Northern Ireland website at: http://www.psni.police.uk/index/departments/statistics_branch.htm

Military Task 2.1: Military Aid to the Civil Authorities

This covers aid to the civil power, other Government Departments and the community at large. Military Aid to the Civil Power is the provision of military assistance to the police and other law enforcement organizations in its maintenance of law, order and public safety. This includes Explosive Ordnance Disposal tasks.
Military Aid to other Government Departments is the use of military forces for non-military Government tasks of national importance, maintenance of supplies and services essential to human life. This includes fishery protection and hydrographic tasks.
Military Aid to the Civil Community is the provision of Service personnel and equipment, to assist the community at large in emergency situations.

Table 7.5 shows the numbers of vessels boarded by the Royal Navy Fishery Protection Squadron within British fishery limits, and convictions arising, in each financial year.

Table 7.6 shows examples of Service assistance to the Civil Community, the civil power and other Government Departments.

Conflict Prevention Activities

The MOD also contributes to the Government's cross-departmental initiative for Conflict Prevention, which cuts across many existing Military Tasks (MT), for example, MT4.3 Peacekeeping, and MT4.4 Peace Enforcement, and MT 3.3 Defence Diplomacy, Alliances and Support to Wider British Interests.

Table 7.7 shows examples of when and where the MOD provided support to the UK's Conflict Prevention Initiative during 2007/08.

Key Points:

Northern Ireland

- As of 1 April 2008, there were 3,220 service personnel committed to Northern Ireland. This is a decrease from 6,170 personnel committed in 2007, continuing the trend of steady decrease in recent years (see **Table 7.1**).
- Of the 3,220 personnel committed to Northern Ireland, 2,610 are from the Army, and the remaining 610 from the RAF (see **Table 7.2**).
- In 2007/08, 16 bombs were neutralized, and 69 persons were charged with terrorist and serious public order offences (see **Table 7.3**).
- There were no Service personnel deaths or injuries in Northern Ireland in 2006 or 2007 (see **Table 7.4**).

Military Aid to Civil Authorities

- 1,309 vessels were boarded and 58 convictions arose as a result of these boardings in 2007/08 (see **Table 7.5**).

CHAPTER 7 - NORTHERN IRELAND, MILITARY AID TO THE CIVIL AUTHORITIES AND CONFLICT PREVENTION

Table 7.1 Number of Service personnel committed to Northern Ireland and in the Royal Irish Regiment (Home Service), and numbers of Army units, at 1 April each year

Numbers of UK armed forces committed to Northern Ireland

With effect from 1 Aug 07 there were fewer than 5000 troops resident in Northern Ireland, trained and available for deployment worldwide. The military will retain some limited but specific responsibilities with the capability to deploy in situations of extreme public disorder in support of the PSNI in a new operation to be known as Operation HELVETIC. In addition, provision of Explosive Ordnance Disposal will continue. As of 1 April 2007, the GOC NI TLB became an IHLB under the Land Command TLB.

	1990	1997	2003	2004	2005	2006	2007	2008
Service personnel committed to NI [1]	18 230	16 790 [2]	14 320	14 030	10 780 [3]	9 330	6 170	3 220

Source: MOD Policy Branch, Civil Secretariat, HQ Northern Ireland

Royal Irish Regiment (Home Service)[4] Full Time and Part Time personnel by sex

The Royal Irish Regiment was formed on 1 July 1992 by the merger of the Ulster Defence Regiment and the Royal Irish Rangers. The Home Service element of the Royal Irish Regiment corresponds to the former Ulster Defence Regiment. These figures exclude long-term sick.

	1990	1997	2003	2004	2005	2006	2007	2008
Full time personnel	2 940	2 760	2 110	2 110	2 010	1 920	1 430	-
Males	2 700	2 510	1 920	1 920	1 830	1 750	1 290	-
Females	240	250	190	190	180	170	140	-

	1990	1997	2003	2004	2005	2006	2007	2008
Part time personnel	3 300	2 010	1 390	1 300	1 210	1 170	-	-
Males	2 820	1 780	1 260	1 190	1 100	1 070	-	-
Females	480	230	130	110	100	100	-	-

Source: MOD Policy Branch, Civil Secretariat, HQ Northern Ireland

Numbers of Army General Service major combat units deployed by length of tour

The numbers of Army General Service units serving in Northern Ireland include Royal Marine Commandos in the Infantry role, but exclude the Royal Irish Regiment (Home Service). The size of units shown may vary according to their primary role. The numbers of major combat units show those on Long Tours (normally, two years) and Short Tours (normally, six months), and exclude temporary deployments.

	1990	1997	2003	2004	2005	2006	2007	2008
Army major combat units	10	12	10	10	5	4	3	2
Long Tour units	6	6	6	6	4	4	3	2
Short Tour units	4	6	4	4	1	-	-	-

	1990	1997	2003	2004	2005	2006	2007	2008
Total units which served in the calendar year	25	28	20	16	10	7	4	..

Source: MOD Policy Branch, Civil Secretariat, HQ Northern Ireland

The numbers of personnel have been rounded to the nearest ten.
1. Includes personnel temporarily deployed to Iraq under Op TELIC.
2. Data as at 1 June 1997 as 1 April 97 data not available in the required format.
3. Includes 85 Army and 51 RAF personnel deployed on Rest of the World operations.
4. This Regiment was disbanded on 1 August 2007. The part time personnel were phased out before 1 April 2007.

CHAPTER 7 - NORTHERN IRELAND, MILITARY AID TO THE CIVIL AUTHORITIES AND CONFLICT PREVENTION

Table 7.2 Number of Service personnel committed to, and deployed in Northern Ireland, at 1 April each year

Service personnel committed to Northern Ireland

Prior to 1 April 2007, the GOC NI HLB was the GOC NI TLB.

	1990 [1]	1997 [2]	2003	2004	2005	2006	2007	2008
Personnel committed to NI [3]	**18 230**	**16 790**	**14 320**	**14 030**	**10 780**	**9 330**	**6 170**	**3 220**
funded by GOC NI HLB	..	13 610	10 900	10 820	9 160	7 880	5 250	2 580
not funded by GOC NI HLB	..	3 170	3 420	3 210	1 620	1 450	920	640
Army	..	**15 340**	**13 340**	**13 030**	**9 800**	**8 380**	**5 400**	**2 610**
funded by GOC NI HLB	..	**12 160**	**10 420**	**10 320**	**8 680**	**7 400**	**4 790**	**2 250**
Resident General Services Forces [4]	..	7 410	6 920	6 920	5 470	4 310	3 360	2 250
R Irish Home Service Full Time	..	2 760	2 110	2 110	2 010	1 920	1 430	-
R Irish Home Service Part Time	..	1 990	1 390	1 300	1 210	1 170	-	-
not funded by GOC NI HLB	..	**3 170**	**2 930**	**2 700**	**1 120**	**980**	**610**	**360**
Roulement General Services Forces (GSF) [5]	..	3 170	2 300	2 080	540	30	-	-
other Army personnel not funded by GOC NI HLB [6]	..	-	630	620	570	950	610	360
Royal Navy / Royal Marines	..	**320**	**30**	**30**	**30**	**10**	**10**	**-**
funded by GOC NI HLB	..	320	30	30	30	10	10	-
Royal Air Force	..	**1 130**	**950**	**970**	**960**	**940**	**760**	**610**
funded by GOC NI HLB	..	1 130	450	470	450	470	440	330
not funded by GOC NI HLB	..	-	490	500	510	470	320	280

Source: MOD Policy Branch, Civil Secretariat, HQ Northern Ireland

Service personnel deployed in Northern Ireland

	1990	1997	2003	2004	2005	2006	2007	2008
Personnel deployed in NI [7]	..	**16 550**	**13 690**	**12 090**	**10 570**	**9 080**	**5 900**	**3 090**
Army	..	15 100	12 730	11 090	9 630	8 150	5 170	2 550
Royal Navy / Royal Marines	..	320	30	30	30	10	10	-
Royal Air Force	..	1 130	930	970	900	920	720	540

Service personnel committed to Northern Ireland, but deployed elsewhere

	1990	1997	2003	2004	2005	2006	2007	2008 [8]
Personnel committed to NI but not deployed in NI [9]	..	**230**	**630**	**1 940**	**220**	**250**	**270**	**130**
Army	..	**230**	**610**	**1 940**	**160**	**230**	**230**	**60**
Forces rear-based in GB [10]	..	230	560	1 900	80	10	-	..
GSF deployed on Op TELIC	..	-	50	40	50	60	160	..
GSF deployed on other ROW operations	..	-	-	-	40	160	70	..
Royal Navy / Royal Marines	..	-	-	-	-	-	-	-
RAF	..	-	**20**	**-**	**50**	**20**	**40**	**70**
Personnel deployed on Op TELIC	..	-	20	-	40	20	30	..
Personnel deployed on other ROW operations	..	-	-	-	10	-	10	..

Source: MOD Policy Branch, Civil Secretariat, HQ Northern Ireland

The numbers of personnel have been rounded to the nearest ten.

1. Detailed breakdown not available for 1990.
2. Data as at 1 June 1997 as 1 April 1997 data not available in the required format.
3. Personnel committed to NI include those rear-based in GB and those temporarily deployed elsewhere, notably under Op TELIC.
4. Resident forces include Army General Service major combat units on long tours (normally for 2 years).
5. Roulement forces are Army General Service or Royal Marine Commando major combat units on short tours (normally 6 months).
6. Full TLB funding allocation information not available for 1997 data.
7. Personnel deployed in NI are those committed to NI less those deployed elsewhere, plus reinforcements deployed for security.
8. As of 2008, figures for personnel committed to NI but not deployed to NI are no longer distinguished between Op TELIC and ROW deployments. Figures are now recorded as deployed overseas without location information.
9. Individual reinforcements for operations outside NI, e.g. Op TELIC, are individual volunteers, not part of a formed unit or sub-unit.
10. Units rear-based in GB are under the command of the GOC NI for deployment in NI if the police need military support.

CHAPTER 7 - NORTHERN IRELAND, MILITARY AID TO THE CIVIL AUTHORITIES AND CONFLICT PREVENTION

Table **7.3** Numbers of Service personnel deaths and injuries, persons charged with terrorist offences and serious public order offences, and the weight of explosives and numbers of weapons and ammunition found in Northern Ireland, by financial year

Numbers of Service personnel killed or injured because of the security situation

	1990/91	1997/98	2002/03	2003/04	2004/05	2005/06	2006/07	2007/08
Service personnel deaths	15	-	-	-	-	-	-	-
of which: Royal Irish Regiment (Home Service)	8	-	-	-	-	-	-	-
Service personnel injured	227	143	67	13	15	2	-	-
of which: Royal Irish Regiment (Home Service)	28	10	37	1	1	-	-	-

Source: Central Statistics Unit, Police Service of Northern Ireland, Lisnasharragh

Numbers of persons charged with terrorist offences and serious public order offences[1,2]

	1990/91	1997/98	2002/03	2003/04	2004/05	2005/06	2006/07	2007/08
Persons charged	351	423	359	279	242	322	185	69
Murder	21	32	3	10	3	2	5	-
Attempted murder	62	15	16	10	6	12	9	3
Firearms and explosive offences	126	69	77	67	75	43	57	26
Armed robbery	40	37	63	30	40	17	11	1
Other offences[3]	102	270	200	162	118	248	103	39

Explosives and weapons

	1990/91	1997/98	2002/03	2003/04	2004/05	2005/06	2006/07	2007/08
Bombs neutralised	94	40	84	50	56	44	27	16

Weight of explosives (kg)

	1990/91	1997/98	2002/03	2003/04	2004/05	2005/06	2006/07	2007/08
Neutralised (ready to detonate)	6 577	383	81	581	5	4	18	2
In explosions (estimated)	4 096	1 168	30	27	22	5	4	2

Amounts of explosives and ammunition, and numbers of weapons found

	1990/91	1997/98	2002/03	2003/04	2004/05	2005/06	2006/07	200708
Explosives (kg)	477	662	18	35	25	28	142	1
Weapons[4]	201	115	127	133	61	349	40	191
Ammunition	18 860	9 984	17 399	19 925	21 425	115 690	4 563	1 570

Source: MOD Policy Branch, Civil Secretariat, HQ Northern Ireland

1. Statistics include only the most serious offence with which a person is charged.
2. Statistics refer to those brought against a person after the original period of detention (including extensions). Subsequent changes, additions or deletions, to original charges are not included.
3. "Other offences" includes hijacking, petrol bomb offences, membership, withholding information, arson, rioting.
4. Covers a range of armaments such as mortars, grenade and rocket launchers and firearms.

Table 7.4 Number of Army personnel deployed to Northern Ireland and numbers of Service personnel deaths and injuries since 1969

The IRA announced a "complete cessation of military operations" on 31 August 1994.
The Combined Loyalist Military Command announced a ceasefire on 13 October 1994.
The IRA announced the end of their ceasefire on 9 February 1996, and an unequivocal restoration of the ceasefire on 19 July 1997.
The Good Friday Agreement (also known as the Belfast Agreement) was signed on 10 April 1998.

Army personnel deployed at 1 April

	Total [1]	of which: Royal Irish Regiment (HS) [2]	
		Full Time	Part time
1969	2 280	..	..
1970	6 230	..	..
1971	10 170	..	..
1972	14 780 [3]	..	..
1973	16 550	..	..
1974	15 940	..	..
1975	13 940	1 410	6 280
1976	14 750	1 530	6 140
1977	13 690	1 670	5 960
1978	13 210	2 190	5 670
1979	15 080	2 470	5 150
1980	19 170	2 550	4 820
1981	13 110	2 740	4 740
1982	17 100	2 740	4 390
1983	16 520	2 790	4 340
1984	15 670	2 680	4 090
1985	15 100	2 720	3 730
1986	17 860	2 790	3 770
1987	16 910	2 790	3 720
1988	16 370	2 860	3 510
1989	17 660	2 920	3 420
1990	16 350	2 940	3 300
1991	16 970	2 980	3 120
1992	18 460	3 000	2 990
1993	17 710	2 920	2 700
1994	17 010	2 900	2 490
1995	16 370	3 060	2 260
1996	15 360	3 010	2 120
1997	15 380	2 760	2 010
1998	14 920	2 700	1 960
1999	13 780 [4]	2 600	1 910
2000	13 070	2 530	1 780
2001	12 310	2 190	1 680
2002	12 530	2 200	1 500
2003	12 730	2 110	1 390
2004	11 090	2 110	1 300
2005	9 630	2 010	1 210
2006	8 150	1 920	1 170
2007	5 170 r	1 430	-
2008	2 550	-	-

Service personnel killed or injured because of the security situation, by calendar year

	Deaths	Injuries
1969	-	54
1970	-	620
1971	48	390
1972	131	578
1973	66	548
1974	37	483
1975	20	167
1976	29	264
1977	29	187
1978	21	135
1979	48	153
1980	17	77
1981	23	140
1982	28	98
1983	15	88
1984	19	86
1985	6	33
1986	12	55
1987	11	104
1988	33	229
1989	14	190
1990	15	214
1991	13	253
1992	6	320
1993	8	173
1994	3	126
1995	-	13
1996	1	55
1997	1	150
1998	1	87
1999	-	36
2000	-	27
2001	-	55
2002	-	77
2003	-	12
2004	-	16
2005	-	4
2006	-	-
2007	-	-
2008	..	..

Source: MOD Policy Branch, Civil Secretariat, HQ Northern Ireland

Source: Police Service of Northern Ireland

The numbers of deployed personnel have been rounded to the nearest ten.

1. The numbers of personnel deployed fluctuate throughout the year as shown in **Table 7.2**.
2. The Royal Irish Regiment was formed on 1 July 1992. Earlier figures are for the former Ulster Defence Regiment.
3. About thirty thousand troops were deployed in Northern Ireland in the summer of 1972.
4. Data have been revised following an in-depth review for the International Monitoring Commission. Data before 1999 were not able to be reviewed because the source data are no longer available.

Table **7.5** Number of vessels boarded by the Royal Navy Fishery Protection Squadron within British fishing limits and convictions arising from these boardings each financial year

This shows the activities of the Royal Navy Fishery Protection Squadron operating within British fishery limits under contract to the Department for Environment, Food and Rural Affairs (DEFRA). Boardings carried out by vessels of the Scottish Executive Environment Directorate and the Department of Agriculture and Rural Development for Northern Ireland are not included.

	1990/91	1997/98	2002/03	2003/04	2004/05	2005/06	2006/07	2007/08
Vessels boarded	**1 803**	**1 715**	**1 375**	**1 709**	**1 747**	**1 371**	**1 335**	**1 309**
by sea areas:								
North Sea	825	743	498	601	502	360	343	367
Faroes, Rockall and West of Scotland	-	-	-	-	-	-	-	-
Bristol Channel, Celtic Sea, English Channel, Irish Sea and Western Approaches	978	972	877	1 108	1 245	1 011	992	942

Source: Department for Environment, Food and Rural Affairs

Convictions arising from Royal Navy boardings

Convictions arising from Royal Navy boardings are convictions of infringements detected by the Royal Navy Fishery Protection vessels in that year operating under contract to DEFRA. Actual figures may change retrospectively as some cases may not be heard in court for a year or more after the initial Royal Navy boarding.

	1990/91	1997/98	2002/03	2003/04	2004/05	2005/06	2006/07	2007/08
Convictions arising from boardings	**49**	**44**	**29**	**28**	**30**	**44**	**49**	**58**
by nationality:								
Belgium	15	2	5	6	6	1	10	24
Denmark	1	-	-	-	-	-	-	-
Eire	1	-	-	4	4	5	10	6
Faeroes	-	-	-	-	-	-	-	-
France	8	5	3	6	12	9	14	15
Germany	-	-	-	-	-	3	-	-
Holland	4	3	1	-	5	10	4	-
Norway	-	-	-	-	-	-	-	-
Russia	-	-	-	-	-	-	-	-
Portugal	5	-	-	-	-	-	-	-
Spain	11	1	-	4	-	-	-	-
United Kingdom	4	33	20	8	3	16	11	13

Source: Department for Environment, Food and Rural Affairs

CHAPTER 7 - NORTHERN IRELAND, MILITARY AID TO THE CIVIL AUTHORITIES AND CONFLICT PREVENTION

Table **7.6** Military Aid to the Civil Power, to other Government Departments and to the Civil Community - examples of assistance provided

Annually, Defence provides operational support to the civil powers on over 70 different occasions on a range of operations. The military provide specialist niche capabilities unavailable to the civil power and always acts in support of the civil power.

		Location	Number of personnel	Type of assistance
1999	19 Sept	Co. Antrim, N. Ireland		Flood relief.
2000	30 Oct -14 Nov	Various	Up to 1,286	Flood relief.
2001	16 Mar-12 Oct	Various	Up to 2,126	Assistance to deal with the Foot and Mouth Disease outbreak.
2002	13-15 Nov	}		
2002	22-30 Nov	}		
2003	21-22 Jan	} Across UK	Up to 18,800	Provided fire service during industrial dispute under Operation Fresco, deploying 177 Red Goddesses and 671 Green Goddesses.
2003	28-30 Jan	}		
2003	1-3 Feb	}		
2004	11 May	Glasgow	20	Movement of rescue equipment and provision of aerial photography after an explosion at the Stocklines Plastic Factory in Glasgow
2004	12-13 Aug	Gloucester	30	Assisted Police searching for missing person
2004	16-20 Aug	Boscastle	50	Search and Rescue helicopter evacuation, helicopter heavy lift and Royal Engineer search assistance following a flash flood
2004	August	Moreton-in-Marsh	1500	Training to provide a fire service during industrial dispute (called off before deployment)
2004	09 Dec	Linton-on-Ouse	12	Defence Fire Service assisted after a civilian airplane crashed
2005	08-10 Jan	Carlisle	30	Search and Rescue evacuation and 20 RAF personnel assisting post flooding
2005	15 Mar	West of Kintyre	44	HMS Penzance located the wreckage of downed Scottish Air Ambulance helicopter
2005	Jul-Aug	Suffolk	90	Provided fire service during industrial dispute under Operation Fresco
2005	Sep-Oct	West Midlands	329	Provided fire service during industrial dispute under Operation Fresco
2005	24 Nov	Leicester	5	Flew a patient by C130 Hercules aircraft from Republic of Ireland to Leicester Hospital
2006	03 Mar	N Ireland	4	Rescuing of a woman by helicopter, who required immediate medical attention and was stranded on Rathlin Island off the Northern Ireland coast.
2006	09 May	Paris	11	A Tri-STAR re-routed via Orly with 3 x Gt Ormond St Hosp doctors to conduct heart transplant operation in Paris.
2006	25 May	London	4	A C130 moved 4 x surgeons to Aldergrove Airport to collect a heart for a transplant at Gt Ormond Street hospital.
2007	18 Jan	Thames Valley	60	Household Cavalry Regiment deployed 60 personnel to support Thames Valley Police during severe weather.
2007	26 Feb	Cumbria	10	Provision of imagery in support of the Grayrigg train crash rescue.
2007	27 Jun	Yorkshire	100	Flood relief
2007	20-31 July	Gloucestershire	1000+	Evacuation following flooding and distribution of bottled / bulk water
2007	14 Nov	Glasgow	4	A C130 moved a critically ill patient from London to specialist facilities in Glasgow.
2008	02 Feb	North West	4	Search and Rescue aircraft assisted with evacuation of personnel from MV Riverdance.

Source: MoD

CHAPTER 7 - NORTHERN IRELAND, MILITARY AID TO THE CIVIL AUTHORITIES AND CONFLICT PREVENTION

Table **7.7** MOD support to the UK's Conflict Prevention Initiative: examples (excluding operations) of activities undertaken in 2007/08

The Global and Africa Conflict Prevention Pools embody a coherent, joined-up approach by MoD, FCO and DFID. Their aim is to improve the effectiveness of the UK contribution to conflict prevention by addressing long-term structural causes of conflict, managing tension and violence and supporting post-conflict reconstruction and stabilisation in a variety of regions and countries where the UK can have most impact. In 2007/08, the pools ran conflict prevention programmes in a diverse range of areas. The Africa pool focused its activity in sub-Saharan Africa and the Global pool covered eight regions including those as diverse as South Asia and the Balkans. The Global pool also operated three thematic programmes on building the capacity of the United Nations, on the control of small arms and light weapons and on enhancing and deploying UK excellence in security sector reform. Through the pools, MoD also made progress in encouraging partner countries to coordinate efforts to maximise the effectiveness of the assistance provided to unstable and conflict-ridden countries.

The types of conflict prevention activity undertaken by MoD through the pools are wide ranging. These examples include some of the non-operational types of activity that MoD performs through the pools. Key activities include our support to international efforts to reduce small arms proliferation and organising weapons collection, management and destruction programmes. MoD also provides security sector reform assistance, training and education programmes, both in the UK and overseas. These provide countries with the knowledge and skills they need to reform their security sectors. Through assisting the process of defence reform in partner states, the MoD helps to improve the effectiveness, efficiency and democratic accountabilities of their defence organisations and Armed Forces, and will enhance their ability to participate in peace support operations.

Date	Location	Type of activity / assistance
2007-08	Worldwide	Through the Global Conflict Prevention Pool, the MOD supports NGOs and UN partners with an annual budget of £500k. This included projects in Guinea-Bissau, Belarus and Montenegro to collect and destroy weapons and improve weapons storage facilities.
Jan 08 - Dec 08	Royal College of Defence Studies (RCDS), United Kingdom	RCDS course prepares senior officers and officials of the UK and other countries for high levels of responsibility in their organisations, by developing their analytical powers, knowledge of defence and international security issues, and strategic vision. Of the 80 places, 50 were filled by foreign students from 46 countries, of which 26 were UK sponsored.
29 May - 13 July 07 & 10 Mar - 25 Apr 08	Defence College of Management and Technology & Cranfield University, United Kingdom	Failing and malfunctioning states not operating according to democratically accountable norms can be a source of conflict. The course enhances knowledge, understanding and the necessary analytical skills to improve governance and management of defence and security systems. All 41 places on this course were UK sponsored and went to international students from 32 countries.
Sep 07 - Jul 08	Joint Service Command and Staff College (JSCSC), United Kingdom	The Advanced Command and Staff Course covers the management of Defence in the United Kingdom, and addresses problems, such as terrorism and the asymmetric threats which are encountered across the wider security sector. Out of the 330 places, 96 foreign students from 56 countries attended, 27 of which were UK sponsored.
Apr 07 - Mar 08	Security Sector Development Advisory Team (SSDAT), World Wide	SSDAT liaises directly with the host nation's armed forces/government on issues of defence reform, restructuring, finance and security. SSDAT is working in 18 countries (Algeria, Antigua Armenia, Azerbaijan, Belize, Bosnia, Czech Rep, Democratic Rep Congo, Georgia, Guatemala, Indonesia, Nepal, Latvia, Macedonia, Moldova, Poland, Sri Lanka and Ukraine).
5 - 9 Nov 07	Regional Exclusive Economic Zone (EEZ) Course Overseas, Indonesia	Regional personnel (Brunei x 2, Indonesia x 39, Malaysia x 5 and Singapore x 3) were trained in the art of maritime security and supporting techniques, thereby improving the ability of other navies to contribute to effective counter-terrorist and counter-narcotics activities. This course has also been delivered overseas in countries such as Kenya, Ghana and Jamaica.
3 - 14 Dec 07	Defence Diplomacy Scholarship Scheme Export Course, Nepal	This course is delivered by Cranfield University, in partnership with MOD's Defence College of Management and Technology, and provides a knowledge, understanding and analysis of: a) Recent UN Peace Support Operations and the supporting role of military forces. b) Key defence management issues, at the strategic and operational level. The course took place in Kathmandu and was attended by 23 students from 5 countries (Afghanistan x 3, Bangladesh x 3, Nepal x 8, Pakistan x 6 and Sri Lanka x 3).
Apr 07 - Mar 08	British Military Advisory Training Team (BMATT) Vyskov, Czech Republic	BMATT delivers military training courses, training assistance and advice to partner nations in order to further develop professional and efficient military forces under democratic civil control. BMATT trains up to 350 Officer, Warrant Officer and senior Sergeant instructors each year at its base at Vyškov, and up to 550 instructors per year in partner countries.
Apr 07 - May 08	Peacekeeping English Project (PEP), World Wide	PEP projects work with the military and police services of 23 countries throughout the world including Armenia, Bosnia, China, Ethiopia, Georgia, Jordan, Kazakhstan, Libya, Macedonia, Mongolia, Mozambique, Turkey, Ukraine and Vietnam. Funded by the Conflict Prevention Pools, the training is project managed by the British Council.
Apr 07 - Mar 08	Vystrel Academy, Russia	Vystrel Academy is the Central Training Academy of the Russian Armed Forces and graduates approximately 220 blue berets annually. 3 courses take place each year with 4 x UK students and 2 x UK instructors participating on each course.
Dec 07 - Jun 08	Palestine	A security advisor and team (1 Brigadier plus 5 contractors) provides the Palestinian Minister of the Interior (MoI) with advice and guidance to enable an effective security policy, thus improving their Command and Control (C2) and Crisis Management (CM) in support of the Rule of Law.
16 Apr-4 May 07	Nigeria, British Defence Advisory Team (BDAT)	A Short Term Training Team of 2 men for 3 weeks has assisted Peacekeeping Wing at Jaji to conduct battalion level pre-deployment training package for a Nigerian Army unit since the end of 2006. The Nigerian requirement is to train 4,000 peacekeepers annually.

Source: MOD

GLOSSARY OF TERMS AND ABBREVIATIONS

1SLsee First Sea Lord.

2SL/CNH Second Sea Lord and Commander-in-Chief Naval Home Command. See **Chief of Naval Personnel/ Commander-in-Chief Naval Home Command.**

ABI see **Annual Business Inquiry**.

ABRO see **Army Base Repair Organisation**.

Adjutant General The AG performs a similar function for the Army to that which the Chief of Naval Personnel performs for the Navy, as well as providing education services to children of all members of the Services on long-term foreign postings.

AFPAA see **Armed Forces Personnel Administration Agency**.

AG see **Adjutant General**.

AINC see **Army Incident Notification Cell.**

Air Command On 1 April 2007, Air Command was formed when RAF's Personnel and Training Command and Strike Command were merged to create a single Command, with a single fully integrated Headquarters, which would better equip the RAF to provide a coherent and coordinated single Air focus to the other Services, MOD Head Office, the Permanent Joint Headquarters and the rest of MOD.

AME see **Departmental Annually Managed Expenditure.**

AMP Air Member for Personnel. In full, Air Officer Commanding-in-Chief RAF Personnel and Training Command. See **Royal Air Force Personnel and Training Command**.

Annual Business Inquiry The ABI is a business survey which gathers data from businesses to produce estimates of employee jobs by industry and geography. It also offers a breakdown of businesses by type.

APC see **Army Personnel Centre**.

Apprentices Apprentices are entrants from civil life to the other ranks of the Armed Forces who undertake training in particular skilled trades.

Appropriation Accounts Appropriation accounts report the expenditure outturn on a cash basis for the previous financial year for each vote. Under resource accounting, from 2000-01 they were replaced by **Resource Accounts Codes**.

Appropriations-in-aid Appropriations-in-aid are receipts used to offset expenditure. They generally arise from the provision of repayment services, the sale of surplus goods or of equipment purchased on behalf of the Defence Sales Organisation.

Armed Forces Personnel Administration Agency AFPAA provided pay and personnel administration services for the Armed Forces, including service pensions. War Pensions paid to widows and other dependants were handled by the Veterans Agency (formerly the War Pensions Agency). AFPAA was merged with the Veterans Agency on 1 April 2007 to form the Service Personnel and Veterans Agency.

Army Base Repair Organisation As of 1 April 2008, ABRO and DARA have merged to form the **Defence Support Group**.

Army Incident Notification Cell Army system for reporting and collating health and safety incidents.

Army Personnel Centre The APC is the administrative centre for Army personnel records.

Army Reserve See **Regular Reserves**.

Army Training and Recruitment Agency ATRA is responsible for each stage of an officer cadet or recruit's progress from the recruiting office, through a Recruit Selection Centre, into recruit training, through specialist courses before they are finally posted to their regiment in the Field Army. The ATRA's mission is to deliver trained and motivated individuals to meet the operational requirements of the Army and defence. ATRA's agency status was removed on 1 April 2006.

Assets Assets can be financial or non-financial. Financial assets include monetary gold, bank deposits, IMF Special Drawing Rights. Loans granted bonds, shares, accounts receivable, and the value of the government's stake in public corporations. Non-financial assets consist of fixed capital (such as buildings and vehicles); stock, land and valuables.

ATRA see **Army Training and Recruitment Agency**.

GLOSSARY OF TERMS AND ABBREVIATIONS

AUC Assets Under Construction.

AWE see **Atomic Weapons Establishment**.

Balance Sheet The balance sheet is a financial statement showing the assets, liabilities, and net worth of a business on a specified date.

Battalion see **Regiment**.

BERR The Department for Business, Enterprise and Regulatory Reform.

BFPO see **British Forces Post Office**.

BMATT see **British Military Advisory Training Team**.

Brigade An Army Brigade is a collection of different Regiments and supporting units that have been grouped together for a specific purpose. A fighting Brigade will traditionally contain Infantry, Armoured Corps, and Artillery Regiments together with many supporting cap badges. The composition of each Brigade will differ depending on its responsibility but could often contain 5,000 soldiers.

British Forces Post Office British Forces Post Office formally ceased to be a Defence Agency as at 1 April 2007 and now reports to DE&S. The BFPO provides mail and Post Office counter services to Forces personnel, their dependants, and authorised civilians, whilst serving outside Great Britain, and a secure service for protectively marked material for the MOD, other Government departments and Defence related Organisations in the United Kingdom (UK).

British Military Advisory Training Team BMATT provides military training courses and assistance, and advises partner nations across the region, to further develop professional and efficient military forces under democratic civil control. It also develops interoperability and a regional capacity for multinational Peace Support Operations.

Capital consumption Capital consumption is also called depreciation and represents the amount of fixed capital used up each year.

Central Health and Safety Project the MOD system to record and analyse health and safety accident/illness at work trends throughout the department and monitor compliance with health and safety legislation.

Central TLB Central TLB has responsibility for the MOD Head Office, covering Defence policy as well as Departmental policy on the equipment programme, resources, finance, personnel and security. However, a significant proportion of Central TLB involves non-Head Office functions. Central TLB provides a diverse range of corporate services for the MOD as a whole. These include pay, bill payment, consultancy services, accountancy, some training, statistical analysis, central IT systems, public relations, defence exports and policing. Central TLB's remit also encompasses the provision of medical services, and our Special Forces.

CHASP see Central Health and Safety Project.

Chief of Joint Operations With a few exceptions, CJO is responsible for running all military operations from his headquarters (the Permanent Joint Headquarters) in Northwood. Military assets are assigned to CJO only for the duration of the operation. In addition to his operational responsibilities, CJO is responsible for the Sovereign Base Areas in Cyprus and British forces in Gibraltar and the Falkland Islands.

Chief of Naval Personnel/ Commander-in-Chief Naval Home Command The CNH is responsible for providing the 'raw material' of trained naval officers, sailors and Royal Marines to CINCFLEET, to allow him to meet his commitment to CJO, and to other TLBs. Chief of Naval Personnel deals with recruitment into the Navy and individual training. Bringing individuals together into coherent ships' crews remains the responsibility of CINCFLEET. This TLB merged with CINCFLEET's TLB to form the Fleet Joint TLB on 1 April 2006.

Chief of the Air Staff Chief of the Air Staff is the professional head of the Royal Air Force. The position is currently held by an officer of the rank of Air Chief Marshal.

Chief of the Defence Staff Chief of the Defence Staff is the professional head of the UK Armed Forces and the principal military adviser to the Secretary of State for Defence and the Government. The position is currently held by an officer of the rank of Air Chief Marshal.

Chief of the General Staff Chief of the General Staff is the professional head of the Army. The position is currently held by an officer of the rank of General.

CI see **Confidence Interval**.

GLOSSARY OF TERMS AND ABBREVIATIONS

CINCFLEET see **Commander-in-Chief Fleet**.

CINCLAND see **Land Command**.

Civilian Level 1 Permanent and casual civilian personnel and Royal Fleet Auxiliaries, but excludes Trading Funds and Locally Engaged Civilians. This will generally be used for MOD internal reporting and planning.

Civilian Level 0 This contains all those at Level 1 plus Trading Funds and Locally Engaged Civilians. This will be used for external reporting, including National Statistics publications CPS1 and UKDS, and Parliamentary Business.

CJO see **Chief of Joint Operations**.

CNH see **Chief of Naval Personnel/ Commander-in-Chief Naval Home Command**.

Commander-in-Chief Fleet The CINCFLEET is responsible for delivery of warships and trained crews to CJO at agreed readiness states. The CINCFLEET maintains an operational command and control capability, in particular for the nuclear deterrent force. The CINCFLEET TLB merged with Chief of Naval Personnel/Commander-in-Chief Naval Home Command TLB to form the Fleet Joint TLB on 1 April 2006.

Commission Commission is the terms under which an Officer is recruited to the Armed Forces. The exact terms vary according to Service and specialisation within each Service.

Communications Service Agency The CSA provides telecommunications and related services to the MOD and is part of the DLO. Not to be confused with the DSCA.

Company A company is a sub-unit of some Regiments, usually Infantry Regiments, and usually commanded by a Major.

Confidence Interval An upper and lower limit, within which there is a stated level of confidence (e.g. 95%) that the true mean lies.

Conflict Prevention consists of early warning, crisis management, conflict resolution, peacemaking, peacekeeping, and peace-building activity and associated strengthening of international and regional systems and capacity. It includes expenditure in both programme and operational expenditure.

Constant prices "at constant prices" indicates a quantity from which the effects of inflation have been removed. The constant prices will refer to a year as the basis for the calculation, e.g. "constant 2001/02 prices".

Corporate Science Innovation and Technology formerly **Corporate Science & Technology** CSIT, headed by the Chief Scientific Adviser, was formed on 1 April 2004 from a merger of two existing budgetary areas. The prime output of this TLB is the delivery of expert advice and the development of scientific and technological solutions to satisfy the MOD's needs and problems.

Corps A Corps is a term used to describe a collection of Regiments or small groupings of soldiers that share a common area of specialist expertise. It is an organisation that has been developed to ensure that common practice is generated across all members of the groupings and to ensure that common interests can be catered for efficiently.

Cost of Capital Charge Cost of Capital Charge is an annual non-cash charge applied to each department's budget. It is currently 3.5% of the net assets of the department and is used to make departments aware of the full cost of holding assets.

CSA see **Communications Service Agency**.

CSIT see **Corporate Science Innovation and Technology**.

Current expenditure Current expenditure on goods and services is the sum of expenditure on pay, and related staff costs, plus spending on goods and services. It is net of receipts from sales. It excludes capital expenditure, but includes expenditure on equipment that can only be used for military purposes since that is counted as current expenditure. It differs from final consumption in that capital consumption is not included.

Current prices See **Outturn prices**.

DARA see **Defence Aviation Repair Agency**.

DASA see **Defence Analytical Services and Advice**.

DBA see **Defence Bills Agency**.

DCSA see **Defence Communications Service Agency**.

GLOSSARY OF TERMS AND ABBREVIATIONS

DDA see **Defence Dental Agency**.

DE see **Defence Estates**.

DE&S see **Defence Equipment & Support**.

Defence Analytical Services and Advice DASA was created in July 1992 and provides National Statistics on Defence and other corporate information, forecasting and planning and consultancy, advice and research services to the MOD. It ceased to be an Agency on 1 April 2008 and was renamed Defence Analytical Service and Advice.

Defence Aviation Repair Agency As of 1 April 2008, ABRO and DARA have merged to form the **Defence Support Group**.

Defence Bills Agency The DBA is primarily responsible for paying bills submitted to the Ministry of Defence by defence contractors. The DBA formally ceased to be a Defence Agency as at 1 April 2007 and forms part of the **Financial Management Shared Service Centre**.

Defence budget Under Cash Accounting, the amount of money planned to be spent during a financial year is the defence budget. Under RAB, the sum of resources planned to be consumed during a financial year is the defence budget. This *excludes* the additional expenditure on current operations that are funded from year to year by HM Treasury. See **Resource budgeting**.

Defence Communications Service Agency Defence Communications Service Agency formally ceased to be a Defence Agency as at 1 April 2007 and was incorporated into **Information Systems and Services.**

Defence Dental Agency Military personnel and their families overseas receive dental care from the Defence Dental Agency.

Defence Equipment & Support At 1 April 2007, Defence Logistics Organisation and Defence Procurement Agency merged to form Defence Equipment & Support. DE&S equips and supports the UK's armed forces for current and future operations. It acquires and supports through-life, including disposal, equipment and services ranging from ships, aircraft, vehicles and weapons, to electronic systems and information services. DE&S satisfies ongoing requirements including food, clothing, medical supplies, maintenance and temporary accommodation, as well as operating HM Naval Bases and the joint supply chain for land, sea and air.

Defence Equipment and Support Incident Notification Cell Defence Equipment and Support system for reporting and collating health and safety incidents.

Defence Estates DE became a TLB on 1 April 2005 with the merger of Defence Estates with the Defence Housing Executive. DE is responsible for managing the defence estate and ensuring that it is managed and developed in a sustainable manner, in line with acknowledged best practice and Government policy.

Defence Logistics Organisation At 1 April 2007, Defence Logistics Organisation and Defence Procurement Agency merged to form **Defence Equipment & Support**.

Defence Medical Services DMS comprises the Defence Medical Services Department, and the three single Service medical directorates.

Defence Medical Services Department The DMSD owns the Defence Dental Agency and the Defence Medical Education and Training Agency.

Defence Medical Education and Training Agency The DMETA was created on 1 April 2003 from the former Defence Medical Training Organisation and the training elements of the Defence Secondary Care Agency. It was owned by the Defence Medical Services Department. From 1 April 2008 it ceased to be an Agency, and is now incorporated within **Joint Medical Command.**

Defence Mission The defence mission are the objectives of the Ministry of Defence, which are to provide the capabilities needed: to ensure the security and defence of the United Kingdom and Overseas Territories, including against terrorism; to support the Government's foreign policy objectives particularly in promoting international peace and security.

Defence Procurement Agency At 1 April 2007, Defence Procurement Agency ceased to be an Agency, and merged with **Defence Logistics Organisation** to form **Defence Equipment & Support**.

Defence Science and Technology Laboratory The DSTL is an Agency of the MOD created on 2 July 2001. It supplies impartial scientific and technical research and advice to the MOD and other government departments.

Defence Secondary Care Agency The DSCA provided hospital and other secondary medical care for members of the Armed Forces. On 1 April 2003, its education functions were transferred to DMETA and its remaining functions to Defence Medical Services. Not to be confused with the DCSA.

GLOSSARY OF TERMS AND ABBREVIATIONS

Defence Storage and Distribution Agency The DSDA provides the Armed Forces with storage and distribution services.

Defence Supply Chain Operations and Movements DSCOM was launched on the 1st October 2005 to combine the enhanced functions of the original organisation with those of the DLO Operations Centre (DLOC). It provides Defence and other authorised users with agreed transport and movements services world-wide in peace, crisis and war in order to support current and future military capability.

Defence Support Group as of 1 April 2008, ABRO and DARA merged to form the Defence Support Group. DSG is a Trading Fund established to support the Armed Forces and deliver wider defence objectives in support of the key Defence Industrial Strategy requirements. DSG's key aim is to provide expert in-house maintenance, repair, overhaul and upgrade services for the through life support of the air, land and maritime systems of the UK Armed Forces. Its mission is to be the preferred supplier of Fleet Management Services to its Customers. It provides engineering support and fleet management services for land based equipment used by the MOD, ranging from radios to main battle tanks. It covers the whole of the UK from a number of strategically located sites and use large numbers of mobile support teams to cover customers in the UK and worldwide.

Defence Transport and Movements Agency Defence Transport and Movements Agency formally ceased to be a Defence Agency as at 1 April 2007. It is now incorporated within Defence Supply Chain Operations and Movements (DSCOM).

Defence Vetting Agency The DVA is responsible for carrying out, and maintaining, national security checks on military and civilian staff employed by the MOD, private sector personnel employed on defence related work, and staff in a number of other government departments.

DEL see **Departmental Expenditure Limit**.

Departmental Annually Managed Expenditure Departmental Annually Managed Expenditure is spending that is outside the **DEL**, but included in departmental budgets. This includes the provision for Armed Forces Pensions and non-cash items such as depreciation, cost of capital charges, and provision. Non-cash items were not subject to the same controls and are included in AME, but from 2003/04 they were included as part of the DEL.

Departmental Expenditure Limit The DEL is a firm plan for three years for a specific part of a department's expenditure. In general the DEL will cover all running costs and all programme expenditure except, in certain cases, spending is included in departmental AME because it cannot be reasonably be subject to close control over a three year period. DELs are divided into current resource and capital budgets.

Departmental Resource Accounts The Department is required to prepare resource accounts for each financial year detailing the resources acquired, held, or disposed of during the year, and the way it has used them during the year.

Depreciation Depreciation is also termed capital consumption. TME includes public sector expenditure gross of the depreciation of capital assets used to produce non-market services. Public sector net investment deducts an aggregate charge for all depreciation (market and non-market) from gross capital spending.

DGII Defence Geographical and Imagery Intelligence.

DINC see **Defence Equipment and Support Incident Notification Cell**.

DIFD Department for International Development.

Direct Entry (DE) Officers DE Officers are army officers (previously called Mainstream officers) who either come direct from civilian life or from the ranks of the Army, commissioned on completion of the 11 month Royal Military Academy Sandhurst (RMAS) Commissioning Course. They will normally be under the age of 29 on entry to RMAS.

DISC Defence Intelligence and Security Centre. Dissolved as an Agency on 1 April 2005.

Disposal Sales Agency The DSA supports and advises on the disposal phase of the through life management of equipment within the Department. The DSA formally ceased to be a Defence Agency as at 1 April 2007 and now reports to DE&S.

Division An Army Division would traditionally be made up of 3 or 4 Brigades depending on the specific role it is to undertake and is configured in a similar fashion to a Brigade but on a larger scale. 1 (UK) Division and 3 (UK) Division are fighting Divisions whereas 2, 4 and 5 Division provide administrative support of specific geographical areas.

DLO see **Defence Logistics Organisation**.

DMETA see **Joint Medical Command**.

DMS see **Defence Medical Services**.

GLOSSARY OF TERMS AND ABBREVIATIONS

DMSD see **Defence Medical Services Department**.

DMTO see **Joint Medical Command.**

DPA see **Defence Procurement Agency**.

DRAc see **Departmental Resource Accounts**.

DSA see **Disposal Sales Agency**.

DSCA see **Defence Secondary Care Agency**.

DSDA see **Defence Storage and Distribution Agency**.

DSG see **Defence Support Group**.

DSTL see **Defence Science and Technology Laboratory**.

DTMA see **Defence Transport and Movements Agency**.

DVA see **Defence Vetting Agency**.

Estimated prices The prices used in the Estimates presented to Parliament. They are forecasts of the prices expected to pertain when the expenditure occurs.

Ethnic Minority Before new classifications were introduced in the 2001 Census of Population, "Ethnic Minority" was defined as anyone who had classified themselves in any category other than "White". It is known that some in the "Other" category had white skin colour but used the category to indicate that they were non-English. One reason that the nationality classification was introduced was so that national as well as ethnic origin or affiliation could be reflected.

Ethnic origin Ethnic origin is the ethnic grouping to which a person has indicated that they belong. The classifications used were revised for the 2001 Census of Population when a classification of nationality was also collected. These revised definitions were also used to re-survey members of the Armed Forces and the Civil Service in 2001-02.

Existing use basis An opinion of the best price at which the sale of an interest in property would have been completed unconditionally for cash consideration on the date of valuation.

FAF see **Forward Available Fleet**.

FCO Foreign & Commonwealth Office.

Financial Management Shared Service Centre The FMSSC was established in April 2007, bringing together several existing MoD back-office finance processes including the former Defence Bills Agency (DBA). Based at sites in Liverpool and Bath, the FMSSC is customer focused and has responsibility for overseeing end-to-end accounting processes. Its mission is to deliver high quality financial management services to support the Department's decision making, internal and statutory reporting activities.

First Sea Lord The 1SL is the professional head of the Naval Service. The position is currently held by an officer of the rank of Admiral. Also known as Chief of the Naval Staff.

Fleet Joint TLB The Fleet Joint TLB is the TLB for the Naval Service. It was formed on 1 April 2006 by the merger of the Commander-in-Chief Fleet and the Chief of Naval Personnel/ Commander-in-Chief Naval Home Command.

Flight A flight is a group of aircraft normally commanded by a Lieutenant Commander (Royal Navy), a Major (Royal Marines or Army) or a Squadron Leader (Royal Air Force).

FMSSC see **Financial Management Shared Service Centre**.

Forward Available Fleet From 2006 onwards the term Required Operating Fleet is no longer used and has been replaced by Forward Available Fleet. This is a new way of managing aircraft resources with the aim to enable the optimal level of availability to the Royal Navy, and the actual number of overall aircraft has not been reduced. Forward Available Fleet is defined as the number of aircraft required to undertake the mandated task; including aircrew and ground crew training, 'in-work' rectification and operational / tactical trials. Also known as Forward Fleet.

Frascati Manual The Frascati Manual is an internationally recognised methodology for collecting and using R&D statistics. It includes definitions of basic concepts, guidelines for collecting data and the classifications to be used in compiling statistics, which in turn allow

GLOSSARY OF TERMS AND ABBREVIATIONS

for international comparisons to be made. See also SSAP 13.

FTE see **Full-time equivalent**.

FTRS see **Full-Time Reserve Service**.

Full-Time Equivalent FTE is a measure of the size of the workforce that takes account of the fact that some people work part-time. Prior to 1 April 1995 part-time employees were assumed to work 50 per cent of normal hours, but since then actual hours worked has been used in DASA's statistics. The average hours worked by part-timers is about 60 per cent of full-time hours. See also **Headcount**.

Full-Time Reserve Service Those on FTRS fill Service posts on a full-time basis while being a member of one of the reserve services, either as an ex-regular or as a volunteer. In the case of the Army and the Naval Service, these will be posts that would ordinarily have been filled by regular service personnel, in the case of the RAF, FTRS personnel also fill posts designated solely for them.

GCHQ see **Government Communications Headquarters**.

GDP see **Gross Domestic Product**.

General Officer Commanding Northern Ireland GOC NI was responsible for military aid to the civil power and counter terrorist operations in Northern Ireland. Although it was a joint-Service TLB, GOC NI was mainly staffed by the Army which provides the bulk of the Service personnel committed to Northern Ireland. At 1 April 2007, GOC Northern Ireland ceased to be a TLB and all staff transferred into Land Command.

GNP see **Gross National Product**.

GOC NI see **General Officer Commanding Northern Ireland**.

Government Communications Headquarters   an intelligence and security organisation reporting to the Foreign Secretary, which works closely with the UK's other intelligence agencies (commonly known as MI5 and MI6). GCHQ's primary customers are the Ministry of Defence, the Foreign and Commonwealth Office and law enforcement authorities, but it also serves a wide range of other Government Departments.

GROS General Register Office for Scotland.

Gross Domestic Product GDP (at market prices) is the value of goods and services produced within a country's borders in a year. Economic data are often quoted as a percentage of GDP to give an indication of trends through time and to make international comparisons easier.

Gross National Product GNP is the total value of goods and services produced in a year by a country's nationals including profits from capital held abroad.

Gurkhas Gurkhas are recruited and employed in the British and Indian Armies under the terms of the 1947 Tri-Partite Agreement (TPA) on a broadly comparable basis. This agreement protects the Gurkhas' status as Nepalese subjects throughout their service. They remain Nepalese citizens but in all other respects are full members of HM Forces. All Gurkhas are discharged in Nepal.

Headcount The headcount is a measure of the size of the workforce that counts all people equally regardless of their hours of work. See also **Full-Time Equivalent**.

Holding Company Refers to companies which are full or part owners of other companies (subsidiaries and joint ventures).

HLB Higher Level Budget.

HQ Headquarters.

Hydrographic Office see **UK Hydrographic Office**.

ICD-10 International Statistical Classification of Diseases and Health-related Problems, 10th revision. ICD is a coding system for diseases and signs, symptoms, abnormal findings, complaints, social circumstances and external causes of injury or diseases, as classified by the World Health Organisation.

IHLB Intermediate Higher Level Budget.

IMPACT Information management system for the Provision of Accident Costs and Trends.

GLOSSARY OF TERMS AND ABBREVIATIONS

Industrial Staff Industrial staff (also known as skill zone staff) are civilian personnel employed primarily in a trade, craft or other manual labour occupation. This covers a wide range of work such as industrial technicians, air freight handlers, storekeepers, vergers and drivers.

Information Systems and Services ISS is a 2* Cluster within Defence Equipment and Support (DE&S), reporting through Chief of Material (Air). ISS is responsible for the delivery and support of information systems and services to operations and to all parts of the UK defence community, including other areas of government.

Intake The intake are those entering the Armed Forces or Civilian workforce. This includes new recruits, re-entrants and transfers from other Forces. If taken over a sufficiently long time, intake figures may include the same individuals more than once, if they were re-entrants.

Intangible Assets Most if not all of MOD's intangible assets are development costs. Under Statement of Standard Accounting Practice 13 (SSAP 13), pure research costs, and applied research costs which are not immediately linkable to a product cannot be put in the Balance Sheet as assets. Only development costs which lead to the introduction into service of new products or systems can be put on the Balance Sheet. SSAP 13 defines "development" as "use of scientific or technical knowledge in order to produce new or substantially improved materials, devices, products or services, to install new processes or systems prior to the commencement of commercial production or commercial applications, or to improving substantially those already produced or installed."

JCCC see **Joint Casualty and Compassionate Cell**.

Joint Casualty and Compassionate Cell provides a joint casualty and compassionate casualty reporting centre for all the Armed Forces.

Joint Medical Command JMC was established from 1 April 2008. The Defence Medical Education and Training Agency (DMETA) ceased to be an executive agency of the MOD and The Joint Medical Command (JMC) was established. The JMC incorporates the Defence Medical Education and Training Agency (DMETA), which ceases to be an Agency on 31 March and will take on additional responsibilities, notably for Healthcare and the Defence Dental Services, in due course.

Joint Personnel Administration JPA is the system used by the armed forces to deal with matters of pay, leave and other personal administrative tasks. Implemented on 20 March 2006, replacing a number of single-service IT systems.

JPA see **Joint Personnel Administration**.

Land Command Commander-in-Chief Land Command. Land Command performs a similar role to CINCFLEET within the context of trained Army formations and equipment.

LEC Locally engaged civilian, see **Locally Entered/Engaged Personnel.**

LEP see **Locally Entered/Engaged Personnel**.

Locally Entered/Engaged Personnel A civilian employee recruited overseas exclusively for employment in support of the UK Armed Forces deployed in a particular overseas theatre (or in support of the Sovereign Base Areas Administration in Cyprus) and on terms and conditions of service applicable only to that overseas theatre or Administration, including the dependents of UK military personnel or UK-based civilian staff employed in that overseas theatre (who are sometimes separately identified as UK Dependents). LECs are not civil servants.

LTA Land Transport Accident.

Location Location statistics may be compiled based on stationed location or deployed location. Stationed location is where an individual is permanently based. Deployed location is where an individual is physically located at a particular point in time and is typically used for short tours of duty.

Major war vessels Major war vessels are Royal Navy vessels of the following types: aircraft carriers, helicopter landing platforms, battleships, cruisers, destroyers, frigates, submarines.

Market Exchange rate The Market Exchange Rate is a currency exchange rate determined largely by market forces.

MDP see **Ministry of Defence Police**.

Meteorological Office The Meteorological Office provides weather forecasting services in the UK and worldwide.

Ministry of Defence The Ministry of Defence (MOD) is the United Kingdom government department responsible for implementation of government defence policy and is the headquarters of the British Armed Forces. The principal objective of the MOD is to defend the United Kingdom and its interests. The MOD also manages day to day running of the armed forces, contingency planning and

GLOSSARY OF TERMS AND ABBREVIATIONS

defence procurement.

Ministry of Defence Police The MDP is responsible for providing effective policing of the Defence Estate.

Minor war vessels Minor war vessels are Royal Navy vessels of the following types: monitors, minehunters, offshore patrol craft, patrol craft, survey ships, ice patrol ships.

MOD see **Ministry of Defence**.

NAO see **National Audit Office**.

NARO see **Defence Aviation Repair Agency**.

National Audit Office The NAO scrutinises public spending on behalf of Parliament. It is totally independent of Government. It audits the accounts of all government departments and agencies as well as a wide range of other public bodies, and report to Parliament on the economy, efficiency and effectiveness with which government bodies have used public money.

National Health Service Central Register contains details of all people registered with a General Practitioner on or since 1 January 1991.

National Statistics Quality Review The Programme of NSQR was established in early 2000 to ensure that National Statistics and other official statistical outputs are fit for purpose and that there is a process to support the continuing improvement in the quality and value of the outputs.

NATO North Atlantic Treaty Organisation.

NATO Eurofighter and Tornado Management Agency NETMA is the prime contractor for the Eurofighter Weapon System. The arrangements for the management of the Eurofighter programme were set out in the NATO Charter dated 18 December 1995 in which the international management agencies of the Tornado and Eurofighter programmes were integrated into a single agency, the NATO Eurofighter and Tornado Management Agency (NETMA). This NATO agency is essentially a multi-nation HQ project office for these two collaborative projects involving the UK, Germany, Italy and Spain. In the UK, Eurofighter is now called "Typhoon".

Naval Manning Agency The NMA was created on 1 July 1996 and dissolved as an agency on 1 April 2004. Its mission was: to ensure that sufficient manpower is available on the trained strength and deployed effectively in peace, transition to war or war.

Naval Recruiting and Training agency The NRTA was established as a Defence Agency of the Ministry of Defence on 1 April 1995. Its role since launch has been to recruit to the Royal Naval and Royal Marines, and to train and develop personnel for their individual tasks as and when appropriate throughout their subsequent careers. The NRTA's agency status was removed on 1 April 2006.

Naval Service The Naval Service is comprised of the Royal Navy (including QARNNS) and the Royal Marines together. The role of the Royal Navy is to contribute to a peaceful environment in which the UK's foreign policy and trade can flourish and in which the security of the UK and her Overseas Territories is assured.

Naval Service Incident Notification Cell Naval Service system for reporting and collating health and safety incidents.

NBSA Naval Bases and Supplies Agency. Now part of the Warship Support Agency.

NCO see **Non-commissioned officer**.

NCR see **Net cash requirement**.

NDA see **Nuclear Decommissioning Authority**.

Net Cash Requirement The NCR is the amount of actual money that MOD requires from the government in order to fund its activities. The NCR takes account of the movements in working capital levels (debtors, creditors and stocks) but not non-cash costs.

NETMA see **NATO Eurofighter and Tornado Management Agency**.

NHSCR see **National Health Service Central Register**.

NISRA Northern Ireland Statistics and Research Agency.

NMA see **Naval Manning Agency**.

GLOSSARY OF TERMS AND ABBREVIATIONS

Non-cash items Non-cash items in Annually Managed Expenditure (AME) include various notional transactions such as **depreciation** and **cost of capital** that appear in the operating cost statement under RAB and which are recorded in AME for the period of Spending Review 2000, rather than in DEL.

Non-Commissioned Officer Non-commissioned officers are ratings of Leading Hand and above in the RN, other ranks of lance corporal and above in the Army and other ranks of corporal and above in the Royal Marines and RAF.

Non-industrial Staff Non-industrial staff are civilian personnel who are not employed in a position where trade, craft or labour experience and knowledge is an essential requirement. Non-industrial staff are primarily office based and perform administrative functions.

NOTICAS see **Notification of Casualty**.

Notification of Casualty the formalised system for casualty reporting within the UK Armed Forces used to inform Chain of Command and next of kin of an individual's condition.

NRTA see **Naval Recruiting and Training Agency**.

NSINC see **Naval Service Incident Notification Cell**.

NSQR see **National Statistics Quality Review**.

Nuclear Decommissioning Authority The NDA is a non-departmental public body created in April 2005 under the Energy Act 2004 to take strategic responsibility for the UK's nuclear legacy. The NDA's main purpose is the decommissioning and clean-up of civil nuclear sites.

Nursing Services The Nursing Services consists of Queen Alexandra's Royal Naval Nursing Service, Queen Alexandra's Royal Army Nursing Corps, and Princess Mary's Royal Air Force Nursing Service.

OECD Organisation for Economic Co-operation and Development.

Office for National Statistics The ONS is responsible for the production of a wide range of independent economic and social statistics, to improve our understanding of the United Kingdom's economy and society, and for planning the proper allocation of resources, policy-making and decision-making. It is the executive office of the UK Statistics Authority, a non-ministerial department which reports directly to Parliament. ONS is the UK Government's single largest statistical producer.

Officer An officer is a member of the Armed Forces holding the Queen's Commission. This includes ranks from Sub-Lt/2nd Lt/Pilot Officer up to Admiral of the Fleet/Field Marshal/Marshal of the Royal Air Force, but excludes NCOs.

Officer Cadet An officer cadet is an entrant from civil life to the officer corps of the Armed Forces.

ONS see **Office for National Statistics.**

Operating Cost Statement The Operating Cost Statement is the statement in departmental resource accounts that shows the current income and expenditure on an accrual basis. It is similar to the profit and loss statement on commercial accounts.

Operational Conversion Unit Operational Conversion Units are training establishments used for converting aircrew to particular aircraft types.

Operational TLBs Operational TLBs are the TLBs directly responsible for the planning and management of military operations and the delivery of front-line capability. They are Air Command, Land Command, and Fleet Joint Command. Operational personnel are those working in these TLBs plus some other small groups.

Other Ranks Other ranks are members of the Royal Marines, Army and Royal Air Force who are not officers. The equivalent group in the Royal Navy is known as "Ratings".

Outflow The outflow are those leaving the Armed Forces or Civil Service for any reason. Those who rejoin and then leave again will be counted twice if the time period includes both exit dates.

Outturn and **estimated outturn** Outturn describes expenditure actually incurred, whereas estimated outturn describes estimated expenditure on the basis of actual expenditure to date.

Outturn prices Outturn prices are the prices of the period when the expenditure actually occurred; also described as current prices.

GLOSSARY OF TERMS AND ABBREVIATIONS

Part-time Part-time civil servants are those working fewer than 37 hours a week (36 hours in London), excluding meal breaks.

PE Procurement Executive. See **Defence Procurement Agency**.

People, Pay and Pensions Agency The PPPA provides pay and personnel administration services for MOD's civilian staff.

PES Public Expenditure Survey.

PESA see **Public Expenditure Statistical Analyses**.

PFI see **Private Finance Initiative**.

Pink Book Detailed annual estimates of the UK balance of payments including estimates for the current account (trade in goods and services, income and current transfers), the capital account, the financial account and the International Investment position.

PJHQ Permanent Joint Headquarters. See **Chief of Joint Operations**.

PMRAFNS see **Princess Mary's Royal Air Force Nursing Service**.

PPO see **Principal Personnel Officer**.

PPPA see **People, Pay and Pensions Agency**.

PPP see **Purchasing Power Parity**.

Princess Mary's Royal Air Force Nursing Service The PMRAFNS provides a range of nursing services to the Royal Air Force. It was founded as the RAF Nursing Service, and was given its present name in 1923.

Principal Personnel Officer Each of the three Services has a PPO who manages all personnel within their Service. The three PPO's are: the Second Sea Lord, the Adjutant General, and the Air Member for Personnel.

Private Finance Initiative The PFI is a system for providing capital assets for the provision of public services. Typically, the private sector designs, builds and maintains infrastructure and other capital assets and then operates those assets to sell services to the public sector. In most cases, the capital assets are accounted for on the balance sheet of the private sector operator.

Procurement Executive see **Defence Procurement Agency**. Formed in 1971.

PSNI Police Service Northern Ireland.

PTC see **RAF Personnel and Training Command**.

Public Expenditure Statistical Analyses PESA is a compendium that gathers recent outturn data, estimated outturns for the latest year, and spending plans over the entire range of UK public expenditure.

Purchasing Power Parity PPA is a method of measuring the relative purchasing power of different countries' currencies over the same types of goods and services. Because goods and services may cost more in one country than in another, PPP allows us to make more accurate comparisons of standards of living across countries. PPP estimates use price comparisons of comparable items but since not all items can be matched exactly across countries and time, the estimates are not always "robust."

QARANC see **Queen Alexandra's Royal Army Nursing Corps**.

QARNNS see **Queen Alexandra's Royal Naval Nursing Service**.

QinetiQ Formerly part of DERA, from 2 July 2001 a limited company, QinetiQ is still partially owned by the MOD. Its staff numbers ceased to be included in DASA's MOD civilian statistics after July 2001.

Queen Alexandra's Royal Army Nursing Corps QARANC provides a range of nursing services to the Army. It was founded in 1902 as Queen Alexandra's Imperial Military Nursing Service, and was merged into the regular Army and renamed QARANC in 1949.

Queen Alexandra's Royal Naval Nursing Service QARNNS provides a range of nursing services to the Naval Service. QARNNS was founded in 1902 and merged with the Royal Navy on 1 April 2000.

R&D Research and Development.

RAB see **Resource accounting**, **resource budget**, and **Resource budgeting**.

GLOSSARY OF TERMS AND ABBREVIATIONS

RAF see **Royal Air Force**.

RAF PTC see **Royal Air Force Personnel and Training Command**.

RAFR Royal Air Force Reserve. See **Regular Reserves**.

RAF Training Group Defence Agency TGDA is responsible for the recruitment and selection of all RAF personnel and delivery of all RAF non-operational training including flying training to Navy and Army personnel. Its mission is to underpin the military effectiveness of the RAF and other services by timely provision of appropriately trained military and civilian personnel. The RAF Training Group Defence Agency's agency status was removed on 1 April 2006.

Rank A rank is a grade within the Military structure – see **Table 2.28** for equivalents among the Services.

Rate A rate is a Naval term for rank when referring to non-officers.

Ratings The ratings are the designation of Other Ranks in the Royal Navy.

RAuxAF Royal Auxiliary Air Force, see **Volunteer Reserves**.

RCDS see **Royal College of Defence Studies**.

Real terms Real terms figures are amounts adjusted for the effect of general price inflation relative to a base year, as measured by the GDP market price deflator.

Regiment The Regiment is often considered to be the most important unit in the British Army. It carries the spirit of the people who have gone before and would usually contain approximately 650 soldiers depending on its cap badge and role. Sometimes Infantry Regiments have more than one unit of this size and they should be correctly referred to as a Battalion and be numbered in ascending order. An example being the 1st Battalion of The Parachute Regiment which like the 2nd Battalion and the 3rd Battalion contains an identical structure and number of posts.

Regular Reserves Former members of the UK regular forces who have a liability for service with the Reserve forces. Includes the Royal Fleet Reserve, Army Reserve and Royal Air Force Reserve as well as other individuals liable to recall.

Reporting of Injuries, Diseases and Dangerous Occurrences Regulations Guidance on the reporting of work-related deaths, major injuries or over-three-day injuries, work related diseases, and dangerous occurrences.

Resource Accounting Resource accounting is the accounting system that will henceforth be used to record expenditure in the departmental accounts instead of cash accounting. It applies generally accepted accounting practice (GAAP) used in private industry and other Government departments to departmental transactions. Spending is measured on an accruals basis.

Resource Budget The resource budget is the sum of a department's resource Departmental Expenditure Limit and resource Annually Managed Expenditure. It is the budget for current expenditure on an accruals basis.

Resource Budgeting Resource budgeting is the budgeting regime adopted for the spending plans set in the 2000 Spending Review. It is derived from resource accounting rules, but there are several differences in treatment between resource accounts and resource budgets. See Introduction to Chapter 1.

RFA see **Royal Fleet Auxiliary Service**.

RFR Royal Fleet Reserve. See **Regular Reserves.**

RfR Request for Resources: RfR1 = Provision of Defence Capability, RfR2 = Net additional cost of operations, RfR3 = War Pensions and Allowances.

RIDDOR see **Reporting of Injuries, Diseases and Dangerous Occurrences Regulations**.

RM see **Royal Marines**.

RMR see **Royal Marines Reserve**.

RN see **Royal Navy**.

RNR see **Royal Naval Reserve**.

Royal Air Force The RAF's mission is: "To generate air power to meet the Defence Mission."

GLOSSARY OF TERMS AND ABBREVIATIONS

Royal Air Force Personnel and Training Command RAF PTC was amalgamated with Strike Command on 1 April 2007 to form Air Command.

Royal Auxiliary Air Force Founded 1924, see **Volunteer Reserves**.

Royal College of Defence Studies The RCDS forms part of the UK Defence Academy. It prepares senior officers and officials of the United Kingdom and other countries, and future leaders from the private and public sectors for high responsibilities in their respective organisations.

Royal Fleet Auxiliary Service Constituted in 1905, this is a civilian manned fleet, owned by the Ministry of Defence. Its main task is to supply warships of the Royal Navy at sea with fuel, food, stores and ammunition which they need to remain operational while away from base. It also provides aviation support for the Royal Navy, together with amphibious support and secure sea transport for Army units and their equipment. Its employees are full-time civil servants, but who come under the Naval Discipline Act when deployed to sea under naval command.

Royal Marines Royal Marines are sea-going soldiers who are part of the Naval Service. RM officer ranks were aligned with those of the Army on 1 July 1999.

Royal Marines Reserve Approximately 10% of the RMR are working with the Regular Corps on long term attachments, mostly FTRS. The remainder are Volunteer Reserves

Royal Naval Reserve Formed in 1859 it was merged with the Royal Navy Volunteer Reserve (RNVR) in 1958, and also incorporates the former Women's Royal Navy Volunteer Reserve (WRNVR) and QARNNS (Reserve). See **Volunteer Reserves**.

Royal Navy The sea-going defence forces of the UK, including ships, submarines, and Naval aircraft and their personnel, but excluding the Royal Marines and the Royal Fleet Auxiliary Service (RFA). From 1 April 2000 the Royal Navy incorporated Queen Alexandra's Royal Naval Nursing Service (QARNNS).

SAS see **Special Air Service**.

SBS see **Special Boat Service**.

SCS see **Senior Civil Service**.

SSAP 13 Statement of Standard Accounting Practices No.13 gives guidance on the accounting policies to be followed in respect of research and development expenditure. This guidance aligns to the OECD Frascati definitions for measuring Research & Experimental Development. See also **Frascati Manual**.

Security Sector Development Advisory Team The SSDAT are defence diplomacy staff based in Shrivenham, provides in-country advice to foreign countries for Security Sector Reform, Defence Reform and Justice/Police Reform. SSDAT is currently undertaking work in 12 countries such as Sierra Leone, Ethiopia, Iraq, and Serbia.

Senior Civil Service Senior Civil Service is the top grades within the Civil Service, that is, Management Levels 1 to 3. Formerly Grades 1 to 5, that is, Permanent Under Secretary to Assistant Secretary.

Senior Non-commissioned officer Senior members of the Ratings/Other Ranks, including Warrant Officer (all classes), Charge Chief Petty Officer, Chief Petty Officer, Colour sergeant, Staff Sergeant, Flight Sergeant/Chief Technician, Petty Officer, Sergeant.

Seriously Ill/Injured/Wounded a NOTICAS medical listing used when an individual's condition is of such severity that there is cause for immediate concern, but there is no imminent danger to life.

Service Personnel and Veterans Agency SPVA was formed on 1 April 2007, by the merger of AFPAA and the Veterans Agency. The SPVA mission is to "deliver reliable, trusted and efficient personnel services to the serving and veterans communities".

SI see **Seriously Ill/Injured/Wounded**.

SIC see **Standard Industrial Classification**.

Single Use Military Equipment Single use military equipment are MOD held assets which are only suitable for military purposes (such as warships), as opposed to dual-use equipment which can also be used for non-military purposes.

SMR see **Standardised Mortality Ratio**.**Special Air Service** Part of the Special Forces, usually drawn from the Army.

Special Boat Service Part of the Special Forces, usually drawn from the Naval Service.

GLOSSARY OF TERMS AND ABBREVIATIONS

Specialist Policing Wg Organised in five divisional commands, located at York, Aldershot, Aldermaston, Foxhill and Clyde Naval Base. Deployed at around 120 MOD sites requiring police officers and an armed security capability, including the guarding of Britain's nuclear deterrent.

SPVA see Service Personnel and Veterans Agency.

Squadron In the Naval Service (i) a group of vessels, normally commanded by a Commander; (ii) a group of naval aircraft, normally commanded by a Commander; (iii) a group of particular personnel, such as divers, commanded by a Commander; (iv) a group of Royal Marines on board ship or an amphibious assault group, normally under the command of a Lt Col (Royal Marines); (v) a sub-unit of the Special Boat Service, normally commanded by a Major (Royal Marines) or Lieutenant Commander (Royal Navy).
In the Army, a sub-unit of some regiments, normally commanded by a Major.
In the Royal Air Force (i) a unit of a number of aircraft larger than a Flight and smaller than a Group; (ii) a unit of personnel, including sub-units of the RAF Regiment. An RAF squadron is usually commanded by a Wing Commander.
See **Table 2.28** for rank equivalents among the Services.

SSDAT see **Security Sector Development Advisory Team**.

STANAG NATO Standardisation Agreement. STANAGs are administered by the NATO Standardisation Agency.

Standard Industrial Classification SIC classifies business establishments and other statistical units by the type of economic activity in which they are engaged. The classification is maintained by the ONS.

Standardised Mortality Ratio the ratio of the number of deaths observed in the study population to the number of deaths expected if the study population had the same age group and year specific rates as the standard population.

STC see **Strike Command**.

Strike Command Strike Command was merged with RAF's Personnel and Training Command on 1 April 2007, to form **Air Command**.

SUME see **Single Use Military Equipment**.

Supply expenditure Supply expenditure is expenditure financed by money voted by parliament in the annual Supply Estimates: also termed Voted in Estimates.

TA Territorial Army. See **Volunteer Reserves**.

TAVR Territorial Army Volunteer Reserve, see **Volunteer Reserves**.

Territorial Army see **Volunteer Reserves**.

Territorial Army Volunteer Reserve see **Volunteer Reserves**.

TGDA see **RAF Training Group Defence Agency**.

Time Expiry A term used to describe those in the Armed Services who reach the end of their engagement or commission and then leave.

TLB see **Top Level Budget**.

TME see **Total Managed Expenditure**.

Top Level Budget The TLB is the major organisational grouping of the MOD. See also **Operational TLBs**.

Total Managed Expenditure TME is a definition of aggregate public spending derived from notional accounts. It is the consolidated sum of current and capital expenditure of central and local government, and public corporations. TME is the sum of the Departmental Expenditure Limit and Annually Managed Expenditure.

Trading Agency see **Trading Fund**.

Trading Fund Trading Funds were introduced by the Government under the Trading Funds Act 1973 as a 'means of financing trading operations of a government department which, hitherto, have been carried out on Vote'. They are self-accounting units that have greater freedom, than other government departments, in managing their own financial and management activities. They are also free to negotiate their own terms and conditions with their staff and for this reason their grading structures do not always match that of the rest of the Ministry, and this is reflected in some of the tables. Examples include the Defence Support Group, DSTL, the

GLOSSARY OF TERMS AND ABBREVIATIONS

Meteorological Office, and the UK Hydrographic Office.

UK Hydrographic Office The UK Hydrographic Office is responsible for surveying the seas around the UK and other areas to aid navigation.

UK Statistics Authority The UK Statistics Authority is an independent body, and is directly accountable to Parliament. It was established on 1 April 2008. The Authority's overall objective is to promote and safeguard the quality of official statistics that serve the public good. It is also required to safeguard the comprehensiveness of official statistics, and ensure good practice in relation to official statistics. The UK Statistics Authority has three main functions: oversight of the Office for National Statistics (ONS) (its executive office), monitoring and reporting on all UK official statistics, and independent assessment of official statistics.

University cadet A university cadet is an entrant from civil life to the officer corps of the Armed Forces who is accepted into one of the Forces prior to starting a university course. They usually receive some form of financial assistance with their course.

USAF United States Air Force.

VAT Value Added Tax.

Very Seriously Ill/injured/wounded A NOTICAS medical listing used when an individual's illness or injury is of such severity that life is imminently endangered.

Veterans Agency Formerly the War Pensions Agency, the Veterans Agency was responsible for veterans' affairs, including war and service pensions, service records, military graves, medals and welfare issues. It was merged with AFPAA on 1 April 2007 to form **Service Personnel and Veterans Agency**.

Voluntary Release Those who leave the Armed Forces voluntarily before the end of their agreed engagement or commission period are said to leave on VR (Voluntary Release).

Volunteer Reserves and Auxiliary Forces Volunteer Reserves and Auxiliary Forces are civilian volunteers who undertake to give a certain amount of their time to train in support of the Regular Forces. They include the Royal Naval Reserve, the Royal Marines Reserve, Territorial Army and the Royal Auxiliary Air Force but do not include Royal Fleet Auxiliary Service (RFA). Some Volunteer Reservists undertake (paid) Full-Time Reserve Service.

Vote A vote was an individual Supply Estimate. Under RAB, from 2001, votes have been replaced by Requests for Resources.

VR see **Voluntary Release**.

VSI see **Very Seriously Ill/Injured/Wounded**.

War Pensions Agency see **Veterans' Agency**.

WHO World Health Organisation.

Women's Royal Naval Service ("Wrens") Founded in 1917 it was merged with the Royal Navy in 1991.

WRNS see **Women's Royal Naval Service** ("Wrens").

WSA Warship Support Agency, dissolved 1 April 2005.

BIBLIOGRAPHY

Additional information may be found in the following publications. The Guide to Official Statistics published by the Office for National Statistics also gives relevant sources.
Annual Abstract of Statistics 2008: TSO (The Defence chapter includes longer runs of data for some of the tables included here).

Appropriation Accounts: Class I Defence (Volume 1):	HMSO/TSO	1995-96 HC 11-I	5 February 1997
	HMSO/TSO	1996-97 HC 251-I	5 February 1998
	HMSO/TSO	1997-98 HC 1-I	26 November 1998
	HMSO/TSO	1998-99 HC 11-I	19 January 2000
Armed Forces' Pay Review Body Reports: HMSO/TSO	1999	Twenty-eighth	Cm 4242
	2000	Twenty-ninth	Cm 4565
	2001	Thirtieth	Cm 4993
	2002	Thirty-first	Cm 5361
	2003	Thirty-second	Cm 5717
	2004	Thirty-third	Cm 6113
	2005	Thirty-fourth	Cm 6455
	2006	Thirty-fifth	Cm 6740
	2007	Thirty-sixth	Cm7016
	2008	Thirty-seventh	Cm7315

Annual Report and accounts and equivalent previous documents

Consolidated Departmental Resource Accounts	2000-01	HC 443	18 December 2001
	2001-02	HC 47	21 November 2002
Ministry of Defence Performance Report	2001/02	TSO	Cm 5661
Ministry of Defence Annual Report and Accounts	2003/04	TSO	HC 1080
	2004/05	TSO: 28 Oct 2005	HC 464
	2005/06	TSO	HC 1394
	2006/07	TSO	HC697
	2007/08	TSO	HC850-I & II
The Meteorological Office Annual Report and Accounts		TSO	Annual
United Kingdom Hydrographic Office: annual report		UKHO	Annual
Obtainable from the United Kingdom Hydrographic Office, MOD, Taunton Somerset.. TA1 2DN			
Civil Service Statistics:		HMSO/TSO	Annual
Deaths in the Armed Forces 2005		DASA	
Defence Professionals in the UK and France		DASA/ SGA(France)	2006
The Government's Expenditure Plans 2007/08: Ministry of Defence		TSO	Cm 7098
Guide to the Classification for Overseas Trade Statistics		HMSO/TSO	Annual
Overseas Trade Statistics of the United Kingdom		HMSO/TSO	Monthly & Annual
International Classification of Diseases and Related Health Problems: Tenth Revision		World Health Organisation 1992	
Major Projects Report 2008: Ministry of Defence		TSO	HC 23 I&II
Managing Resources: Analysing Resource Accounts: An Introduction		HM Treasury	June 2001
Ministry of Defence: Claims Annual Report		DS&C (Claims)	
The Military Balance: Institute for International Strategic Studies		OUP	Annual
Navy, Army and Air Force Institutes (NAAFI); annual report and accounts;		TSO	Cm 6811
obtainable from NAAFI, London Road, Amesbury Wiltshire SP4 7EN			
Public Expenditure: Statistical Analyses 2008		*TSO*	HC 489
Suicide and Open Verdict Deaths among Males in the UK Regular Armed Forces.		DASA	
Suicide and Open Verdict Deaths among Males in the UK Regular Armed Forces, 1984-2005: Methods Used to Commit Suicide.		DASA	
Supply Estimates: Class I Defence:		HMSO	1994-95: HC 276-1
became part of the Main Estimates from 1996-97)			1995-96: HC 271-1
Supply Estimates: Main Estimates:	HMSO/TSO	1996-97: HC 261-1	2002-03: HC 795
		1997-98: HC 235-1	2003-04: HC 648
		1998-99: HC 635-1	2004-05: HC 487
		1999-00: HC 336-1	2005-06: HC 2
		2000-01: HC 377-1	2006-07: HC 1366
		2001-02: HC 348-1	2007/08: HC 835
United Kingdom National Accounts		HMSO/TSO	Annual
United Kingdom Standard Industrial Classification of Economic Activity:		HMSO	(i) Revised 1980
			(ii) Revised 1992
White Papers: *Defence White Paper 2003:*		TSO	Cm 1048
Delivering Security in a Changing World: Future Capabilities		TSO	Cm 6269
Strategic Defence Review (renamed the Defence White Paper)		TSO	Cm 3999

BIBLIOGRAPHY

Note: The MOD is not responsible for the contents or reliability of the listed non-MOD web sites and does not necessarily endorse the views expressed therein. Listing should not be taken as endorsement of any kind. We have no control over the availability of these sites. Users access them at their own risk. The information given was correct at the time of going to press.

Organisation	*Address*
Defence Support Group	http://www.dsg.mod.uk/
British Army	http://www.army.mod.uk
Canada: Department of National Defence	http://www.dnd.ca
Defence Analytical Services and Advice	http://www.dasa.mod.uk
Financial Management Shared Service Centre (formerly Defence Bills Agency)	http://www.fmscc.mod.uk
Defence Manufacturers' Association of Great Britain	http://www.the-dma.org.uk/
Defence Equipment & Support	http://www.mod.uk/DefenceInternet/Microsite/DES/
Defence Science and Technology Laboratory	http://www.dstl.gov.uk
Department for Environment, Food and Rural Affairs	http://www.defra.gov.uk
Department for International Development	http://www.dfid.gov.uk/
Department for Transport	http://www.dft.gov.uk
European Union (in English)	http://www.europa.eu.int/index_en.htm
Eurostat	http://europa.eu.int/comm/eurostat/
Foreign and Commonwealth Office	http://www.fco.gov.uk
France: Ministère de la Défense (in English)	http://www.defense.gouv.fr/sites/defense/english_contents
Germany: Bundesministerium der Verteidigung (English)	http://eng.bmvg.de/
International Institute for Strategic Studies	http://www.iiss.org
Jane's Information Group	http://www.janes.com
Japan Defence Agency (in English)	http://www.mod.go.jp/e/index.html
Meteorological Office	http://www.metoffice.gov.uk
Ministry of Defence	http://www.mod.uk
NAAFI	http://www.naafi.co.uk/
National Statistics	http://www.statistics.gov.uk
North Atlantic Treaty Organisation	http://www.nato.int
Northern Ireland Statistics and Research Agency	http://www.nisra.gov.uk
Organisation for Economic Co-operation & Development	http://www.oecd.org/home/
Organisation for Security and Co-operation in Europe	http://www.osce.org
Royal Air Force	http://www.raf.mod.uk
Royal Fleet Auxiliary Service	http://www.rfa.mod.uk
Royal Navy and Royal Marines	http://www.royal-navy.mod.uk
Royal United Services Institute for Defence Studies	http://www.rusi.org
Statistics Commission	http://www.statscom.org.uk/
Stockholm International Peace Research Institute	http://www.sipri.org
The Stationery Office (TSO)	http://www.tso.co.uk
UK Defence Forum	http://www.ukdf.org.uk/
UK Government	http://www.direct.gov.uk/Homepage/fs/en
UK Hydrographic Office	http://www.hydro.gov.uk
United Nations Economic Commission for Europe	http://www.unece.org
US Department of Defense	http://www.pentagon.mil/
Western European Union	http://www.weu.int
World Health Organisation (in English)	http://www.who.int/en/